Pombo
a man of
Che's *guerrilla*

Harry Villegas

Pombo
a man of
Che's *guerrilla*

**With Che Guevara in Bolivia
1966-68**

PATHFINDER

NEW YORK   LONDON   MONTREAL   SYDNEY

Edited by Mary-Alice Waters

ISBN 0-87348-833-4 paper; ISBN 0-87348-834-2 cloth
Library of Congress Catalog Card Number 97-65977

Manufactured in the United States of America

First edition, 1997

COVER DESIGN: Eric Simpson
COVER PHOTO: Ernesto Che Guevara and Harry Villegas (*Pombo*) in
    Bolivia, late 1966 or early 1967. Courtesy Richard Dindo.
BACK COVER PHOTO: Harry Villegas, 1995. Luis Madrid/*Militant*

Pathfinder
410 West Street, New York, NY 10014, U.S.A.
Fax: (212) 727-0150
CompuServe: 73321,414 • Internet: pathfinder@igc.apc.org

PATHFINDER DISTRIBUTORS AROUND THE WORLD:
Australia (and Asia and the Pacific):
    Pathfinder, 19 Terry St., Surry Hills, Sydney, N.S.W. 2010
    Postal address: P.O. Box K879, Haymarket, N.S.W. 1240
Canada:
    Pathfinder, 4581 rue St-Denis, Montreal, Quebec, H2J 2L4
Iceland:
    Pathfinder, Klapparstíg 26, 2d floor, 101 Reykjavík
     Postal address: P. Box 233, 121 Reykjavík
New Zealand:
    Pathfinder, La Gonda Arcade, 203 Karangahape Road, Auckland
    Postal address: P.O. Box 8730, Auckland
Sweden:
    Pathfinder, Vikingagatan 10, S-113 42, Stockholm
United Kingdom (and Europe, Africa except South Africa, and Middle East):
    Pathfinder, 47 The Cut, London, SE1 8LL
United States (and Caribbean, Latin America, and South Africa):
    Pathfinder, 410 West Street, New York, NY 10014

To the Heroic Guerrilla,
Commander Ernesto Che Guevara

To the comrades in struggle, especially
Ñato, Inti, Darío, Elmo Catalán (Elías), Maya,
and all the others who, after Che's death in combat
in Bolivia, raised the banner of struggle with
courage, determination, and total
confidence in the future.

They were prepared to – and did – give their lives
for such sacred ideals.

Contents

MAPS

Photo sections can be found after pages 104, 200, and 312.

Harry Villegas (Pombo)

HARRY VILLEGAS WAS BORN MAY 10, 1940, in a small village in the foothills of the Sierra Maestra mountains in eastern Cuba, near the city of Manzanillo, in what is now the municipality of Yara. The youngest of ten children, his father was a carpenter and his mother owned a couple of small shops and a bakery.

As a teenager he joined the struggle against the U.S.-backed dictatorship of Fulgencio Batista, participating in clandestine activities in Manzanillo as a member of an Action and Sabotage cell of the July 26 Movement, the revolutionary organization led by Fidel Castro. In late 1957 he joined the Rebel Army and was incorporated into Column no. 4 under the command of Ernesto Che Guevara. When Guevara was assigned to establish the first military training school of the Rebel Army at Minas del Frío, Villegas accompanied him. Villegas subsequently participated in numerous combat actions in the Sierra, among them the battles of Las Mercedes, Las Vegas de Jibacoa, and El Jigüe. In September–October 1958, as a member of Guevara's Column no. 8, Villegas participated in the Rebel Army campaign known as the "invasion," the westward march of two columns from the Sierra Maestra to the central province of Las Villas to open a new front in the Escambray Mountains. At the end of 1958 he fought in the battles of Fomento, Cabaiguán, Placetas, Remedios, and finally the taking of Cuba's third-largest city, Santa Clara. That campaign cut the island in two and sealed the fate of the dictatorship. After thirteen months in the Rebel Army, at the end of the war Villegas held the rank of first lieutenant and was a member of Guevara's personal escort.

With the defeat of the Batista dictatorship on January 1, 1959, and the consequent deepening of the revolutionary struggle, Villegas assumed new responsibilities, serving as head of Guevara's escort. By the end of 1960, in response to Washington's escalating efforts to sabotage the Cuban economy and overturn the workers and farmers regime, all major foreign- and domestic-owned industry had been nationalized by the Cuban government. When Guevara became minister of industry in early 1961, Villegas joined him in the pressing task of restructuring industrial production and placing it on a new foundation. He participated in an intensive training course for administrators of industrial enterprises and served as head of a ceramics factory producing sanitation and other fixtures, and of a unit of the Paper and Cardboard Recycling Enterprise.

Returning to active military duty in 1962, he helped organize the Western Army and served as chief of personnel. He was part of the organizing commission for the formation of the Communist Party of Cuba, and in 1965 became a founding member.

That same year Villegas volunteered to take part in an internationalist mission in the Congo led by Guevara. From April to November 1965 the Cuban volunteers assisted revolutionary forces in that country fighting a pro-imperialist regime backed by South African and Belgian mercenary forces. During that time Guevara gave Villegas the pseudonym Pombo Pojo, meaning "green nectar" in Swahili. Pombo remained his nom de guerre through the Congo and Bolivia campaigns and later in Angola.

At the end of 1965 Villegas volunteered to join Guevara in preparing the Bolivia campaign. In July 1966 he left for La Paz as part of the advance team organizing the Latin America–wide effort that was to begin in Bolivia.

As a member of the general staff of Guevara's guerrilla unit in Bolivia in 1966–67, he served as head of services (supplies, medicine, transportation) and fought in numerous battles.

Following Guevara's death in October 1967, Villegas commanded the group of combatants that was able to elude the encirclement jointly organized by the Bolivian army and U.S. military and intelligence forces.

Upon reaching Cuba in March 1968 he rejoined the Revolutionary Armed Forces and was assigned to the Eastern Army Corps.

In line with the pledge made by the survivors of the Bolivian campaign to continue the struggle begun together with Che, Villegas resumed military training and prepared to go back to Bolivia. He was selected to be military leader under the command of Inti Peredo. Peredo's death in La Paz in 1969 at the hands of Bolivian army and police ended these plans.

In 1970 Villegas participated in Operation Mambí, part of the unsuccessful effort to achieve a historically unprecedented ten-million-ton sugar harvest in Cuba and gain the resources for more rapid economic diversification and development. Villegas also served as head of the Infantry Regiment of the Tank Division and later head of the Political Group of the Artillery Reserves of the high command of Cuba's Revolutionary Armed Forces.

In the early 1970s Villegas was named commander of the Border Brigade of Guantánamo, assigned to protect the island's territory at its border with the U.S. naval base at Guantánamo Bay, a piece of Cuba occupied by Washington against the wishes of the Cuban people since the beginning of the twentieth century. He held that responsibility for most of the decade.

Following a request in 1975 by the newly independent government of Angola for military assistance to combat a South African invasion, Villegas volunteered for the internationalist mission there, serving as commander of the Northern Front. From 1981 to 1990 he served in Angola almost continuously, during which time he participated in a number of actions, among them the battles of Cangamba and Cuito Cuanavale. While in Angola his responsibilities included acting as a liaison between the mission and the armed forces command in Havana, and later head of operations. He helped plan and organize the return of Cuban troops at the conclusion of the mission.

Harry Villegas currently holds the rank of brigadier general in the Revolutionary Armed Forces and is director of political education of the Western Army. He has received numerous decorations, among them four orders of valor and the medal of Hero of the Republic of Cuba, the country's highest honor. He is vice president of the National Commission organizing the commemoration of the thirtieth anniversary of the death of Ernesto Che Guevara and his fellow combatants.

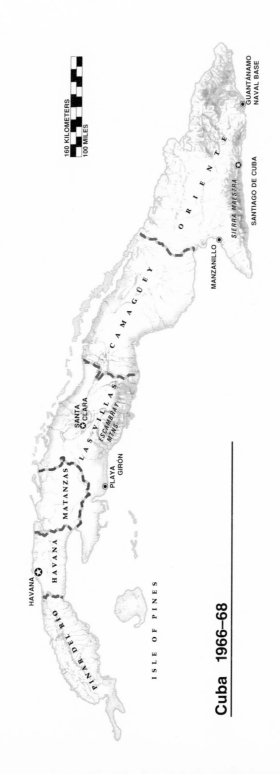

Cuba 1966–68

160 KILOMETERS
100 MILES

GUANTÁNAMO
NAVAL BASE

O R I E N T E

SANTIAGO DE CUBA

SIERRA MAESTRA

MANZANILLO

C A M A G Ü E Y

SANTA
CLARA

L A S   V I L L A S

ESCAMBRAY
MTNS.

PLAYA
GIRÓN

MATANZAS

HAVANA

HAVANA

PINAR DEL RÍO

ISLE OF PINES

Publisher's preface
to the English-language edition

Pombo: A Man of Che's guerrilla is "the story of an epic chapter in the history of the Americas," says Harry Villegas in these pages. The story tells us even more about the present and future than about the past. It needs to be told and retold today, because the importance of the struggle waged in the mid-1960s by the men and women of Che's *guerrilla* in Bolivia — the necessity of the socialist future for which they fought — has not receded with time. To the contrary, it has become more urgent than ever and to an even larger portion of humanity.

This is the story of several dozen men and women — Bolivian, Cuban, Peruvian, Argentine — whose struggle helped shape the closing decades of the twentieth century and create the foundations for the titanic battles that will mark the twenty-first. It is told through the eyes of a Cuban then still in his twenties, but already a veteran of a decade of struggle around the globe. The combatants, regardless of nationality, had all been deeply affected by the Cuban revolution and sought to emulate its example. They were fighters whose life experience, acquired habits of organization and discipline, and political understanding of history convinced them that working people little different than they can remake the world and, by the many millions, transform themselves in the process.

As Washington's bombs rained down on the people of Vietnam with ever greater destructiveness, the men and women of Che's guerrilla had the confidence to up the ante against the mightiest empire in the world and act on the intention of creating "two, three, many Vietnams." They knew the weaknesses as well as the brutal power of what Che Guevara calls "the great enemy of the human race," the imperialist government of the United States of America. Fully conscious of what they were doing, they sought to accelerate the struggle for national liberation in Latin America that culminated a few years later in massive revolutionary upsurges throughout the Southern Cone of that continent. They knew their acts would help determine the course of history.

The title of the book accurately conveys the story to be told.

This is Pombo's story, his firsthand account of the 1966–68 revolutionary campaign in Bolivia led by Ernesto Che Guevara. Harry Villegas — Pombo — today a brigadier general in Cuba's Revolutionary Armed Forces, was a member of Guevara's general staff in Bolivia. He commanded the six combatants who fought their way out of the encirclement by the U.S.-aided Bolivian armed forces in which Guevara and many others were killed. Of the two Bolivians and three Cubans who lived to continue the revolutionary struggle, he was the only one who kept a campaign diary, on which this book is based.

Aside from the extensive notes kept by Guevara, published in 1968 as his *Bolivian Diary*,[1] the only other firsthand account, which was written soon after the events, is *My Campaign with Che* by Inti Peredo, the central leader of the combatants who was Bolivian. Like Pombo, he was a member of the general staff. Peredo wrote the account in 1969 while living clandestinely in La Paz, helping to reorganize the ELN, the National Liberation Army of Bolivia, to continue the struggle. He was aided in this work by ELN combatant and Chilean journalist Elmo Catalán (*Elías*). *My Campaign with Che* was published in Bolivia and several other countries of Latin America soon after Peredo, betrayed by an informer, was wounded, captured, and murdered by the Bolivian police in September of that

---

1. *The Bolivian Diary of Ernesto Che Guevara*, Pathfinder Press, 1994.

year. It is published for the first time in English as an appendix to Pathfinder's edition of *The Bolivian Diary of Ernesto Che Guevara*. Peredo's account, however, was necessarily silent on numerous details of the combatants' escape. To have told the story then would have cost the lives of many who had aided them.

Now, with Pombo's account, we learn much more: the months of preparation, including the sharp conflicts with leaders of the Bolivian Communist Party; the aid and support from dozens of Bolivians who risked their lives to help the surviving revolutionaries as they eluded the more and more massive concentration of forces determined to bring them in dead or alive. We learn the bitter story of Ñato's death, and how the three Cuban veterans finally fought their way across the border to Chile, and from there made their way literally around the world in order to regain their homeland and continue their internationalist fight.

In October 1967, near the village of La Higuera in Bolivia, when the fact of Guevara's death was inescapably confirmed for Pombo and his co-combatants, they took an oath — each to himself, as well as to each other — to fight to stay alive in order to continue the struggle they had begun together with Che. "Your banners, which are ours, will never be lowered. Victory or death." That pledge has not only continued to guide the actions of Harry Villegas, but it embodies the internationalist commitment evident through the entire course of the leadership of the Cuban revolution: from the war against the Batista dictatorship itself, to Venezuela, to Algeria, to Vietnam, to the Congo, to Bolivia, to Angola and the battle against the apartheid invaders at Cuito Cuanavale, to Nicaragua, Grenada, and many others, to today. The most intransigent foes of the Cuban revolution in Washington and elsewhere have no doubt that if conditions allow, the revolutionary leadership of Cuba, from Fidel Castro on down, will not hesitate to act again with exactly the same internationalist selflessness.

■

Pombo's account is also a book about Ernesto Che Guevara, the Argentine-born revolutionary recruited by Fidel Castro in Mexico City in 1955 to the July 26 Movement and the nucleus of the new Rebel Army. Guevara had graduated from medical school in Buenos Aires two years earlier and spent the intervening months traveling the Americas. In the course of these travels, Guevara became a more and more serious student of Marxism and was increasingly drawn toward action consistent with his revolutionary convictions.

In Guatemala Guevara met some Cuban veterans of the July 26, 1953, assault on the military garrisons of Moncada and Bayamo. In 1954, when U.S.-organized mercenaries overthrew the regime of Guatemalan president Jacobo Arbenz after limited steps towards land reform threatened the vast interests of the U.S.-owned United Fruit Company, Guevara volunteered to join the armed resistance.

Forced to flee from Guatemala, Guevara was introduced to Castro in Mexico City and became the third confirmed member — Raúl Castro had been the second — of the expeditionary force that landed in eastern Cuba in December 1956 to relaunch the insurrectional struggle against the Batista dictatorship. Originally recruited as the troop doctor, Guevara rapidly proved himself an outstanding soldier and leader. Within months he became the first combatant selected by Castro to command a separate column.

The Cuban revolutionary war was the practical experience that transformed Guevara from a young revolutionary intellectual, in the best sense of that term, to a seasoned communist, a combat leader of men and women. As he fought side by side with the men and women of the Sierra, the Rebel Army became his school of Marxism. Through the war, working with and learning from Fidel Castro, who became increasingly recognized throughout the Americas as the central political and military leader of the struggle, Che developed the capacities that enabled him to become one of the most capable communist leaders of the twentieth century. The war, and his own discipline and study, prepared him to assume a broad range of responsibilities in the new revolutionary government that emerged following the January 1, 1959, victory over the Batista tyranny — from military commander, to president of the National Bank, to minister of industry, to international spokesperson, to organizer of volunteer work brigades, to educator, communist theorist, journalist, and party organizer.

The story of the revolutionary war and how it educated and transformed the men and women of the Rebel Army, including Che Guevara, is told with humor and eloquence in *Episodes of the Cuban Revolutionary War*, originally written by Guevara as a series of articles published in Cuba and elsewhere in the early 1960s. A new, and for the first time complete, English-language edition of that work was published by Pathfinder Press in 1996. It is indispensable reading to understand the story told by Harry Villegas in these pages. Not only Guevara and Villegas, but every one of the Cuban combatants who participated in the Bolivian campaign, were veterans of Cuba's revolutionary war, graduates of the Rebel Army's school of life, leadership, and revolutionary training.

Harry Villegas volunteered for the Rebel Army and was recruited by Guevara when he was seventeen years old. He has spent the last forty years of his life as a revolutionary determined to live up to the high standards of conduct and discipline Guevara demanded of himself and those around him. Pombo's story can be found in the pages of *At the Side of Che Guevara: Interviews with Harry Villegas*, published in English and Spanish by Pathfinder Press, 1997.

Villegas fought at Guevara's side in every campaign commanded by Che from 1957 on. He belonged to Rebel Army column no. 4 in the Sierra Maestra mountains of eastern Cuba; he took part in the 1958 march across several provinces of eastern and central Cuba by Rebel Army column no. 8 to establish a new front in the Escambray mountains; he fought in the battles that ended January 1, 1959, with the capture of Santa Clara, Cuba's third-largest city, and sealed the fate of the Batista dictatorship; he joined Guevara in the 1965 internationalist mission to aid the anti-imperialist forces in the Congo, and he was part of the general staff of the 1966–68 revolutionary campaign in Bolivia.

For more than half a decade, Villegas commanded the troops that guard Cuba's border with the U.S.-held Guantánamo naval base in eastern Cuba.

Between 1975 and 1990 Villegas volunteered for three tours of duty in Angola, where Cuban military forces, at the request of the newly independent government, helped turn back repeated invasion attempts by the apartheid regime of South Africa and armed assaults by imperialist-backed counterrevolutionary groups.

Pombo's story — written through the eyes and experiences of an individual combatant — *is* the story of the Cuban revolution.

■

"Let it be known that we have measured the scope of our acts and that we consider ourselves no more than a part of the great army of the proletariat." Those words of Guevara, part of his "Message to the Tricontinental," penned as he prepared to leave for Bolivia, are reprinted in this volume. It was his last major political writing, in which he examines the world political situation and explains the course of revolutionary action he and his comrades will follow in Bolivia.

Che's *guerrilla* — like the Rebel Army and militias before it, and the Red Army born of the October Revolution — was a nucleus of the international proletarian army referred to in the "Message to the Tricontinental."

In Guevara's as yet unpublished "Notes on the Revolutionary War in the Congo" he explains this even more precisely. The volunteers from Cuba who went to the Congo to fight along-

side and help train the anti-imperialist fighters there, Che
writes, were drawn by nothing except ties of proletarian internationalism. He then adds: "They were initiating something
new in modern wars of liberation: *the creation of an international
proletarian army*, through having experienced people fighting
alongside [less seasoned combatants] in battles for liberation
and, later on, against reaction."

"We never envisioned a sectarian undertaking," Villegas
states in his introduction. "Such a conception would have
been impossible not only on a Bolivian scale, but above all on
a continental scale. Our idea was to create a broad revolutionary movement that would draw in all honest individuals prepared to struggle for social justice, together with all revolutionary organizations, parties, and sectors of the people."

"Che's *guerrilla*" invites an easy but misleading translation
into English as simply "Che's guerrillas." But for Che, *la
guerrilla* was more than an armed unit or the summation of
individual fighters. It was the organic political nucleus
through whose actions and example — as well as actions related to it — the entire revolutionary movement and its cadres
would be differentiated, reconstructed, and transformed, in
the cities, towns, and countryside as well as within the guerrilla nucleus. That political content is subtly lost in the translation, "Che's guerrillas." For the title of this English edition
of Pombo's account, therefore, we decided to use the familiar
and understandable term Villegas chose for the original
Spanish: *Pombo: un hombre de la guerrilla del Che*.

Most readers of this English-language edition who will find
themselves devouring the pages of Pombo's account were not yet
born when the events recorded here took place. Those readers
especially will find themselves drawn to the record that Pombo's
account supplements, *The Bolivian Diary of Ernesto Che Guevara*,
together with its "Necessary Introduction" by Fidel Castro.[2]

---

2. Pathfinder Press, 1994.

■

The first notebook of Pombo's Bolivian diary fell into the hands of Bolivian military forces on October 8, 1967, when Guevara was wounded and taken prisoner. He was murdered in cold blood by his captors the following day. In his introduction, Villegas describes how a typed transcript of his first notebook was sent to Cuba in March 1968. Along with a microfilm copy of Guevara's captured diary, it had been smuggled out of Bolivia with the knowledge and aid of Bolivian interior minister Antonio Arguedas.

The transcript of Pombo's notes was translated and published in English in July 1968 as part of a book entitled *The Complete Bolivian Diary of Ché Guevara and Other Captured Documents*. Stein and Day, the U.S. publishers of the book, claimed they had been granted "exclusive literary rights" by Bolivia's military dictatorship. In light of the document's origins, obvious distortions, and incongruous passages, the version made public by Bolivian and U.S. military intelligence, later published in Spanish in Bolivia and elsewhere, was of limited use to those who sought the truth about the events in Bolivia.

With the publication of *Pombo: un hombre de la guerrilla del Che*, those obstacles are cleared away. The first part of this volume is the text of the diary, revised and corrected by the author himself, who used, among other things, the typed version released in 1968, his own notes and recollections, and other documents and reports of the time — but still without ever having had access to his original handwritten notes. Fighters who seek to learn from the strengths and victories of the revolutionaries who fought in Bolivia, as well as from their errors, now have a document on which they can rely.

■

The Pathfinder English-language edition could not have been prepared without the generous collaboration of Gen. Harry

Villegas, who gave many hours of his time to review maps, identify photos, explain words and phrases that were difficult to translate, and answer numerous questions.

Rodolfo Saldaña, one of the Bolivian revolutionaries who carried central responsibilities in the clandestine urban support network, provided invaluable help.

Aleida March, Che's widow and comrade-in-arms, clarified a number of details. Information provided by Manuel Piñeiro, Armando Campos, and Rafael Salas (*Santiago*) of the Americas division of the Department of International Relations of the Central Committee of the Cuban Communist Party enabled the editors to provide annotation that is more complete and thus more accurate than would have otherwise been possible.

The assistance of Editora Política, the publishing house of the Central Committee of the Communist Party of Cuba, was indispensable, especially the care and attention to detail of Iraida Aguirrechu, editor-in-chief of the current affairs department. Ana Rosa Gort reviewed portions of the translation.

Many of the historic photos came from the archives of Editora Política; others were located by Delfín Xiqués, director of the archives of the newspaper *Granma*.

Pathfinder is also appreciative of the photos provided by Richard Dindo, director of the film *Ernesto Che Guevara: The Bolivian Diary*. A number of these, including the photo of Guevara and Pombo used on the cover of this edition, were taken by the revolutionary combatants in Bolivia themselves and subsequently seized by the Bolivian military, some of whose officers have trafficked in these murderously acquired goods for three decades.

Translation of the English-language edition was supervised and edited by Michael Taber, who also drafted the extensive annotation, chronology, and glossary. Michael Baumann organized production of the book. The team of translators who volunteered their skills and efforts included Marty Anderson, Susan Apstein, Seth Galinsky, Mariposa

Geller, Joya Lonsdale, Harvey McArthur, Aaron Ruby, and Matilde Zimmermann.

Book, photo-signature, and cover design are by Eric Simpson, who, together with Harvey McArthur, also prepared the many maps.

■

In the closing months of the Bolivian campaign, as the weeks passed and still the Bolivian and Cuban combatants managed to elude the manhunt organized by the regime's U.S.-trained forces, the stature of the revolutionaries grew. In the popular culture of Bolivia, as well as in the minds of their military foes, the guerrillas who had fought their way out of the encirclement assumed mythic proportions. Pombo himself, we learn in the pages that follow, was believed to be "a Black man of tremendous size who fought with two machine guns, one in each hand."

As with many popular myths, this one was not without foundation.

"You are alive because you were aggressive, because you fought," Fidel Castro told the three Cuban combatants when they arrived back in Havana in March 1968. "Had you been scared, had you shown fear, you would have perished. It is precisely your ability to resist, your capacity to fight, that shows your revolutionary strength and conviction."

That example, the example of the Cuban revolution, is what *Pombo: A Man of Che's guerrilla*, has to offer to new generations of fighters around the world. Now those millions of workers and youth whose reading language is English can make this chronicle their own.

Mary-Alice Waters
May 1997

Introduction

THIS INTRODUCTION to the English-language edition of my diary and account of the Bolivian campaign is appearing more than thirty years after the first entry was written. I began keeping the diary in July 1966, and the last entry of the first notebook is dated May 28, 1967. I later continued my diary in other notebooks, until my return to Cuba in March 1968.

On April 19, 1967, Commander Ernesto Che Guevara ordered that all the diaries kept by members of the guerrilla unit, together with other documents, be collected and held for safekeeping in a knapsack I carried. (On that day a British journalist had given us a false report that very dangerous internal information had leaked out. The cause of this, the journalist said, was Braulio's diary, supposedly found in the main camp by the Bolivian army.) The diaries would then be taken out, updated, and in a disciplined manner returned to the place Che ordered them kept. In fairness, it should be said that Che was visibly irritated to have to take this step. But he did not want those personal notebooks to endanger the rigorous security measures the initial guerrilla force needed to maintain under extremely adverse circumstances.[1]

In his "Necessary Introduction" to *The Bolivian Diary of Ernesto Che Guevara*, Commander in Chief Fidel Castro re-

---

1. For Guevara's account of this incident see *The Bolivian Diary Diary of Ernesto Che Guevara* (New York: Pathfinder, 1994), pp. 175–78.

ferred to these measures in commenting on the rigor and discipline that were essential at those moments, as well as the
criticisms, often severe and frank, that are a necessary part of
the first stage of creating a small nucleus of combatants such
as ours. It was necessary to prevent the slightest act of carelessness, Fidel said, however insignificant it might appear. At
the same time, criticism would serve to educate the combatants, while appealing — as Che always did — to the honor
and dignity of each one of us.[2]

On October 8, 1967, the first booklet containing my notes
was captured together with Che's diary and other documents.
It was transcribed in Bolivia. In 1968 Antonio Arguedas, Bolivia's minister of the interior at the time, sent a typed copy of
the notes to Cuba. The original, which I did not receive a
photographic copy of, remained in Bolivia, in the custody of
the army high command.

Almost thirteen years later, on July 17, 1980, Division General Luis García Meza seized power in a military coup and assumed the presidency of a junta that lasted until the end of
1981, when it was succeeded by other military governments
that ruled Bolivia until October 1982. During the time he held
power, García Meza sold the original of Che's diary and the
first notebook of mine to British dealer Erick Galantiere, who
was given the diaries on December 15, 1980, along with
"exclusive written authorization . . . to sell the diaries of Che
and Pombo." The British businessman closed the deal on February 25, 1981, with "a certified check for the total agreed
amount."[3]

In 1984 Galantiere sold the documents to the British firm
Sotheby's, which informed the world that the documents
were in its possession and would be put up for public auction,
with a minimum asking price of approximately $400,000.

---

2. Castro's "A Necessary Introduction" is contained in the Pathfinder edition of
   The Bolivian Diary, pp. 51–70.
3. From letter of Div. Gen. Luis García Meza to Erick Galantiere, December 15,
   1980, and letter of Galantiere to García Meza, February 25, 1981.

Bolivian journalist Humberto Vacaflor denounced both the illegal sale and the subsequent announcement they would be auctioned off. Faced with charges of illegal possession of the documents and international indignation over these events, plans for the auction stalled. In 1986, following measures taken during a trip to Britain, Bolivia's minister of foreign relations, Guillermo Bedregal Gutiérrez, succeeded in getting the diaries back through official diplomatic channels — an event that was noted by the international press at the time. The originals of the diaries were then placed in box A-73 of the vault of the Central Bank of Bolivia, under the custody of the Bolivian foreign ministry.

From May 28, 1967, through the end of the Bolivian campaign, I was able to continue my diary. I kept it up until the arrival of the group of survivors in Chile, on whose fraternal soil we were warmly received. Later, through the determined and valiant efforts of the late president Salvador Allende — then a senator of the Socialist Party of Chile — comrades in Chile sent me the three notebooks I had kept during the latter stage.

Many years lapsed between those events and the publication of the first Cuban edition of this book, brought out by Editora Política at the beginning of 1996. A number of clarifications are therefore necessary to help place the diary in context.

After returning to Cuba, I gave a series of talks in the La Cabaña military fortress to my comrades in arms, using as a guide and reference my diary of nearly twenty months of guerrilla and clandestine struggle. For part two of the present edition, I have based myself on those talks, with the aim of rounding out these historical recollections. I have summarized part of what I presented at the time. This is the first time the material is being published in its entirety.

Observations and comments written three decades ago in the heat of the struggle may appear harsh and full of passion. I am indeed struck by this today when I reread and relive some of the passages. At all times, however, the diary reflects

the critical spirit, expressed in language that is frank and direct, straight to the point, in which we were educated by
Commander Che Guevara. This was undoubtedly among the
greatest lessons we received in his incomparable school.

In making revisions to the transcript of the first notebook of
my diary previously published outside Cuba — based on my
notes and on documents of the time — I am not attempting to
alter or modify what was written in the heat of struggle. My
aim, rather, is to clarify the words, commentaries, and ideas
that were misunderstood, or were deliberately distorted,
when the diary was transcribed. By doing so, I hope that the
comments recorded in the diary can be seen in accurate historic dimension, reflecting the reality, grandeur, and truth of
the events themselves. Distortions of historic reality in previous editions of the diary have been corrected.

It is necessary to make a few comments on the political and
historical circumstances that existed at the time the diary was
written. On the international level, the years 1966 and 1967
were marked by an escalation of one of the most horrendous
crimes humanity has ever witnessed: the aggression against
the people of Vietnam, a small but unflinchingly heroic
country, by the strongest imperialist power on earth.

This genocide expressed, in all its cruelty, the U.S. government course of using force to impose its criminal interests of
domination, plunder, and exploitation wherever in the world
these interests were seriously threatened.

In Vietnam they applied a new strategy of military intervention known as "flexible response." The old doctrine of "massive
retaliation," which included the threat or use of atomic weapons, had ceased being effective in a world characterized by nuclear parity with the Soviet Union and by the advance of
struggles for national liberation on an international scale. The
triumph of the Cuban revolution on January 1, 1959, and its
influence in the hemisphere, foretold new victories.

The empire then tried to develop and apply a new mode of aggression providing for appropriate differentiated responses to

small conflicts, to local wars, to struggles for national liberation, and even to a possible nuclear confrontation and holocaust.

In the end, "flexible response" was simply another term for imperialism's efforts to continue unleashing all its power in acts of extermination against movements for national liberation and their leaders, which by then were active in the underdeveloped countries of Asia, Africa, and Latin America. There has been nothing new under the sun since the term "thieving eagle" was coined by our national hero José Martí at the end of the last century to refer to the U.S. policy of expansion, intervention, and conquest. Cubans are quite familiar with these acts by the empire. With regard to Cuba, the first U.S. moves toward annexation date back to 1803, when the United States had barely established itself as an independent state.

In his 1966 "Message to the Tricontinental,"[4] Che made a thorough and deep-going analysis of this policy of imperialist domination. At the same time he expounded, in all their strategic and continental dimensions, his anti-imperialist ideas and course of action that by then were already being put into practice through his own personal example. In that message, Che proclaimed: "Our every action is a battle cry against imperialism and a call for the unity of the peoples against the great enemy of the human race: the United States of North America."

This deep conviction of the Heroic Guerrilla concerning the role played by the United States was rooted in the innumerable acts of imperial aggression that make up the history of contemporary colonialism and neocolonialism in this hemisphere. To mention only a few examples of bloody interventions in our century, there are the cases of Mexico, Guatemala, the Dominican Republic, Panama, Haiti, and Cuba.[5]

---

4. Reprinted in this volume on pages 37–55.
5. U.S. military operations took place against Mexico in 1914, 1916, and 1918; Guatemala in 1904, 1920, and 1954; the Dominican Republic in 1904, 1912–14, 1916–24, and 1965; Panama in 1903, 1908, 1912, 1918, 1919–20, 1925, and 1989; Haiti in 1914, 1915–34, and 1994; and Cuba in 1898–1902, 1906–9, 1912, 1961, and 1962.

The continent as a whole has experienced the varied forms through which this imperialist policy has been systematically implemented. Neocolonialism has left its imprint of economic and political domination and deep social crisis, with its resulting hunger, poverty, unemployment, marginalization, and devastation. An entire region has been ravaged by foreign control over its natural resources and products, the exploitation of its workers, and the sharp impoverishment of its economies. Tribute is exacted in ways that violate the sovereignty of the nations of Latin America, pillage their material and spiritual patrimony, deepen their dependence and subjugation to imperialism, and close off possibilities of development and progress.

Together with a handful of heroic Bolivian, Peruvian, and Cuban combatants who accompanied him to Bolivia, Che fought to change this reality of the 1960s — a reality whose cruel mechanisms of plunder have since been deepened and refined. Che's death resounds vividly in his stirring message to revolutionaries around the world:

"Wherever death may surprise us, let it be welcome if our battle cry has reached even one receptive ear, if another hand reaches out to take up our arms, and other men come forward to join in our funeral dirge with the rattling of machine guns and with new cries of battle and victory."[6]

With the new century virtually upon us, this image of Che remains present in the revolutionary dreams of Latin Americans. Among them are receptive ears.

The apostle of Cuba's independence, José Martí, also conceived of a continent-wide anti-imperialist struggle. On the eve of his death in combat, in his last letter to a Mexican friend, Martí was unambiguous:

"I am in danger each day now of giving my life for my country and for my duty — because I understand that duty and am eager to carry it out — of preventing the United States, as Cuba

6. See page 55.

obtains her independence, from extending its control over the Antilles and consequently falling with that much more force upon our countries of America. Whatever I have done till now, and whatever I shall do, has been with that aim."

Simón Bolívar, Miranda, O'Higgins, San Martín, and other great figures of Latin America's independence struggle also raised the ideal of a free and united Latin America.

Che's dream was the dream of Martí and Bolívar. In elaborating his strategy, given the struggles already under way in different countries of the continent, Che envisioned the possibility of forming a guerrilla nucleus, a mother column that would pass through the necessary and difficult stage of survival and development. Later on it would give birth to new guerrilla columns extending outward toward the Southern Cone of Latin America,[7] giving continuity to a battle that would become continent-wide in scope. He took into account the experience of the mother column in Cuba's Sierra Maestra mountains, which gave rise to new guerrilla columns and fronts, culminating in the defeat of the Batista dictatorship and the victory of the Cuban revolution.

Totally convinced that the political conditions were ripening and that this perspective was realizable, Commander Che Guevara carried out his plans and initiated actions to open a path toward victory. In his view, victory was certain to the degree that the struggle extended as far as possible throughout Latin America.

Never has such a small group of individuals undertaken an enterprise of such gigantic proportions. That small detachment of heroic combatants was Che's "sling of David." As our commander in chief pointed out, Che did not outlive his ideas, he enriched them with his blood.[8]

Following the conclusion of his internationalist activity in

7. The countries of the Southern Cone are Argentina, Bolivia, Chile, Paraguay, and Uruguay.
8. Fidel Castro, "A Necessary Introduction" to the Bolivian Diary, p. 58.

the Congo, and given the confrontation unfolding in Latin America at the time, Che chose Bolivia as the place from which to inititate his strategic course in Latin America.

One factor behind Che's selection was his analysis of the Bolivian people's combative traditions going all the way back to the fight of the indigenous peoples against the royalists, to the so-called little republics.[9] (We learned about this epoch initially through the book *Santa Juana de América*, which vividly describes the battles by the Indians with primitive weapons against much more powerful forces.) With its mixture of victories and defeats, courage and fears, this chapter in history resembled Bolivia in the 1960s. Students, peasants, miners, and workers all fought heroically, under the noteworthy leadership of the Central Organization of Bolivian Workers (COB), against the new version of the conquistadors, and the growing poverty, misery, and marginalization of the majority of the people. Bolivia's geographic characteristics and continental location figured in the selection, as well.

Another factor that weighed heavily for Che was the nature of the Bolivian Communist Party, which had shown signs of determination during the popular battles taking place in those days. The party had also demonstrated its solidarity with revolutionary efforts for national liberation in neighboring countries. This included its backing for the Peruvian ELN (National Liberation Army), which began actions in Puerto Maldonado; its support to the combatants in Argentina led by Jorge Ricardo Masetti (*Comandante Segundo*); and its solidarity with the young Cuban revolution.[10]

---

9. During Bolivia's independence war of the early nineteenth century, the largely indigenous guerrilla fighters set up six enclaves that became known as the "little republics."

10. In May 1963 a group of fighters led by Javier Heraud entered Peru from Bolivian territory, where they had received assistance from members of the Bolivian CP. After making their way to Puerto Maldonado in Peru, the guerrillas were crushed by the Peruvian police and Heraud was killed.

The Bolivian Communist Party was assigned an important role in the complex preparatory stage of organizing our efforts in that country. Under those difficult circumstances, different points of view were being debated within the party over the conception held by the leadership regarding the struggle and the possible forms it would assume. These differences are reflected in the discussions we were compelled to have with them on this subject, given our responsibilities during that initial time and because that organization's participation and support were essential to us.

For these reasons, the observations I made in my diary on these discussions recorded the justifiable condemnation of conduct by party leaders that appeared to us improper given the historic moment in which we were living. Such was the case with Mario Monje, the party's general secretary, whose conduct contrasted with that of true communists like Coco and Inti Peredo, among others. The diary also reflects the firm conviction and internationalist fervor of our efforts for the national liberation of Latin America, as well as the real possibilities that existed for achieving that objective. The diary reflects our conviction that the struggle we were initiating would increasingly widen those possibilities. The precondition for this was to overcome the hard and difficult stage in which the guerrilla unit struggled to survive, in order to develop later on along the lines conceived by Che.

We never envisioned a sectarian undertaking. Such a conception would have been impossible not only on a Bolivian scale, but above all on a continental scale. Our idea was to create a broad revolutionary movement that would draw in all honest individuals prepared to struggle for social justice, together with all revolutionary organizations, parties, and sectors

---

A guerrilla nucleus in the Salta mountains of northern Argentina functioned from late 1963 to early 1964, led by Jorge Ricardo Masetti (*Comandante Segundo*). Members of the Bolivian CP provided logistical support along the border. In early 1964 the Argentine guerrillas were wiped out by government troops. Masetti was killed.

of the people. This was the basis on which the ELN (National Liberation Army) was formed, as is made clear by its five public communiqués, containing information and appeals addressed to the Bolivian people.[11]

Examining the events recorded in Che's Bolivian diary and in my own, one can see how relations were established not only with different political forces within Bolivia and their representatives, but also with leaders and representatives of other political organizations of the continent. These contacts and relations would inexorably lead to an expansion of ties with other progressive forces in the region provided that the struggle intensified and succeeded in surviving the initial phase, which imposed severe restrictions on contacts and communications.

My only hope is that the recollections contained in my diary give a true picture of the war in Bolivia. This was a confrontation carried out by a group of men true to their ideas. They fought a professional army equipped by the United States and aided by the CIA — starting with the country's president René Barrientos and extending to phony journalists, officers, soldiers, and peasant infiltrators. The participation of U.S. Rangers and agents from the CIA's station in La Paz and its general headquarters in the United States was, of course, direct and open.

I present these materials for the consideration of the reader. They tell the story of an epic chapter in the history of the Americas. I believe they will be of use to young people who wish to study the life and work of the Heroic Guerrilla. It is my hope that these youth get a better understanding and appreciation of the times we are living through and of the greatness of the human values embodied in Che's life, expressed through his early and lifelong decision to fight for humanity.

Che taught us many lessons, which were passed on to us through his practical activity. In Cuba he, also, had the pos-

11. These are printed elsewhere in this volume.

sibility of learning, of self-improvement. One of the virtues he acquired from contact with our people was confidence in victory, faith in human beings, and the deepest sense of loyalty. I am certain that he was true to what he stated in his letter of farewell,[12] and that his last thoughts were of our commander in chief, Fidel Castro.

Brigadier General Harry Villegas
February 1997

---

12. Guevara's 1965 letter to Fidel Castro, written right before he left Cuba, is published in Pathfinder's edition of Guevara's *Bolivian Diary* on pages 71–73.

Create two, three . . . many Vietnams – that is the watchword

Ernesto Che Guevara

*"It is the hour of the furnace,
and the light is all that can be seen."*

José Martí

TWENTY-ONE YEARS HAVE ELAPSED since the end of the last world conflagration, and various publications in every language are celebrating this event, symbolized by the defeat of Japan. A climate of optimism is apparent in many sectors of the different camps into which the world is divided.

Twenty-one years without a world war in these days of maximum confrontations, of violent clashes and abrupt turns, appears to be a very high number. All of us declare our readi-

---

In April 1965 Guevara resigned his political, military, and government posts and responsibilities in Cuba in order to lend his experience and leadership abilities to revolutionary struggles in other parts of the world — from the Congo to Bolivia. This message, Guevara's last major political article, was written prior to the opening of the revolutionary campaign in Bolivia in November 1966. It was addressed to the Organization of Solidarity of the Peoples of Asia, Africa, and Latin America (OSPAAAL, also referred to as the Tricontinental), which was established at a January 1966 conference in Havana. It was published on April 16, 1967, in a special inaugural edition of Tricontinental *magazine, published by the Executive Secretariat of OSPAAAL. It appeared there under Guevara's title, "Create Two, Three . . . Many Vietnams — That Is the Watchword."*

ness to fight for this peace. But without analyzing its practical results (poverty, degradation, constantly increasing exploitation of enormous sectors of humanity), it is appropriate to ask whether this peace is real.

The purpose of these notes is not to write the history of the various conflicts of a local character that have followed one after another since Japan's surrender. Nor is it our task to recount the numerous and growing instances of civil strife that have occurred in these years of supposed peace. It is enough to point to the wars in Korea and Vietnam as examples to counter the boundless optimism.

In Korea, after years of ferocious struggle, the northern part of the country was left submerged in the most terrible devastation in the annals of modern war: riddled with bombs; without factories, schools, or hospitals; without any kind of housing to shelter 10 million inhabitants.

Dozens of countries intervened in that war, led militarily by the United States, under the false banner of the United Nations, with the massive participation of U.S. troops and the use of the conscripted South Korean people as cannon fodder. On the other side, the army and people of Korea and the volunteers from the People's Republic of China received supplies and advice from the Soviet military apparatus. The United States carried out all kinds of tests of weapons of destruction, excluding thermonuclear ones, but including bacteriological and chemical weapons on a limited scale.

In Vietnam a war has been waged almost without interruption by the patriotic forces of that country against three imperialist powers: Japan, whose might plummeted after the bombings of Hiroshima and Nagasaki; France, which recovered its Indochinese colonies from that defeated country, disregarding the promises made at a time of duress; and the United States, in the latest phase of the conflict.

There have been limited confrontations on all continents, even though on the Latin American continent there were for a long time only attempts at freedom struggles and military coups d'état, until the Cuban revolution sounded its clarion call, signaling the importance of this region and attracting the wrath of the imperialists, compelling Cuba to defend its coasts first at Playa Girón and then during the October crisis.[1]

The latter incident could have touched off a war of incalculable proportions if a U. S.-Soviet clash had occurred over the Cuban question.

Right now, however, the contradictions are clearly centered in the territories of the Indochinese peninsula and the neighboring countries. Laos and Vietnam were shaken by conflicts that ceased to be civil wars when U.S. imperialism intervened with all its power, and the whole region became a lit fuse, leading to a powder keg. In Vietnam the confrontation has taken on an extremely sharp character. It is not our intention to go into the history of this war either. We will just point out some milestones.

In 1954, after the crushing defeat [of the French forces] at Dien Bien Phu, the Geneva accords were signed, dividing

---

1. On April 17, 1961, 1,500 Cuban mercenaries invaded Cuba at the Bay of Pigs on the southern coast. The mercenaries, organized and financed by Washington, aimed to declare a provisional government to appeal for direct U.S. intervention. However, the invaders were defeated within seventy-two hours by Cuba's militia and its Revolutionary Armed Forces. On April 19 the last invaders surrendered at Playa Girón (Girón Beach), which is the name Cubans use to designate the battle. The day before the abortive invasion, at a mass rally called to honor those killed or wounded in U.S.-organized air attacks on Havana, Santiago de Cuba, and San Antonio de los Baños, Fidel Castro had proclaimed the socialist character of the revolution in Cuba and called the people of Cuba to arms in its defense.

Amid escalating preparations by Washington for a new invasion of Cuba in the spring and summer of 1962, the Cuban government signed a mutual defense agreement with the Soviet Union. In October 1962 President Kennedy demanded removal of Soviet nuclear missiles installed in Cuba following the signing of that pact. Washington ordered a naval blockade of Cuba, stepped up its preparations to invade, and placed U.S. armed forces on nuclear alert. Cuban workers and farmers mobilized in the millions to defend the revolution. Following an exchange of communications between Washington and Moscow, Soviet premier Nikita Khrushchev, without consulting the Cuban government, announced his decision to remove the missiles on October 28.

Vietnam into two zones with the stipulation that elections would be held in eighteen months to determine who would govern the country and how it would be reunified. The United States did not sign that document, but began maneuvering to replace Emperor Bao Dai, a French puppet, with a man who fit their aims. He turned out to be Ngo Dinh Diem, whose tragic end — that of a lemon squeezed dry by imperialism — is known to everyone.[2]

In the months following the signing of the accords, optimism reigned in the camp of the popular forces. They dismantled military positions of the anti-French struggle in the southern part of the country and waited for the agreement to be carried out. But the patriots soon realized that there would be no elections unless the United States felt capable of imposing its will at the ballot box, something it could not do even with all its methods of electoral fraud.

The struggles in the southern part of the country began once again, and these have been gaining in intensity. Today the U.S. army has grown to almost a half-million invaders, while the puppet forces decline in number and, above all, have totally lost the will to fight.

It has been about two years since the United States began the systematic bombing of the Democratic Republic of Vietnam in yet another attempt to halt the fighting spirit in the South and to impose a conference from a position of strength. At the beginning, the bombings were more or less isolated occurrences, carried out in the guise of reprisals for alleged provocations from the North. Then their intensity and regularity increased, until they became one gigantic onslaught by the U.S. air force carried out day after day, with the purpose of destroying every vestige of civilization in the northern zone of the country. It is one episode in the sadly notorious escalation.

2. South Vietnamese dictator Ngo Dinh Diem was assassinated on November 1, 1963, at the instigation of Washington, which was dissatisfied with his regime's inability to counter the military and political successes of the National Liberation Front.

The material aims of the Yankee world have been achieved in good part despite the valiant defense put up by the Vietnamese antiaircraft batteries, the more than 1,700 planes brought down, and the aid in military supplies from the socialist camp.

This is the painful reality: Vietnam, a nation representing the aspirations and hopes for victory of all the world's disinherited, is tragically alone. This people must endure the pounding of U.S. technology — in the south almost without defenses, in the north with some possibilities of defense — but always alone.

The solidarity of the progressive world with the Vietnamese people has something of the bitter irony of the plebeians cheering on the gladiators in the Roman Circus. To wish the victim success is not enough; one must share his fate. One must join him in death or in victory.

When we analyze the isolation of the Vietnamese, we are overcome by anguish at this illogical moment in the history of humanity. U.S. imperialism is guilty of aggression. Its crimes are immense, extending over the whole world. We know this, gentlemen! But also guilty are those who at the decisive moment hesitated to make Vietnam an inviolable part of socialist territory — yes, at the risk of a war of global scale, but also compelling the U.S. imperialists to make a decision. And also guilty are those who persist in a war of insults and tripping each other up, begun quite some time ago by the representatives of the two biggest powers in the socialist camp.

Let us ask, seeking an honest answer: Is Vietnam isolated or not, as it tries to maintain a dangerous balancing act between the two quarreling powers?

And what greatness has been shown by this people! What a stoic and courageous people! And what a lesson for the world their struggle holds.

It will be a long time before we know if President Johnson ever seriously intended to initiate some of the reforms needed by his people — to sandpaper the class contradictions that are appearing with explosive force and mounting frequency. What is certain is that the improvements announced under the pompous title of the Great Society have gone down the drain in Vietnam. The greatest of the imperialist powers is feeling in its own bowels the bleeding inflicted by a poor, backward country; its fabulous economy is strained by the war effort. Killing has ceased to be the most comfortable business for the monopolies.

Defensive weapons, and not in sufficient number, are all these marvelous Vietnamese soldiers have besides love for their country, for their society, and a courage that stands up to all tests. But imperialism is bogged down in Vietnam. It sees no way out and is searching desperately for one that will permit it to emerge with dignity from the dangerous situation in which it finds itself. The "four points" put forward by the North and the "five" by the South have it caught in a pincers, however, making the confrontation still more decisive.

Everything seems to indicate that peace, the precarious peace that bears that name only because no global con-flagration has occurred, is again in danger of being broken by some irreversible and unacceptable step taken by the United States.

What is the role that we, the exploited of the world, must play?

The peoples of three continents are watching and learning a lesson for themselves in Vietnam. Since the imperialists are using the threat of war to blackmail humanity, the correct re-sponse is not to fear war. Attack hard and without letup at every point of confrontation — that must be the general tactic of the peoples.

But in those places where this miserable peace that we en-dure has not been broken, what shall our task be?

To liberate ourselves at any price.

The world panorama is one of great complexity. The task of winning liberation still lies ahead even for some countries of old Europe, sufficiently developed to experience all the contradictions of capitalism but so weak that they can no longer follow the course of imperialism or embark on that road. In those countries the contradictions will become explosive in the coming years. But their problems, and hence their solutions, are different from those facing our dependent and economically backward peoples.

The fundamental field of imperialist exploitation covers the three backward continents — Latin America, Asia, and Africa. Each country has its own characteristics, but the continents, as a whole, have their own as well.

Latin America constitutes a more or less homogeneous whole, and in almost its entire territory U.S. monopoly capital holds absolute primacy. The puppet — or, in the best of cases, weak and timid — governments are unable to resist the orders of the Yankee master. The United States has reached virtually the pinnacle of its political and economic domination. There is little room left for it to advance; any change in the situation could turn into a step backward from its primacy. Its policy is to maintain its conquests. The course of action is reduced at the present time to the brutal use of force to prevent liberation movements of any kind.

Behind the slogan "We will not permit another Cuba" hides the possibility of cowardly acts of aggression they can get away with — such as the one against the Dominican Republic;[3] or, before that, the massacre in Panama[4] and the clear warning that Yankee troops are ready to intervene anywhere in Latin America where a change in the established order endangers their interests. This policy enjoys almost absolute im-

3. In April 1965 24,000 U.S. troops were sent to the Dominican Republic to crush a popular uprising against the regime there backed by Washington. The Organization of American States later added its support, and a handful of Latin American countries sent troops to join the U.S.-led effort.

4. In January 1964 U.S. forces opened fire on Panamanian students demonstrating in the U.S.-occupied Canal Zone, sparking several days of street fighting. More than twenty Panamanians were killed and three hundred were wounded.

punity. The OAS [Organization of American States] is a convenient mask, no matter how discredited it is. The UN's ineffectiveness borders on the ridiculous or the tragic. The armies of all the countries of Latin America are ready to intervene to crush their own people. What has been formed, in fact, is the International of Crime and Betrayal.

On the other hand, the indigenous bourgeoisies have lost all capacity to oppose imperialism — if they ever had any — and are only dragged along behind it like a caboose. There are no other alternatives. Either a socialist revolution or a caricature of revolution.

Asia is a continent with different characteristics. The liberation struggles against a series of European colonial powers resulted in the establishment of more or less progressive governments, whose subsequent evolution has in some cases deepened the main objectives of national liberation, and in others reverted toward proimperialist positions.

From the economic point of view, the United States had little to lose and much to gain in Asia. Changes work to its favor; it is struggling to displace other neocolonial powers, to penetrate new spheres of action in the economic field, sometimes directly, sometimes utilizing Japan.

But special political conditions exist there, above all in the Indochinese peninsula, that give Asia characteristics of major importance and that play an important role in the global military strategy of U.S. imperialism. The latter is imposing a blockade around China utilizing South Korea, Japan, Taiwan, South Vietnam, and Thailand, at a minimum.

This dual situation — a strategic interest as important as the military blockade of the People's Republic of China, and the ambition of U.S. capital to penetrate those big markets it does not yet dominate — makes Asia one of the most explosive places in the world today, despite the apparent stability outside of the Vietnamese area.

Belonging geographically to this continent, but with its own contradictions, the Middle East is at the boiling point. It is not possible to foresee what the cold war between Israel, which is backed by the imperialists, and the progressive countries of this region will lead to. It is another one of the threatening volcanoes in the world.[5]

Africa appears almost like virgin territory for neocolonial invasion. Changes have occurred that, to a certain degree, have compelled the neocolonial powers to give up their former absolute prerogatives. But when the processes continue without interruption to their conclusion, colonialism gives way without violence to a neocolonialism, with the same consequences in regard to economic domination.

The United States did not have colonies in this region and is now struggling to penetrate its partners' old private preserves. It can be said with certainty that Africa constitutes a long-term reservoir in the strategic plans of U.S. imperialism. Its current investments there are of importance only in the Union of South Africa, and it is beginning its penetration of the Congo, Nigeria, and other countries, where a violent competition is opening up (of a peaceful nature up to now) with other imperialist powers. It does not yet have big interests to defend except its alleged right to intervene any place on the globe where its monopolies smell good profits or the existence of big reserves of raw materials. All this background makes it legitimate to pose a question about the possibilities for the liberation of the peoples in the short or medium term.

If we analyze Africa, we see that there are struggles of some intensity in the Portuguese colonies of Guinea, Mozambique, and Angola, with particular success in Guinea and varying successes in the other two.[6] We are also still witnessing a

5. In June 1967 the Israeli regime, backed by Washington, launched a simultaneous attack on Egypt, Jordan, and Syria. In the course of the war Israel seized and occupied the Sinai Peninsula, the West Bank, and the Golan Heights, leading to further intensification of Palestinian resistance.

6. After years of armed struggle, Guinea was to win independence from Portugal in 1974; Mozambique and Angola followed in 1975.

struggle between Lumumba's successors and the old accomplices of Tshombe in the Congo, a struggle that appears at the moment to be leaning in favor of the latter, who have "pacified" a big part of the country for their benefit, although war remains latent.[7]

In Rhodesia the problem is different: British imperialism used all the means at its disposal to hand power over to the white minority, which now holds it.[8] The conflict, from England's point of view, is absolutely not official. This Western power, with its usual diplomatic cleverness — in plain language also called hypocrisy — presents a facade of displeasure with the measures adopted by the government of Ian Smith. It is supported in this sly attitude by some Commonwealth countries that follow it, but is attacked by a good number of the countries of Black Africa, even those that are docile economic vassals of British imperialism.

In Rhodesia the situation could become highly explosive if the efforts of the Black patriots to rise up in arms were to crystallize and if this movement were effectively supported by the neighboring African nations. But for now all these problems are being aired in bodies as innocuous as the UN, the Commonwealth, or the Organization of African Unity.

Nevertheless, the political and social evolution of Africa does not lead us to foresee a continental revolutionary situa-

7. In January 1961 Patrice Lumumba, central leader of the Congo's independence movement, was murdered by imperialist-backed forces loyal to rightist figure Moise Tshombe. Standing aside while Lumumba was deposed and arrested were United Nations troops he had invited in to halt mercenary attacks backed by Belgium. When Tshombe became the Congo's prime minister in 1964, forces that had previously supported Lumumba revolted; they were defeated with the help of Belgian and South African mercenary armies — politically and militarily backed by Washington — whose assignment was to prevent the vast mineral wealth of the Congo from escaping imperialist control.

8. The white minority settler regime in Rhodesia, headed by Ian Smith, declared independence from Britain on November 11, 1965. After struggle by guerrilla forces intensified in the mid-1970s following the winning of independence by Angola and Mozambique, the white minority regime collapsed in 1980 and Rhodesia became Zimbabwe.

tion. The liberation struggles against the Portuguese must end victoriously, but Portugal signifies nothing on the imperialist roster. The confrontations of revolutionary importance are those that put the whole imperialist apparatus in check, although we will not for that reason cease struggling for the liberation of the three Portuguese colonies and for the deepening of their revolutions.

When the Black masses of South Africa or Rhodesia begin their genuine revolutionary struggle, a new era will have opened in Africa.[9] Or, when the impoverished masses of a country set out against the ruling oligarchies to conquer their right to a decent life. Up to now there has been a succession of barracks coups, in which one group of officers replaces another or replaces a ruler who no longer serves their caste interests and those of the powers that control them behind the scenes. But there have been no popular upheavals. In the Congo these characteristics were fleetingly present, inspired by the memory of Lumumba, but they have been losing strength in recent months.

In Asia, as we have seen, the situation is explosive, and Vietnam and Laos, where the struggle is now going on, are not the only points of friction. The same holds true for Cambodia, where at any moment the United States might launch a direct attack. We should add Thailand, Malaysia, and, of

9. In 1976, as Angolan and Cuban troops turned back the South African invasion of Angola and the Rhodesian regime entered its death agony, an uprising of Black youth in Soweto signaled the opening of the final phase of the struggle against the apartheid regime. Victory in that struggle was registered by the election of Nelson Mandela as president of South Africa in 1994. A decisive role in apartheid's destruction was played by Cuban volunteer troops, who together with the Angolan army stopped South Africa's attempt to militarily overthrow the independent government of Angola between 1975 and 1991. The historic turning point came with the defeat of the South African army at the battle of Cuito Cuanavale in 1988. Mandela told a rally in Matanzas, Cuba, in 1991 that Cuba's role in defeating the apartheid army constituted "a turning point in the struggle to free the continent and our country from the scourge of apartheid." In Nelson Mandela and Fidel Castro, *How Far We Slaves Have Come!* (Pathfinder, 1991), p. 20.

course, Indonesia, where we cannot believe that the final word has been spoken despite the annihilation of the Communist Party of that country after the reactionaries took power.[10] And, of course, the Middle East.

In Latin America, the struggle is going on arms in hand in Guatemala, Colombia, Venezuela, and Bolivia, and the first outbreaks are already beginning in Brazil. Other centers of resistance have appeared and been extinguished. But almost all the countries of this continent are ripe for a struggle of the kind that, to be triumphant, cannot settle for anything less than the establishment of a government of a socialist nature.

In this continent virtually one language only is spoken save for the exceptional case of Brazil, with whose people Spanish-speakers can communicate in view of the similarity between the two languages. There is such a similarity between the classes in these countries that they have an "international American" type of identification, much more so than in other continents. Language, customs, religion, a common master, unite them. The degree and forms of exploitation are similar in their effects for exploiters and exploited in a good number of countries of our America. And within it rebellion is ripening at an accelerated rate.

We may ask: This rebellion — how will it bear fruit? What kind of rebellion will it be? We have maintained for some time that given its similar characteristics, the struggle in Latin America will in due time acquire continental dimensions. It will be the scene of many great battles waged by humanity for its own liberation.

In the framework of this struggle of continental scope, the ones that are currently being carried on in an active way are only episodes. But they have already provided martyrs who

10. On September 30, 1965, Indonesian general Suharto seized power and proceeded to carry out a massacre of members and supporters of the Indonesian Communist Party. In the next several months, hundreds of thousands were killed.

will figure in the history of the Americas as having given their necessary quota of blood for this final stage in the struggle for the full freedom of man. There are the names of Commander Turcios Lima, the priest Camilo Torres, Commander Fabricio Ojeda, Commanders Lobatón and Luis de la Puente Uceda, central figures in the revolutionary movements of Guatemala, Colombia, Venezuela, and Peru.

But the active mobilization of the people creates its new leaders — César Montes and Yon Sosa are raising the banner in Guatemala; Fabio Vázquez and Marulanda are doing it in Colombia; Douglas Bravo in the western part of the country and Américo Martín in El Bachiller are leading their respective fronts in Venezuela.

New outbreaks of war will appear in these and other Latin American countries, as has already occurred in Bolivia.[11] And they will continue to grow, with all the vicissitudes involved in this dangerous occupation of the modern revolutionist. Many will die, victims of their own errors; others will fall in the difficult combat to come; new fighters and new leaders will arise in the heat of the revolutionary struggle.

The people will create their fighters and their leaders along the way in the selective framework of the war itself, and the Yankee agents of repression will increase in number. Today there are advisers in all countries where armed struggle is going on. It seems that the Peruvian army, also advised and trained by the Yankees, carried out a successful attack on the revolutionists of that country.[12] But if the guerrilla centers are led with sufficient political and military skill, they will become

11. In 1965 the Barrientos dictatorship provoked a confrontation with the trade union movement by arresting Juan Lechín, longtime leader of the Central Organization of Bolivian Workers (COB). When workers responded with a general strike and seizure of the country's tin mines, the regime unleashed a wave of repression, arresting union leaders and sending in troops to occupy the mining camps, killing many. After the strike was defeated, a 40 percent wage cut was imposed on large sections of the working class.

12. See note on page 86.

practically unbeatable and will make necessary new reinforcements by the Yankees. In Peru itself, with tenacity and firmness,
new figures, although not yet fully known, are reorganizing the
guerrilla struggle.

Little by little, the obsolete weapons that suffice to repress
the small armed bands will turn into modern weapons, and
the groups of advisers into U.S. combatants, until at a certain
point they find themselves obliged to send growing numbers
of regular troops to secure the relative stability of a power
whose national puppet army is disintegrating in the face of
the guerrillas' struggles.

This is the road of Vietnam. It is the road that the peoples
must follow. It is the road that Latin America will follow, with
the special feature that the armed groups might establish
something such as coordinating committees to make the repressive tasks of Yankee imperialism more difficult and to
help their own cause.

Latin America — a continent forgotten in the recent political
struggles for liberation, which is beginning to make itself felt
through the Tricontinental in the voice of the vanguard of its
peoples: the Cuban revolution — will have a much more important task: the creation of the world's second or third Vietnam, or second *and* third Vietnam.

We must keep in mind at all times that imperialism is a
world system, the final stage of capitalism, and that it must be
beaten in a great worldwide confrontation. The strategic objective of that struggle must be the destruction of imperialism.

The contribution that falls to us, the exploited and backward of the world, is to eliminate the foundations sustaining
imperialism: our oppressed nations, from which capital, raw
materials, and cheap labor (both workers and technicians) are
extracted, and to which new capital (tools of domination),
arms, and all kinds of goods are exported, sinking us into absolute dependence. The fundamental element of that strategic
objective, then, will be the real liberation of the peoples, a liberation that will be the result of armed struggle in the major-

ity of cases, and that, in Latin America, will almost unfailingly turn into a socialist revolution.

In focusing on the destruction of imperialism, it is necessary to identify its head, which is none other than the United States of North America.

We must carry out a task of a general kind, the tactical aim of which is to draw the enemy out of his environment, compelling him to fight in places where his living habits clash with existing conditions. The adversary must not be underestimated; the U.S. soldier has technical ability and is backed by means of such magnitude as to make him formidable. What he lacks essentially is the ideological motivation, which his most hated rivals of today — the Vietnamese soldiers — have to the highest degree. We will be able to triumph over this army only to the extent that we succeed in undermining its morale. And this is done by inflicting defeats on it and causing it repeated sufferings.

But this brief outline for victories entails immense sacrifices by the peoples — sacrifices that must be demanded starting right now, in the light of day, and that will perhaps be less painful than those they would have to endure if we constantly avoided battle in an effort to get others to pull the chestnuts out of the fire for us.

Clearly, the last country to free itself will very probably do so without an armed struggle, and its people will be spared the suffering of a long war as cruel as imperialist wars are. But it may be impossible to avoid this struggle or its effects in a conflict of worldwide character, and the suffering may be as much or greater. We cannot predict the future, but we must never give way to the cowardly temptation to be the standard-bearers of a people who yearn for freedom but renounce the struggle that goes with it, and who wait as if expecting it to come as the crumbs of victory.

It is absolutely correct to avoid any needless sacrifice. That is why it is so important to be clear on the real possibilities that dependent Latin America has to free itself in a peaceful way. For us the answer to this question is clear: now may or may not be the right moment to start the struggle, but we can have no illusions, nor do we have a right to believe, that freedom can be won without a fight.

And the battles will not be mere street fights with stones against tear gas, nor peaceful general strikes. Nor will it be the struggle of an infuriated people that destroys the repressive apparatus of the ruling oligarchies in two or three days. It will be a long, bloody struggle in which the front will be in guerrilla refuges in the cities, in the homes of the combatants (where the repression will go seeking easy victims among their families), among the massacred peasant population, in the towns or cities destroyed by the enemy's bombs.

We are being pushed into this struggle. It cannot be remedied other than by preparing for it and deciding to undertake it.

The beginning will not be easy; it will be extremely difficult. All the oligarchies' repressive capacity, all its capacity for demagogy and brutality will be placed in the service of its cause.

Our mission, in the first hour, is to survive; then, to act, the perennial example of the guerrilla carrying on armed propaganda in the Vietnamese meaning of the term, that is, the propaganda of bullets, of battles that are won or lost — but that are waged — against the enemy.

The great lesson of the guerrillas' invincibility is taking hold among the masses of the dispossessed. The galvanization of the national spirit; the preparation for more difficult tasks, for resistance to more violent repression. Hate as a factor in the struggle, intransigent hatred for the enemy that takes one beyond the natural limitations of a human being and converts one into an effective, violent, selective, cold, killing machine. Our soldiers must be like that; a people without hate cannot triumph over a brutal enemy.

We must carry the war as far as the enemy carries it: into his home, into his places of recreation, make it total. He must be prevented from having a moment's peace, a moment's quiet outside the barracks and even inside them. Attack him wherever he may be; make him feel like a hunted animal wherever he goes. Then his morale will begin to decline. He will become even more bestial, but the signs of the coming decline will appear.

And let us develop genuine proletarian internationalism, with international proletarian armies. Let the flag under which we fight be the sacred cause of the liberation of humanity, so that to die under the colors of Vietnam, Venezuela, Guatemala, Laos, Guinea, Colombia, Bolivia, Brazil — to mention only the current scenes of armed struggle — will be equally glorious and desirable for a Latin American, an Asian, an African, and even a European.

Every drop of blood spilled in a land under whose flag one was not born is experience gathered by the survivor to be applied later in the struggle for liberation of one's own country. And every people that liberates itself is a step in the battle for the liberation of one's own people.

It is time to moderate our disputes and place everything at the service of the struggle.

That big controversies are agitating the world that is struggling for freedom, all of us know; we cannot hide that. That these controversies have acquired a character and a sharpness that make dialogue and reconciliation appear extremely difficult, if not impossible, we know that too. To seek ways to initiate a dialogue avoided by those in dispute is a useless task.

But the enemy is there, it strikes day after day and threatens new blows, and these blows will unite us today, tomorrow, or the next day. Whoever understands this first and prepares this necessary unity will win the peoples' gratitude.

In view of the virulence and intransigence with which each side argues its case, we, the dispossessed, cannot agree with either way these differences are expressed, even when we agree with some of the positions of one or the other side, or when we agree more with the positions of one or the other side. In this time of struggle, the way in which the current differences have been aired is a weakness. But given the situation, it is an illusion to think that the matter can be resolved through words. History will either sweep away these disputes or pass its final judgment on them.

In our world in struggle, everything related to disputes around tactics and methods of action for the attainment of limited objectives must be analyzed with the respect due others' opinions. As for the great strategic objective — the total destruction of imperialism by means of struggle — on that we must be intransigent.

Let us sum up as follows our aspirations for victory. Destruction of imperialism by means of eliminating its strongest bulwark: the imperialist domination of the United States of North America. To take as a tactical line the gradual liberation of the peoples, one by one or in groups, involving the enemy in a difficult struggle outside his terrain; destroying his bases of support, that is, his dependent territories.

This means a long war. And, we repeat once again, a cruel war. Let no one deceive himself when he sets out to begin, and let no one hesitate to begin out of fear of the results it can bring upon his own people. It is almost the only hope for victory.

We cannot evade the call of the hour. Vietnam teaches us this with its permanent lesson in heroism, its tragic daily lesson of struggle and death in order to gain the final victory.

Over there, the soldiers of imperialism encounter the discomforts of those who, accustomed to the standard of living that the United States boasts, have to confront a hostile land; the insecurity of those who cannot move without feeling that they are stepping on enemy territory; death for those who go outside of fortified compounds; the permanent hostility of the entire population. All this is provoking repercussions inside the United States. It is leading to the appearance of a factor that was attenuated by imperialism at full strength: the class struggle inside its own territory.

How close and bright would the future appear if two, three, many Vietnams flowered on the face of the globe, with their quota of death and their immense tragedies, with their daily heroism, with their repeated blows against imperialism, forcing it to disperse its forces under the lash of the growing hatred of the peoples of the world!

And if we were all capable of uniting in order to give our blows greater solidity and certainty, so that the aid of all kinds to the peoples in struggle was even more effective — how great the future would be, and how near!

If we, on a small point on the map of the world, fulfill our duty and place at the disposal of the struggle whatever little we are able to give — our lives, our sacrifice — it can happen that one of these days we will draw our last breath on a bit of earth not our own, yet already ours, watered with our blood. Let it be known that we have measured the scope of our acts and that we consider ourselves no more than a part of the great army of the proletariat. But we feel proud at having learned from the Cuban revolution and from its great main leader the great lesson to be drawn from its position in this part of the world: "Of what difference are the dangers to a man or a people, or the sacrifices they make, when what is at stake is the destiny of humanity?"

Our every action is a battle cry against imperialism and a call for the unity of the peoples against the great enemy of the human race: the United States of North America.

Wherever death may surprise us, let it be welcome if our battle cry has reached even one receptive ear, if another hand reaches out to take up our arms, and other men come forward to join in our funeral dirge with the rattling of machine guns and with new cries of battle and victory.

Chronology

1952

March 10 – Coup d'état brings retired general Fulgencio Batista to power in Cuba. With Washington's support he consolidates brutal military dictatorship. Fidel Castro begins organizing a revolutionary movement to overthrow the Batista tyranny by armed insurrection.

April 9 – Revolutionary upsurge in Bolivia topples country's military government and leads to installation of new regime headed by bourgeois Revolutionary Nationalist Movement (MNR), led by Víctor Paz Estenssoro. The Bolivian trade union movement, led by the tin miners, plays a central role in the uprising. The popular upsurge results in nationalization of the largest tin mines, legalization of the trade unions, initiation of land reform, and enfranchisement of Bolivia's indigenous majority.

1953

July 26 – Some 160 fighters led by Fidel Castro launch insurrectionary attack on the Moncada army garrison in Santiago de Cuba and the garrison in nearby Bayamo, Cuba. The combatants fail to take the garrisons, and over 50 captured revolutionaries are murdered. Castro and 27 other fighters are subsequently captured, tried, and sentenced to up to 15 years in prison.

1954

May – Capping an eight-year war for national liberation, Vietnamese fighters rout French imperialist forces at Dien Bien Phu, ending French colonial rule of Indochina. Following accords reached in Geneva, Vietnam is divided in two and Washington replaces Paris as major imperialist power in South Vietnam, Laos, and Cambodia, setting stage for continuing national liberation struggle.

June-September – Seeking to crush political and social struggles in Guatemala accompanying limited land reform initiated by regime of Jacobo Arbenz, mercenary forces backed by CIA invade the country to oust Arbenz government. Among those volunteering to fight the imperialist-organized attack is Ernesto Guevara, who had been drawn to Guatemala by the upsurge in struggle. Arbenz refuses to arm the people and resigns June 27; mercenary forces enter Guatemala City in August. In September Guevara, forced to flee Guatemala, arrives in Mexico City.

1955

May-July – Fidel Castro and other Moncada prisoners are released in May in response to a growing campaign for amnesty. In June they and their political supporters reorganize themselves as July 26 Movement. In July Castro arrives in Mexico to begin preparations for an expedition to resume armed insurrectionary struggle inside Cuba. Shortly after Castro's arrival he meets Ernesto Guevara, who joins the combatants' nucleus as troop doctor.

1956

December 2 – Fidel Castro and Ernesto Che Guevara are among 82 members of the July 26 Movement who arrive in Cuba aboard the yacht *Granma* to initiate the revolutionary war against Batista dictatorship. Rebel Army is born.

1957

July 21 – Guevara is first combatant promoted by Castro to commander and named head of a second Rebel Army column, Column no. 4.

November-December 1957 – Harry Villegas, later known as Pombo, after volunteering for Rebel Army is accepted by Guevara as member of Column no. 4. Rebel Army continues to consolidate positions, grow in strength and size, and carry out effective guerrilla attacks on Batista army outposts and mobile columns.

1958

January – Popular uprising and general strike in Caracas, Venezuela, overthrows dictator Marcos Pérez Jiménez. New government led by nationalist army officers gives aid to Cuba's Rebel Army.

February – Rebel victory at second battle of Pino del Agua in Sierra Maestra marks decisive shift in military relation of forces, opening several months of expanded operations by Rebel Army, with new fronts and columns.

May-July – Batista launches "encircle and annihilate" offensive, sending 10,000 troops into the Sierra Maestra. Rebel Army, then with 300 fighters and usable rifles, concentrates forces around command post of Fidel Castro's Column no. 1, draws in government troops, and defeats them in course of several decisive battles.

August-December – Rebel Army launches counterattack. Columns commanded by Che Guevara and Camilo Cienfuegos lead westward invasion from Sierra Maestra mountains to Las Villas province in central Cuba. Rebel Army fronts in eastern Cuba led by Fidel Castro, Raúl Castro, and Juan Almeida establish a vast liberated territory. By late December major cities and towns in central and eastern Cuba are cut off and surrounded by Rebel Army, sealing the fate of Batista dictatorship.

1959

January 1 – Fulgencio Batista flees Cuba, ceding power to a military junta. Speaking over Radio Rebelde, Fidel Castro opposes new junta, calls for nationwide general strike, and orders columns led by Guevara and Cienfuegos to march on Havana.

January 2 – Cuban workers respond to call for revolutionary general strike with massive uprising. Rebel columns led by Cienfuegos and Guevara enter Havana and occupy principal army garrisons. Military junta collapses. Led by July 26 Movement and Rebel Army, Cuba's workers and peasants deepen revolutionary struggle, taking first steps toward creating a government in their interests.

March – Street demonstrations by students throughout Bolivia denounce U.S. domination of the country. The protests coincide with a strike by 24,000 tin miners. Workers and youth confront the increasingly corrupt and fractured MNR government.

May 17 – The Cuban revolution initiates a deep-going agrarian reform, confiscating the large landed estates of foreign and Cuban owners, and distributing land titles to hundreds of thousands of peasants.

October 7 – Guevara is named head of Department of Industrialization of National Institute of Agrarian Reform (INRA). Along with other responsibilities he also heads Rebel Army's Department of Education.

November 26 – Guevara is appointed president of Cuba's National Bank, with responsibility for the country's finances.

1960

August 6 – In response to escalating U.S. economic aggression and sabotage actions, the revolutionary government decrees the nationalization of major U.S. companies in Cuba. By October virtually all Cuban-owned industry is also nationalized.

October 19 – The U.S. government decrees a partial embargo against trade with Cuba.

1961

January 17 – Patrice Lumumba, central leader of the independence movement in the former Belgian colony of the Congo, is murdered by imperialist-backed forces loyal to rightist figure Moise Tshombe. Standing aside while Lumumba was deposed and arrested were United Nations troops he had invited in to halt mercenary attacks backed by Belgium.

February 23 – Guevara becomes Cuban minister of industry.

April 16 – At a mass rally to honor victims of U.S.-organized air attacks the previous day, Fidel Castro proclaims the socialist character of the Cuban revolution and calls the people of Cuba to arms in its defense. Guevara is sent to Pinar del Río province to command troops.

April 17 – 1,500 Cuban mercenaries invade Cuba at the Bay of Pigs on the southern coast. The invasion, organized and financed by Washington, aims to declare a provisional government to appeal for direct U.S. intervention. The invaders are defeated within 72 hours by Cuba's militia and its Revolutionary Armed Forces. On April 19 the last invaders surrender at Playa Girón (Girón Beach).

August – The Alliance for Progress is proclaimed at a meeting of the Organization of American States (OAS). The U.S.-sponsored program, established as a response to the Cuban revolution and its example, aims to prop up compliant capitalist regimes and enrich U.S. bankers and investors. It allocates $20 billion in loans to Latin American governments over a ten-year period in exchange for their cooperation in opposing Cuba's revolutionary regime.

1962

January 31 – The OAS votes to expel Cuba.

February 3 – President Kennedy orders a total embargo on U.S. trade with Cuba.

February 4 – Mass rally of one million in Havana's Plaza of the Revolution proclaims the Second Declaration of Havana, underlining support for revolutionary struggle throughout the Americas.

February – A revolutionary movement is formed in Guatemala, led by Marco Antonio Yon Sosa and Luis Augusto Turcios Lima, and begins guerrilla actions.

July 3 – Following an eight-year armed struggle, France recognizes Algeria's independence.

October 22–28 – Washington orders a naval blockade of Cuba and places U.S. armed forces on nuclear alert to demand removal from the island of a Soviet-supplied nuclear missile defense. The missiles had been installed following a mutual defense agreement between Cuba and the Soviet Union in face of Washington's renewed preparations to launch an invasion of Cuba. In response to U.S. aggression, Cuban workers and farmers mobilize in the millions to defend the revolution. Following an exchange of communications between Washington and Moscow, Soviet premier Nikita Khrushchev, without consulting the Cuban government, announces his decision to remove the missiles.

1963

February 20 – Members of Venezuelan Communist Party, dissident military officers, and others form the Armed Forces for National Liberation (FALN) to wage a guerrilla struggle.

April-May – U.S. civil rights fighters in Birmingham, Alabama, conduct mass marches and sit-ins to desegregate public facilities.

May – An attempt to establish a guerrilla movement in Peru is crushed in Puerto Maldonado, and its leader Javier Heraud is killed.

May 29 – Peruvian peasant leader Hugo Blanco is captured and jailed following several years of mass struggle by peasants for land in the valley of La Convención.

August 26 – A quarter of a million march on Washington, D.C., in support of civil rights struggle.

September – A guerrilla nucleus is established in the Salta mountains of northern Argentina, led by Jorge Ricardo Masetti. Logistics and support are coordinated from Bolivia by Cuban internationalist José María Martínez Tamayo, aided by several members of the Bolivian Communist Party.

November 1 – South Vietnamese dictator Ngo Dinh Diem is assassinated at the instigation of Washington, which is dissatisfied with his regime's inability to counter the military and political successes of the National Liberation Front.

1964

January 9 – U.S. forces open fire on Panamanian students demonstrating in the U.S.-occupied Canal Zone, sparking several days of street fighting. More than 20 Panamanians are killed and 300 wounded.

March 31–April 2 – A U.S.-backed military coup d'état in Brazil overthrows the liberal bourgeois government of João Goulart and inaugurates bloody reign of terror.

March-April – The guerrillas in the Salta mountains of Argentina are crushed; Masetti is killed.

April – The Communist Party of Bolivia holds its second congress. A pro-Maoist minority led by Oscar Zamora is excluded from the Central Committee, leading to a split in the party.

August – Following a naval incident manufactured by Washington in the waters off Indochina, the U.S. Congress passes the Gulf of Tonkin resolution, authorizing the bombing of North Vietnam and rapid escalation of the war.

November 4 – Amidst a wave of protests and strikes by workers and students against the corrupt and unpopular government of Víctor Paz Estenssoro, a military coup is carried out by René Barrientos, Bolivia's vice president and head of the air force, and army commander Alfredo Ovando. Barrientos becomes president.

November – Following an uprising by supporters of murdered prime minister Patrice Lumumba, U.S. planes bomb rebel-held

villages in the Congo and ferry Belgian troops and
mercenaries to crush the revolt. Thousands of Congolese are
massacred.

November 18 – Haydée Tamara Bunke (*Tania*) arrives in Bolivia
from Cuba to begin intelligence work in preparation for
initiating a guerrilla front to coincide with deepening popular
struggles throughout South America's Southern Cone.

December 11 – Che Guevara addresses United Nations General
Assembly, where he denounces the escalating U.S. war against
Vietnam, and the imperialist-backed assault in the Congo.

1965

January 7 – The National Liberation Army (ELN) of Colombia
carries out its first armed action.

January-March – Civil rights fighters in U.S. wage campaign for
voting rights for Blacks, centered in Alabama.

February 21 – U.S. revolutionary leader Malcolm X is assassinated
in New York City.

March 8–9 – Washington's first combat units arrive in Vietnam,
joining the 23,000 U.S. troops already there. By 1968 there will
be 540,000 U.S. troops engaged in Vietnam War.

March 13 – Fidel Castro appeals for unity among the world's
progressive forces in support of Vietnam

March 14 – Guevara returns to Cuba following three-month world
trip that included visits to numerous countries in Africa.
Immediately afterward Guevara drops from public view.

April 1 – Guevara, in disguise, leaves Cuba en route to Africa.
Before leaving he writes a letter to Fidel Castro giving up his
leadership posts and Cuban citizenship and announcing his
decision to participate in revolutionary struggles abroad.

April 17 – Twenty thousand march in Washington, D.C., in first
mass demonstration protesting Vietnam War.

April 24 – Guevara arrives in the Congo, where he heads a
contingent of over 100 Cuban volunteers giving assistance to
revolutionary forces fighting that country's proimperialist

regime. Congolese government troops are supported by mercenaries backed by Belgian, South African, and other imperialist forces. Among the Cuban volunteers are Pombo, Tuma, Mbili, Moro, and Braulio, who later go to fight with Che in Bolivia.

April 28 – Some 24,000 U.S. troops invade the Dominican Republic to crush a popular uprising against the military junta there backed by Washington.

May – The Barrientos dictatorship provokes a confrontation with the trade union movement by arresting Juan Lechín, central leader of the Bolivian Workers Federation (COB). Workers respond with a general strike and seizure of the country's tin mines. The regime unleashes a wave of repression, arresting union leaders and sending troops to occupy the mining camps, killing many.

June 19 – Revolutionary government of Ahmed Ben Bella in Algeria is overthrown in military coup.

June-December – A guerrilla front in Peru operates in the department of Junín, organized by the Movement of the Revolutionary Left (MIR). It is annihilated and its leader, Guillermo Lobatón, disappears and is presumed dead.

September-October – A guerrilla front in Peru operates in the department of Cuzco, organized by the MIR. The movement is crushed and its leader, Luis de la Puente, is killed in battle.

September-December – A guerrilla front in Peru operates in the department of Ayacucho, organized by the National Liberation Army (ELN). It is destroyed and its leader, Héctor Béjar, is subsequently captured.

September 30 – Indonesian general Suharto seizes power and carries out a massacre of members and supporters of the Indonesian Communist Party. Hundreds of thousands are subsequently killed.

October 3 – During a public meeting to introduce the Central Committee of the newly founded Communist Party of Cuba, Fidel Castro reads Guevara's letter of farewell.

November 21 – Following a decision by African states and liberation

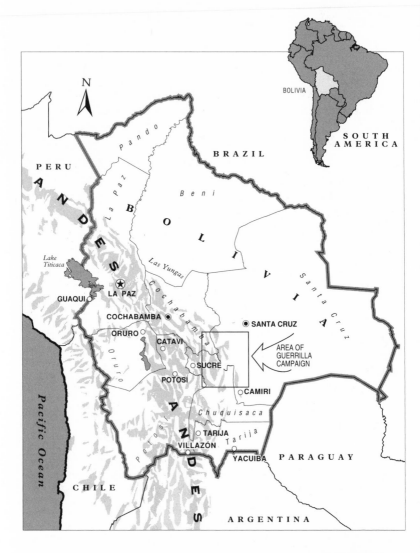

PERU

BRAZIL

BOLIVIA

SOUTH AMERICA

Pando

La Paz

B   *Beni*

O

Las Yungas

L

I

V

Lake
Titicaca

GUAQUI

★ LA PAZ

COCHABAMBA

Cochabamba

I

Santa Cruz

A

⦿ SANTA CRUZ

ORURO

CATAVI

Oruro

SUCRE

POTOSÍ

← AREA OF
GUERRILLA
CAMPAIGN

CAMIRI

Chuquisaca

A

N

D

Potosí

Tarija

TARIJA

VILLAZÓN

E

YACUIBA

PARAGUAY

Pacific Ocean

S

CHILE

ARGENTINA

350 KILOMETERS

220 MILES

Bolivia

movements to halt military aid to the Congolese rebel movement, the Cuban volunteer contingent ends its mission in the Congo; Guevara crosses into Tanzania. Subsequently travels to Prague, Czechoslovakia, where he steps up preparations for revolutionary effort in Southern Cone of Latin America.

1966

January 3–14 – Tricontinental Conference of Solidarity of the Peoples of Asia, Africa, and Latin America is held in Havana, attended by anti-imperialist fighters from around the world.

January – Bolivian CP members Coco Peredo, Rodolfo Saldaña, Jorge Vázquez (*Loro*), and Luis Méndez (*Ñato*) travel to Cuba to receive military training.

February 15 – Colombian guerrilla leader Camilo Torres is killed.

March – Cuban internationalist José María Martínez Tamayo (*Ricardo, Mbili, Papi, Chinchu, Taco*) arrives in Bolivia to organize preparations for a revolutionary guerrilla front to be centered in Peru or Bolivia.

June – Venezuelan FALN leader Fabricio Ojeda is captured and murdered in custody.

June 27 – A 3,000-acre farm in southeastern Bolivia along the Ñancahuazú river is purchased as a possible preliminary staging area for a guerrilla front. Other possible sites include the Alto Beni (Caranavi) and Chapare regions.

July 14 – Cuban internationalists Pombo and Tuma leave Prague en route to Bolivia to help with logistical and political preparations to open a guerrilla front in Bolivia.

July 21 – Pombo and Tuma arrive in Bolivia.

July 27 – Pombo and Tuma reach La Paz.

Late July – Guevara arrives in Cuba to directly supervise organization of revolutionary front in Bolivia and training of Cuban volunteers.

July-September – Main body of Cuban volunteers selected by Guevara for Bolivia mission undergoes training in San Andrés,

Pinar del Río province, in western Cuba.

August-October – Relations between the Cuban team in Bolivia and the Bolivian CP leadership steadily deteriorate. CP general secretary Mario Monje reneges on commitments to support revolutionary front.

September – Exploration of alternate sites in Bolivia being considered for initial guerrilla zone of operations.

September 26 – Guevara sends message giving approval of Ñancahuazú for initial guerrilla training operations.

October 23 – Guevara, in disguise, traveling as an official of the Organization of American States with a Uruguayan passport, leaves Cuba, passing through Moscow, Prague, Vienna, and Brazil en route to Bolivia.

November 3 – Guevara arrives secretly in La Paz.

November 7 – Guevara and several other combatants reach the "zinc house" at the Ñancahuazú site.

November 11 – The combatants establish themselves at their first camp, several miles from the zinc house.

November-December – Cuban internationalists and Bolivian fighters arrive at the camp. Scouting parties explore the area.

December 16 – Guerrilla contingent moves to the site of their main camp.

December 31 – Bolivian CP leader Mario Monje comes to the Ñancahuazú camp and meets with Guevara. When his demand for leadership of the column is refused, he breaks off talks and urges Bolivian cadres to desert.

1967

January 8–10 – Bolivian CP Central Committee endorses Monje's stance. Subsequently Bolivian volunteers are dissuaded from joining the revolutionary front and several fighters are expelled from the leadership of the CP's youth group.

January 26 – Guevara meets with miners' leader Moisés Guevara, who agrees to join the guerrilla movement with 20 members of his group, which had split from the pro-Peking Communist

Party (Marxist-Leninist) over the CP(M-L)'s refusal to support launching of revolutionary front.

February 1 – Guerrillas undertake exploratory and training journey. The trip is planned to last three weeks, but takes seven. A small group remains at camp.

February-March – New recruits continue to arrive at the Ñancahuazú camp, including Moisés Guevara and 11 other members of his group, Peruvian combatants, and individuals who belonged to the Bolivian CP and CP youth. Régis Debray and Ciro Bustos arrive at camp for discussions with Guevara on organizing international solidarity. Tania, who escorts them, remains with column when her cover is blown.

February 26 – Benjamín drowns in the Río Grande, the first fatality among the combatants.

February 28 – The forward detachment led by Marcos gets separated from the rest of the troops while crossing the Río Grande. Their presence in the village of Tatarenda several days later arouses the army's suspicion.

March 11 – Two new recruits from Moisés Guevara's group desert from the base camp. They are captured three days later and inform the army of Che Guevara's presence.

March 12 – The forward detachment led by Marcos arrives back at the Ñancahuazú camp.

March 17 – Carlos drowns while crossing the Río Grande. The Ñancahuazú farm is raided by 60 troops, capturing Salustio, one of the newly arrived recruits acting as a messenger. One soldier is shot.

March 20 – The main guerrilla force returns to camp. Guevara orders an ambush if the army advances on the camp.

March 23 – In first combat action, army troops ambushed along the Ñancahuazú, killing 7. News of the action causes a sensation throughout the country.

March 25 – The combatants adopt the name National Liberation Army of Bolivia (ELN). Four Bolivian recruits are expelled from the column.

March 27 – U.S. Lt. Col. Redmond Weber and Maj. Robert Shelton

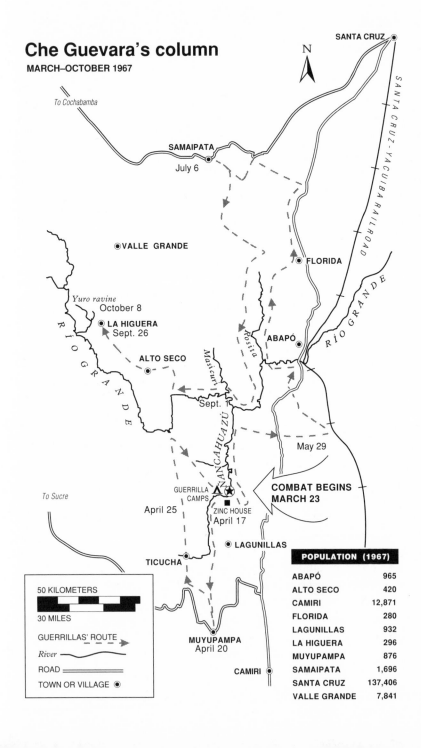

Che Guevara's column

MARCH–OCTOBER 1967

N

SANTA CRUZ

To Cochabamba

SANTA CRUZ-YACUIBA RAILROAD

SAMAIPATA
July 6

VALLE GRANDE

FLORIDA

Yuro ravine
October 8

LA HIGUERA
Sept. 26

RÍO GRANDE

Rosita

ABAPÓ

ALTO SECO

Masicuri

RÍO GRANDE

Sept. 1

ÑANCAHUAZÚ

May 29

COMBAT BEGINS
MARCH 23

GUERRILLA
CAMPS

To Sucre

April 25

ZINC HOUSE
April 17

LAGUNILLAS

TICUCHA

POPULATION (1967)	
ABAPÓ	965
ALTO SECO	420
CAMIRI	12,871
FLORIDA	280
LAGUNILLAS	932
LA HIGUERA	296
MUYUPAMPA	876
SAMAIPATA	1,696
SANTA CRUZ	137,406
VALLE GRANDE	7,841

50 KILOMETERS

30 MILES

GUERRILLAS' ROUTE
River
ROAD
TOWN OR VILLAGE

MUYUPAMPA
April 20

CAMIRI

arrive in Bolivia, followed the next day by 15 U.S. counterinsurgency instructors.

April – U.S. military advisers and CIA personnel continue to arrive in Bolivia. Washington steps up shipment of arms to Bolivian military.

April 10 – An army column is ambushed at the Iripiti river (Monkey Creek), with 10 dead. Rubio is killed, the first combatant to die in action.

April 11 – Bolivian dictatorship bans Communist Party, Communist Party (Marxist-Leninist), and Revolutionary Workers Party (POR) and arrests a number of their leaders.

April 15 – 400,000 demonstrate against the Vietnam War in New York City and 75,000 in San Francisco.

April 16 – Guevara's "Message to the Tricontinental," written in 1966 before he left Cuba and containing Che's assessment of the world political situation, is published in Cuba. The article calls for revolutionary forces everywhere to come to the aid of the Vietnamese fighters and outlines the perspectives for the struggle in Latin America.

April 17 – Main column commanded by Guevara heads south to escort Debray and Bustos to safety. Rear guard led by Joaquín remains behind to care for combatants who are sick. Meant to last three days, the separation of forces becomes permanent.

April 19 – Journalist George Andrew Roth — suspected by the fighters of being an intelligence agent — tracks them to their zone of operations. After interrogation by Inti he is given a written account of recent guerrilla actions prepared by Guevara.

April 19–20 – Debray, Bustos, and Roth are dropped off outside Muyupampa but are arrested hours later. Over the coming months, the imprisonment and trial of Debray and Bustos become a focus of world attention. Roth is released July 8 and disappears.

April 22 – Guerrillas clash with army troops at Taperillas. Loro becomes separated from the column; he is later captured, tortured, and executed. Guevara's pseudonym is changed from Ramón to Fernando.

April 25 – Army column is ambushed at El Mesón. Rolando is killed in the fighting.

May 1 – Communiqué no. 1 of ELN is published in *Prensa Libre* of Cochabamba.

May 8 – Army column is ambushed at the Ñancahuazú. Three soldiers are killed.

Venezuelan fighters joined by Cuban volunteers stage landing by sea in an attempt to join up with MIR (Movement of the Revolutionary Left) guerrilla front in El Bachiller region of Venezuela. The expedition is destroyed. Its leader, Cuban Antonio Briones, is captured and murdered in custody.

May 23 – Pepe, one of the expelled guerrillas being escorted by Joaquín's column, deserts. He is captured by army troops three days later and murdered.

May 30 – Main column ambushes government troops between El Espino and Muchiri. Three soldiers are killed.

May 31 – Main column clashes with army outside of Muchiri, killing one.

June 2 – Víctor and Marcos, members of Joaquín's column, are killed in battle near Bella Vista.

June 10 – Main column clashes with army troops at El Cafetal, killing one.

June 20 – Based on information provided by Paulino, a peasant who has volunteered to join the combatants, three army spies are taken prisoner by the guerrillas in Abapó. Several days later Paulino is sent to Cochabamba to deliver messages, in attempt to renew contacts. He is captured by the army and tortured.

June 23–24 – With resistance to the dictatorship's moves against tin miners growing, Bolivian army troops occupy mining camps at Siglo XX mines and open fire on workers and their families as they sleep; scores are killed.

June 26 – Main column ambushes troops at Florida. Tuma and 3 soldiers are killed.

July 1 – Bolivian dictator Barrientos publicly announces Guevara's presence in the country.

July 6 – A detachment of main column captures Samaipata, capital of Florida province. One soldier is killed and 9 are taken prisoner.

July 9 – Serapio, a member of Joaquín's column, is killed in action.

July 20 – Eusebio and Chingolo, expelled guerrillas under escort of Joaquín's column, desert and are captured. Chingolo subsequently leads the army to combatants' strategic supply caves.

July 27 – Guevara's column ambushes army troops at La Cruz, killing several.

July 30 – Combatants clash with troops at Suspiro river. Ricardo, Raúl, and 4 government troops are killed.

July 31–August 10 – Organization of Latin American Solidarity (OLAS) conference is held in Havana; conference proclaims support for guerrilla movements throughout Latin America; Guevara is elected honorary chair.

August 9 – Joaquín's column clashes with army near Monteagudo. Pedro is killed in the battle.

August 26 – Guevara's column skirmishes with troops at the Río Grande.

August 31 – Betrayed by peasant Honorato Rojas, Joaquín's column is annihilated while fording the Río Grande at the Puerto Mauricio ford. Killed in the ambush are Joaquín, Braulio, Alejandro, Tania, Walter, Polo, and Moisés Guevara. Ernesto is captured and executed. Negro escapes but is captured and executed four days later.

September 3 – One government soldier is killed in skirmish with Guevara's column in the lower Masicuri region.

September 6 – Guerrillas clash with troops.

September 14 – Loyola Guzmán is arrested in La Paz as hundreds of suspected ELN collaborators are rounded up and imprisoned.

September 22 – Guevara's column occupies town of Alto Seco. They hold meeting in local schoolhouse addressed by Guevara and Inti.

September 26 – Forward detachment falls into army ambush at La

Higuera. Coco, Miguel, and Julio are killed. Camba and León desert.

September 27 – León surrenders to Bolivian army and turns informer. Camba is captured while trying to return to the guerrilla unit

October 8 – Guevara's column is cornered in the Yuro ravine. Aniceto, Antonio, and Arturo are killed in the fighting, as well as four soldiers. Pacho and Che Guevara, both wounded, are taken prisoner, along with Willy and Chino, and moved to the schoolhouse at La Higuera. Pacho dies of his wounds during the night.

October 9 – After consulting Washington, the Bolivian government orders Guevara's execution. Willy, Chino, and Guevara are shot.

October 10 – Pombo, Inti, Ñato, Urbano, Benigno, and Darío — one of two groups of combatants to escape following Yuro ravine clash — hear the news of Guevara's murder. They vow to continue the struggle and select Pombo as leader.

October 12 – The other group — Pablito, Eustaquio, Moro, and Chapaco — are killed by troops as they try to escape the encirclement. Group led by Pombo clashes with troops at Naranjal, killing 5, and breaks out of encirclement.

October 18 – A mass rally is held in Havana's Plaza of the Revolution. Fidel Castro delivers political tribute to Guevara and other fallen combatants.

November 15 – Ñato is mortally wounded in combat in Mataral.

November 16 – Debray and Bustos are sentenced to 30 years in prison.

December 4 – The combatants meet peasant Don Víctor near San Isidro. For the next month he and his family shelter them from Bolivian army pursuit.

December 15 – The five combatants agree to divide into two groups to try to establish contact with supporters in the cities. Inti and Urbano depart for Cochabamba, arriving the next day.

December 26 – In line with arrangements made by Inti and Urbano, a team from Cochabamba makes contact with the three other guerrillas to plan for their rescue.

1968

January 5 – Pombo, Benigno, and Darío are picked up in a rescue
operation carried out by urban supporters. They reach
Cochabamba the following day.

January 11–22 – Guerrilla veterans make their way to La Paz with
aid of supporters.

January – Fighters from Vietnam's National Liberation Front mount
the Tet Offensive, taking the fight against the U.S. occupation
army into the heart of South Vietnam's cities.

February 4 – Pombo and Inti discuss perspective for regrouping and
continuing the revolutionary struggle in Bolivia.

February 17 – Pombo, Urbano, and Benigno elude a massive army
presence at the border and cross into Chilean territory. The
two Bolivian veterans, Inti and Darío, remain in Bolivia to
reorganize the ELN.

February 23 – The three Cuban combatants turn themselves in to
Chilean authorities.

February 25 – Cuban veterans of struggle leave Chilean mainland
for Isla de Pascua (Easter Island) accompanied by Chilean
senator Salvador Allende. From there they begin a return trip
to Cuba that takes them around the globe.

March 6 – Pombo, Urbano, and Benigno arrive in Cuba.

Mid-March – Microfilms of Guevara's diary are smuggled out of
Bolivia and brought to Cuba, together with a typed transcript
of the first notebook of Pombo's diary. The copies are secretly
provided by Antonio Arguedas, Bolivia's minister of the
interior.

April 4 – U.S. civil rights leader Martin Luther King is assassinated
in Memphis, Tennessee. Antigovernment outrage erupts in
Black communities across country.

May-June – Student protests in France against the Vietnam War are
violently repressed by the police. Students occupy universities
around the country and barricade streets. Workers join

protests against de Gaulle government and a general strike
paralyzes country for weeks.

July 1 – Guevara's diary is published in Cuba, foiling Bolivian
military's plans to exploit its theft of the document. The
following day diary is published in translation in the U.S., and
a half dozen other editions around the world quickly appear.

July 19 – A manifesto by Inti Peredo is published calling for
resumption of the guerrilla struggle in Bolivia.

August-September – Inti Peredo travels to Cuba, where he
discusses plans to resume the guerrilla struggle together with
Cuban veterans and Bolivian combatant Darío.

October 2 – After more than two months of deepening student
protests against police repression, Mexican police fire on
gathering of 20,000 in Tlatelolco square of Mexico City.
Hundreds are killed.

1969

April 27 – Barrientos is killed in a helicopter crash. Luis Adolfo Siles
Salinas replaces him as president.

May – A general strike erupts in Rosario, Argentina's second-largest
city, followed by a massive uprising in Córdoba, the third-
largest city. The *Cordobazo* ushers in a period of rapidly
sharpening class struggle in Argentina. After workers
movement fails repeatedly to resolve conflict in its interests,
struggle culminates in 1976 military coup and infamous "dirty
war" waged by dictatorship of Gen. Jorge Rafael Videla in
which over ten thousand Argentines are estimated killed or
"disappeared."

September 9 – Inti Peredo is killed in La Paz by Bolivian police and
army forces, tipped off by an informer.

September 26 – Siles Salinas is overthrown in a coup by Gen.
Alfredo Ovando.

November 15 – 750,000 anti–Vietnam War protesters march in
Washington and 250,000 in San Francisco.

December 31 – David Adriazola (*Darío*), remaining Bolivian veteran of the guerrilla front, is murdered by police in La Paz.

1970

May – Following the U.S. invasion of Cambodia and the murder of antiwar protesters at Kent State and Jackson State universities, a massive student strike and occupation of schools sweeps the United States, involving over four million students. Demonstrations of tens of thousands occur in scores of cities across the country as opposition to U.S. government policy broadens.

June – Mass demonstrations in Bolivia protest brutal government murder of ELN organizer Elmo Catalán and his pregnant wife, Jenny Koeller.

July – 75 ELN members attempt to set up a new guerrilla front in Teoponte, north of La Paz under the leadership of Chato Peredo, brother of Inti. Through a hostage exchange they win release of Loyola Guzmán and other imprisoned revolutionaries. Within eight weeks, military offensive annihilates all but a handful of the guerrillas.

August 26 – Over 50,000 demonstrate for women's rights in New York City. Nationwide actions mark the opening of new wave of women's liberation movement in U.S.

August 29 – 30,000 march in Los Angeles in National Chicano Moratorium against Vietnam War. Police attack demonstrators, killing three.

August-September – Class struggle sharpens throughout Bolivia as workers and students press for concessions and a sector of the ruling class demands harsher measures be taken.

September 4 – On the shoulders of rising working-class and peasant militancy, Socialist Party leader Salvador Allende is elected president of Chile. He holds office until September 11, 1973, when a bloody right-wing military coup deals decisive defeat to workers movement.

October 6–7 – General Ovando resigns presidency and turns power over to an ultrarightist military junta. In face of massive

popular mobilizations in the streets to counter this takeover,
the Bolivian army divides and a second coup is carried out
against the rightists by Gen. Juan José Torres.

December 23 – Torres regime issues amnesty for Debray, Bustos,
and others imprisoned for their role in the 1967 guerrilla
movement.

1971

January 10 – An attempted coup against the Torres regime is
defeated by a massive popular mobilization. Thousands
of armed miners arrive in La Paz.

February – Riding the wave of popular mobilization, a People's
Assembly — an incipient workers' parliament — is formed in
Bolivia.

August 19–22 – Following months of wavering and indecision by
workers leaders, right-wing military forces led by Hugo
Banzer overthrow Torres government. A wave of murderous
repression follows.

1975

April 30 – U.S. forces abandon Saigon, and Vietnamese fighters
achieve victory in decades-long battle for national liberation.

PART ONE

July 1966
May 1967

This section contains the first notebook of Harry Villegas's diary of the Bolivian campaign. The notebook, together with other documents, was carried in Pombo's knapsack, which was always kept close to Ernesto Che Guevara at the guerrillas' command post. On October 8, 1967, while retreating under fire during the battle at the Yuro ravine, Guevara retrieved the documents from the knapsack, which the combatants had to leave behind. When Guevara was wounded and captured later that day, the documents fell into the hands of the Bolivian military.

In early 1968 Antonio Arguedas, Bolivia's interior minister at the time, provided microfilm of Guevara's diary to Cuba, along with a typescript prepared in Bolivia of the first part of the diary of Pombo. The text has been reviewed and corrected by the author.

July 1966

July 14

We left Prague by train at 10:00 a.m. via Frankfurt.[1] The only problem we had with the Czechs was when we were leaving (on the border with Germany). They said our visas were for air travel and that we could not leave over land. In Frankfurt we registered at the Royal Hotel. We had quite a fright: as we talked, watching a cook make pizzas, an individual approached and asked if we were Cubans. We told him we were Ecuadorans but he did not believe us, saying we looked like we were from the Caribbean. He was Dominican, and invited us to have some coffee.

July 16

We left for South America via Lufthansa. Our itinerary is Zurich, Dakar, Rio, and São Paulo, our final destination.

July 17

We had a fright at the [São Paulo] airport when my baggage was set aside for a special check. I was informed by a customs officer that I was over the weight limit.[2] We stayed at the Broadway Hotel.

---

1. Pombo was accompanied by Carlos Coello (*Tuma, Tumaine*). For biographical information, see the glossary on pages 326–51.
2. The suitcase had a false bottom in which US$20,000, a Browning pistol, and ammunition for it were hidden. Large books filled the visible part to justify the weight. Guevara personally prepared everything for the suitcase, which had been built for him.

July 19

After going through all the necessary steps to obtain visas for Bolivia, we sent a telegram to Papi[3] informing him we would arrive on the twenty-second.

July 21

We took a Cruzeiro do Sul flight to Santa Cruz de la Sierra, in Bolivia. At the airport we were told there would be an overnight layover in Corumbá. But at the Campo Grande airport we were informed that the plane would continue on, and that the Corumbá-bound passengers would continue our trip on the twenty-second at 4:00 a.m. We met a young Bolivian woman named Sara Polo. (She is very pretty.)

July 22

We continued on to Corumbá. There we were told that there were no flights to Santa Cruz until Monday, the twenty-fifth. We tried to get the airline company to pay for the room and board, but they refused. We are seven passengers in all (two Brazilians, two Bolivians, one German, and we two Ecuadorans[4]). We stayed at the Grand Hotel.

The Bolivians include the young woman referred to earlier, Sara Polo Arivez; she is very interesting. The other one is Mr. Mario Euclides Cardona, representing a German firm. He behaved well but tried to ascertain if we were smugglers. The Brazilians are Mario's wife and daughter. I really like the little girl, Claudia. The way she acts reminds me a lot of Harry Andrés.[5]

That night, as we were eating, another Ecuadoran arrived, named Diego (I don't remember his last name), the son of an ex-minister of his country. He worried us a bit.

3. José María Martínez Tamayo (*Ricardo, Mbili, Papi, Chinchu, Taco*), who had arrived in La Paz in March 1966 to coordinate preparations for the guerrilla effort.
4. Pombo and Tuma were traveling with Ecuadoran passports under the names of Arturo González López and Tomás Suances.
5. Pombo's oldest son, Harry Andrés Villegas Campuzano.

July 23

Our "Latin American Fraternity," as Mario termed us, decided to do what we could to help Sara get home as soon as possible, because she has been expected for four days.

July 24

They invited us to mass, but we decided to go to the movies instead.

July 25

We got up early, because I promised Sara to help her leave in the morning. After that we went to get inoculated against yellow fever. We left at 2:00 p.m. On arriving in Santa Cruz, we were happy to see the familiar face of Mbili[6] waiting for us. The Bolivian comrades took care of our paperwork formalities, etc.

We spoke with Mbili, gave him all the documents we brought for him, and explained to him orally what Ramón[7] had told us regarding his instructions:

1. On Tania.[8] We should avoid all contact with her in order to preserve her cover. Communication with her will be by coded messages. She will need to see us, so she can identify us in the event we have to make direct contact in an emergency.

2. The need to purchase a farm in the north for the possible zone of operations.

3. What is behind the Emiliano matter.[9]

4. Ramón's trip to the island and the duration of his stay there.

---

6. Another nom de guerre of José María Martínez Tamayo.
7. Ernesto Che Guevara, also referred to as *Mongo*. Later on *Fernando* is also used.
8. Haydée Tamara Bunke. On Guevara's instructions, she had been living in Bolivia since 1964, under the identity of Laura Gutiérrez, and had responsibilities related to various intelligence and support tasks.
9. *Emiliano, Francisco, Flaco*. A Cuban combatant who had decided to drop out of the Bolivian campaign.

We were very surprised when Mbili asked us where the thing was going to take place[10] because he had not received any specific instructions on it. We gave him our opinion based on what Ramón had told us, and what we had been instructed to tell Mbili, regarding the location of the farm.[11] We told him that our principal efforts were to be focused on Bolivia,[12] even though we did not have much information on this given the degree of compartmentalization, and that we were only bearers of information. He said that if he had been given more time, everything would have been ready, but now we would have to begin looking for a place for Tuma and me, because the house on Tejada Zorzano Street had been abandoned and he did not want to blow the cover of the one on República Dominicana Street, in case it were necessary for Mongo[13] to use it. He could not go to the farm because it was located practically inside a military camp (about three miles away).

We departed for La Paz with the aim of giving as much assistance as possible. This is necessary, according to what Mbili told us, because nothing has been done and we would have to start from the beginning.

We discussed the new orientation with the representatives of the [Bolivian Communist] Party, starting with the conditions in the country for the struggle. We tried to get a commitment from them to join the struggle, even though Estanislao[14] was opposed to this. They said they planned to raise the matter with Estanislao and that they were certain his position would be to join the armed struggle. If he did not agree, they were prepared to join us. We tried to find out about the plan

10. A reference to where the guerrillas would initially establish their base.
11. Two farms in the Caranavi region, in the the Alto Beni zone, had been selected, one near Santa Ana, the other near Puerto Linares.
12. Peru and Argentina had also been considered.
13. Ernesto Che Guevara.
14. Mario Monje (*Estanislao, Negro, Mario*), general secretary of the Communist Party of Bolivia until December 1967, when he was replaced by Jorge Kolle.

to launch an uprising; it was to have the character of a lightening blow that, if unsuccessful, would serve to raise the people's consciousness. Negro had offered to provide four men to prepare things in Argentina or Peru, and promised us six more.

July 26
We left Santa Cruz very early for La Paz. The road is very mountainous because the climb starts from here and rises up to the vast plateau of the Cordillera Oriental of the Andes. (The area offers good tactical possibilities for operations, although it appears there is not an abundance of water.)

July 27
We arrive in La Paz. It is a provincial city located in a basin completely surrounded by mountains. We went to the house of a man named Tellería,[15] a member of the Central Committee of the Bolivian Communist Party who is in charge of the supplies we need (arms, medicine, food, clothing, etc.). A month ago, Papi told us that this comrade was looking for a house, but for some reason he still has not found one. The only option left is to go and ask Estanislao if the group has a house available where we can put up Camba,[16] a Bolivian comrade who works with Papi. The rest of us are staying in the house on República Dominicana Street.

July 28
Papi discussed the new situation with Estanislao, based on the instructions received from the island. It was agreed to begin the armed struggle immediately, in line with the instructions from Che that I had relayed to Papi. The plan for a gen-

15. Luis Tellería (*Tellería, Facundo*).
16. Julio Méndez (*Ñato, Camba*), a member of the Bolivian CP assigned to assist the guerrilla preparations. Méndez was known as *Camba* until November 11, when he became *Ñato*. After that date, *Camba* refers exclusively to another Bolivian guerrilla, Orlando Jiménez.

eral uprising was to be kept alive, but the guerrillas were to be organized at the same time. The weak point of Estanislao's plan was pointed out to him, in that it depends on the cooperation of sectors of the Bolivian military. Without this, a large number of men would be put in a position of unequal conflict against superior forces. We left the question unresolved, however, to be discussed later when Mongo arrives. According to the commitments made, the guerrilla forces will be able to count on twenty men provided by the PCB.

July 29

We spoke with Sánchez,[17] the Peruvian comrade who acts as courier between us and Chino,[18] and informed him of our government's decision to begin the struggle first in Bolivia and afterwards in Peru. We explained that for the moment conditions are better in Bolivia, given the turn of events in his country following the defeat of the armed struggle there (the death of de la Puente, the imprisonment of Calixto, the disappearance of Lobatón, etc.)[19] He understood the matter perfectly. We asked him to continue collaborating with us and requested that his organization send men, as agreed, to receive training here. They would participate with the Bolivians in some of the

17. Julio Dagnino Pacheco (*Sánchez*), a Peruvian revolutionary working in the guerrillas' clandestine network in La Paz.

18. Juan Pablo Chang (*Chino*), a leader of the Peruvian National Liberation Army (ELN). He later joined the guerrillas in Bolivia.

19. The guerrilla forces in Peru, organized by the Movement of the Revolutionary Left (MIR) and the National Liberation Army (ELN), suffered a series of defeats in 1965.

In October 1965 a MIR guerrilla front in the department of Cuzco, led by Luis de la Puente, was crushed. De la Puente, the MIR's founding leader, was killed in battle on October 22.

In September 1965 an ELN front began operations in the department of Ayacucho, led by Héctor Béjar (*Calixto*). It was destroyed by December, and Béjar was subsequently captured and imprisoned.

A MIR front operating in the department of Junín, led by Guillermo Lobatón and Máximo Velando, was annihilated in clashes that took place in December 1965 and January 1966. Velando was captured and died in the army's custody; Lobatón disappeared, apparently killed in early January 1966.

fighting and would subsequently form the guerrilla nucleus in their country, together with some of our countrymen.

July 30

We spoke with Comrade [Moisés] Guevara. This comrade has an organization that is a faction of the pro-China group. He says he is a supporter of armed struggle. We proposed he join the guerrilla force we are organizing with the idea of forming a united front in the struggle against imperialism in Bolivia. We discussed the points he had raised with Francisco, in which he had not been completely open and sincere, given that all he had asked for up to then was money.

Guevara was asked to prepare another report presenting his group's actual views. We explained that we would not hand over money for arms and equipment because the main command would be in charge of equipping the men. However, he should prepare a detailed report to appraise Manila[20] of everything; a comrade coming through here could take it back with him. These negotiations were conducted by Comrade Sánchez. The report will be delivered within two days.

We sent three comrades to work under the direction of Coco.[21] They will look for a farm within the possible zone of operations where we can train.

We received a report from Ramón requesting details about the situation. We held a discussion with Mbili on the best way to inform him.

ANALYSIS OF THE MONTH
BEGIN REPORT NO. 15 (TRANSCRIPT)

Comrade Ariel,[22]

From my conversation with Pombo, it seems that Flaco did not make an adequate report. I have asked a number of questions

---

20. A reference to Cuba.
21. Roberto Peredo (*Coco*), a member of the Bolivian CP assigned to guerrilla preparations. He later joined the guerrillas.
22. Code name for one of the liaisons in Cuba.

and have not received instructions on the matters of [Moisés] Guevara and Sánchez.

On the situation here, we have run into some difficulties. Estanislao is vacillating a great deal. He vacillated a great deal at the beginning. With the arrival of the four[23] we have been able to exert some pressure through Coco. Everything is going well; the man [Monje] appears determined and he committed himself to carrying the plan out, even though he proposes to do so with an uprising in the capital that would serve as a call to action, simultaneously with armed struggle in the mountains. For the latter we have been promised twenty of their best men to begin the struggle. I went to scout out Pablo's[24] farm. It will not do because it lies within the area of an [army] division. I am looking for one in the indicated zone. I hope to have it within twenty days.

I have been forced to tell Sánchez of our aim to concentrate our main efforts in Bolivia instead of Peru. He understood, for the moment.

I see real possibilities of success. Now is the time to raise with Estanislao the question of Mongo's participation. We have felt him out, and he has told us that if this were to occur, he would fight at Mongo's side to the end.

As regards myself, I am at no risk for the moment. The fellows are safe. It is necessary to find someone to take charge of the work in the city so I can go to the farm. I think more reserve funds should be sent.

An embrace. Taco.[25]

STOP

23. Four Bolivian CP members were assigned by Monje to assist with guerrilla preparations and join in the effort. They were Rodolfo Saldaña; Jorge Vázquez Viaña (*Bigotes, Loro*); Roberto Peredo (*Coco*); and Julio Méndez (*Ñato*). At the request of the Bolivian CP, they had been sent to Cuba to receive military training in January 1966.
24. The owner of one of the Caranavi properties.
25. Another nom de guerre of José María Martínez Tamayo.

August 1966

August 5

We received a message from Manila acknowledging receipt of the news of our arrival. It also mentions bilateral communications beginning on the thirteenth. They are upset that nothing is ready here. Furthermore, they ask for a map of the country to military specifications, and they do not mention the reports. Apparently these have not arrived.

They suggest that Mbili not make contact with Moisés [Guevara]. Sánchez should be the go-between, and Moisés should be told that we are waiting for an answer from our government, which is considering his proposal.

August 6

Two Peruvian comrades arrived with messages from Chino, saying he does not understand why priority is being given to Bolivia. He believes that they have made the decision to begin the struggle, even though work is going slowly, and that whatever conditions are lacking will be created. (In our opinion Ramón cannot go there. Many things need to be cleared up, such as Calixto's capture, de la Puente's death, Lobatón's disappearance, and Gadea's capture. Based on how events have unfolded, it appears that Calixto, using a doctor as an intermediary, might have surrendered, perhaps in exchange for guarantees for his life.)

Tumaine went out with Sánchez to see the school parade, made up of students, civilians, and military personnel (a monumental waste of time and money). It is like the ones in Cuba prior to 1959.

August 7

Today there was a military parade culminating in a ceremony where the draftees and the military academies (army, Red Battalion, navy, military cadets, Rangers, etc.) swore allegiance to the flag. Throughout the parade there was much anti-Chilean propaganda, based on Bolivia's need for access to the sea. Members of the party explained that this is how they distract the masses' attention from domestic problems to international ones.

We are a little concerned about the amount of time we have stayed in this house (twelve days) without having obtained a more secure one.

The speech of General Barrientos[1] was a pack of lies. In it he called for unity based on love of country in order to create a new, industrialized Bolivia, with its own smelting plants. He called on his collaborators to meet their responsibilities to the people, which is why they must work day and night to make Bolivia a great nation, respected by all, with access to the sea.

August 8

In the evening we visited Estanislao at his home. Mbili stressed the need to send some more men in addition to the twenty he had promised. Estanislao then asked, "What twenty?" He didn't remember any such promise. Moreover, he said, he does not have anyone who could head up an intelligence and counterespionage organization, that Coco is the one who should be used. He explained that some high officials in the government have promised to provide him in-

1. Gen. René Barrientos had become Bolivia's president following a military coup in November 1964.

formation. He gave us the names but it is best not to repeat them here. When Mbili reminded him of his commitment to provide twenty men, he responded that he was having problems with the rest of the Central Committee, which was pressuring him not to join in the armed struggle. Their view is that the results of the last elections, where they received 32,000 votes, were a success. Given the little progress we have made, it's obvious something is up. To be more concrete, their decision to join the struggle is very uncertain. In fact, things have come to a halt. We have run up against the problem of lack of enthusiasm and apathy toward the effort. In truth, Mbili has to push them to do anything at all. There is tremendous apathy. We are the ones doing all the organizational work; they are helping us.

August 10

For the second time I had bad stomach pains and diarrhea. We saw Dr. Rhea[2] to get some pills. He told us it was dysentery, but nothing to worry about.

August 12

We received a report from Manila that stated: "Pacho[3] departs on the twentieth with reports and instructions from Mongo. He will arrive around the twenty-fourth." It did not say how he would arrive. They say to send someone to make contact with him in front of the Universo Theater.

August 15

Bigotes[4] arrived with information about the farms they have visited, indicating which is best suited for our purposes. It was decided to send Camba and Tumaine to purchase the most suit-

2. Humberto Rhea, a Bolivian doctor, one of the leaders of the guerrilla movement's urban network.
3. Alberto Fernández (*Pacho*), a Cuban internationalist who later joined the guerrillas.
4. Jorge Vasquez Viaña (*Bigotes, Loro*), a member of the Bolivian CP assigned to assist with guerrilla preparations. He later joined the guerrillas.

able farm, the one belonging to Algarañaz,[5] because Mongo will probably come with Pacho. We argued with Comrade Olivares,[6] one of the men Monje sent us. He stated that he did not want to continue, since the guerrilla struggle had no prospects in the country; moreover, it had not been discussed with him.

August 19

Mbili had a meeting with Estanislao where they discussed some important questions of the moment. Estanislao threatened to withdraw the four men, who he could tell not to take up arms. We told him we knew he could do that, but if he was not willing to keep the promise he made in Manila and repeated here a few days ago, we would have to report this to Manila. He replied that he was a man of his word and would keep his promises, but he wanted it understood that he had to speak with his men again. He would let us know before we were ready to go off to the mountains, because many of the men who had been assigned to us still did not know they had been selected for this work. Regarding Olivares, the young man who refused to participate because he did not think conditions were right, Estanislao said he would discuss it with him, because the man had made a commitment in Manila to go off to the mountains.

August 20

Bigotes traveled to Santa Cruz with the weapons.

August 21

We had a discussion with Comrade Saldaña, who was upset because he thought he had been relegated to the sidelines. We explained that, to the contrary, we intended to incorporate him fully, and that there was no reason for him to think he was being marginalized.

5. Ciro Algarañaz, owner of the property nearest to the Ñancahuazú farm in the department of Santa Cruz, near Camiri.
6. René Roberto Olivares, a member of the Bolivian CP. He did not join the guerrillas.

August 23

We tested Mbili's pistol and a machine gun on the outskirts of the city.

We discussed what to do if it is decided to include [Moisés] Guevara. Sánchez suggested that we not tell Guevara the actual place selected for the zone of operations, etc. He suggested that the best thing, even though it would cost some money, would be to put Guevara's organization to a practical test. With this aim, we would ask him to get his people together in Cochabamba, ready to take up arms. We would give them two weeks to do it and then ask them how much it would cost for tickets, rent for houses, etc. In this way we could be sure if they really have anyone ready to take up arms. Prior to this we would ask them to clarify aspects of their report. This would give us a better idea about how they plan to implement it, and what their real aims are.

August 24

Today we finally obtained the house we had been looking to rent for more than two months. The comrade who raised that he did not want to "go off to the mountains," because he had no confidence in our success, does not believe that conditions in the country are ripe for the struggle. He later said he has faith in the people, that the masses can see through Barrientos's political farce, but that conditions in the party are not ripe for the struggle. He had been told one thing by a leading member of the Central Committee and another by the general secretary. Therefore, as he sees it, there is no unity of aims. Our opinion is that this comrade should speak with Mario and stay and do work in the city, because he could cause unrest among the men in the field, which could force us to take drastic measures (firing squad), which would not be a good beginning to the struggle.

August 26

Mario spoke with Comrade Olivares and asked him to fulfill his commitment. He agreed to go off to the mountains.

August 27

Mbili has now spoken to the comrade. He explained the conditions in which the struggle would unfold, that it will take seven to ten years to reach final victory. Mbili also told him that our position is not to permit negative comments about the struggle. The man responded that he felt we didn't trust him, and that therefore, he would be in a very awkward position in the mountains, because he is a party man and would not be able to adapt himself to our discipline. Therefore, even though he had agreed with Estanislao to go off to the mountains, it would be preferable for him to remain in the city.

August 29

We invited Dr. Rhea to eat some chicken à la madrilène. We discussed the political situation in Bolivia and his opinion about the methods and forms of struggle that the left should employ to take power. First, he said, we must rid ourselves of traditional historic conceptions — that power is attained by a general uprising, a lightning blow — without considering the possibility of a much longer and more difficult struggle, a struggle that could last many years.

Second, we need to create a leader from among the masses, a figure capable of leading this struggle. Mario is a good theoretician but he is not of this calibre. Dr. Rhea did not want this taken as a criticism of his people but it's true. Mario is not a man capable of leading the country following victory and would serve better as minister of education and propaganda.

Third, a careful analysis is needed of the failure in Peru, Argentina, and the current situation in Venezuela. He believes that the errors basically involved military tactics. In order to prevent them in this country, we should learn from the various experiences to help us avoid these errors.

Fourth, an objective assessment of the possible zone of operations must not overlook the search for methods to mobilize the peasant masses. When the struggle begins we should not forget the particular characteristics of the peasantry. We should remember that the fight for land has little weight since there are thousands of hectares of unoccupied land. For example, in the Beni region (not in our zone of operations) a situation is developing that we should be able to take advantage of. The United Nations is trying to get Barrientos to establish control over the coca plantations as a means of curtailing cocaine trafficking. When they implement these measures, discontent among the Indians will increase because for them coca is more than just a stimulant. It is an object of veneration linked to all aspects of their lives. It involves future harvests, hunger, their very lives and the future of their children, the death of their ancestors, etc. In short, it encompasses their entire religious perspective.

There are secret discussions being held about sending a Bolivian contingent to Vietnam. If it is decided to send troops, this could explode on a national level.

Sánchez, the Peruvian comrade working with us here, arrived a little late to a meeting with someone named Roberto, from [Moisés] Guevara's group. This worried us because there is always a lot of drinking at these meetings and they should not say too much to these people. Mbili thinks that Sánchez is not happy about the decision to suspend the effort in his country and is thinking about returning to Peru. We understand that he would like to do this. We will have a frank discussion with him about the matter, and if that is how things really are, we'll send someone to talk to Chino to find out what Sánchez knows about Ramón, and act accordingly.

August 30

I spoke with Sánchez. He stated that he had accepted a proposal to stay and collaborate with us until conditions exist for him to return to Peru voluntarily. When he made this decision, he understood perfectly what he was doing, and he is willing to honor his commitment. However, he wanted us to know that he felt hurt by our lack of confidence in him at times. We tried to tell him that we never doubted him. On the contrary, we have the greatest confidence in him and have faith that he will carry out the duties he has been assigned.

September 1966

September 3

Pacho arrived by train from Chile. He raised the question of the zone selected by Mongo[1] and asked our opinion of it. [Moisés] Guevara will get 500 dollars. Concerning the visit by Danton,[2] his mission will be to make a geopolitical study of the zone selected and discuss Guevara's reports with him. Mongo's plan is to arrive without advance notice. Efforts are to be centered on Guevara's group.

All of this runs counter to the work we have been carrying out, beginning with the effort to place some people in the zone near Camiri, relying primarily upon the group from the party. We have nearly all we need (the farm, forty-five rifles, clothing, etc.). Some of the equipment is already in the Santa Cruz zone. According to Mongo's plan, however, we find ourselves compelled to move everything back to La Paz en route to Beni. We should have someone from the party take charge of the farm and plant crops, to avoid arousing suspicions.

1. Alto Beni.
2. Régis Debray (*Danton, Frenchman*), a French writer assisting the guerrilla effort.

September 5

I went to the movies with Pacho. We talked about a number of things. He knows about Mbili's reaction to the new plans. I explained that, basically, Mbili is unhappy to learn of the decision to pay attention to [Moisés] Guevara. All of his relations have been with the party, which is committed to joining the struggle and has provided the people who have helped us the most in purchasing arms and equipment. Even though the party's plan is for a general uprising, they have promised to provide us with twenty men for the guerrillas. If the thing fails (the general uprising), all of them will go off to the mountains. I also told him how Estanislao has vacillated on the twenty comrades; that he has even gone so far as to threaten to withdraw the four men who, as stipulated in the agreement with Manila, were supposed to have been placed unconditionally at our disposal, regardless of where the struggle would be occurring. Then I told him how Estanislao had said that he did not remember making a promise about twenty men.

But Mbili, who is basically under the party's influence, is biased against Guevara, viewing him as a troublemaker, incapable of really taking up arms. That is what Tellería told me. I also told Pacho about Sánchez's opinion of Guevara, which I think is significant because he gets along with him. None of us have had any contact with him. Sánchez believes that Guevara is of some value, that he has shown himself capable of organizing his group, which has decided to join the struggle. Sánchez thinks Guevara has no other alternative but to accept our aid or to fight alone, given the fact that he is a dissident from the official party and from Zamora's group, the pro-Chinese party.[3]

3. Oscar Zamora was the leader of a group that split from the Communist Party of Bolivia in 1964, and later founded the pro-Peking Communist Party of Bolivia (Marxist-Leninist). Moisés Guevara and his supporters had been part of Zamora's group after the split but were expelled from it.

September 6

Together with Sánchez and Mbili, we discussed the situation created by our new instructions and how best to resolve the matter. The most complicated question is our relations with the party, now that we have decided to organize things with [Moisés] Guevara and have been given orders to virtually sever our relations with the party, at least temporarily. The other problem is that we now need to get rid of the farm that was purchased near Santa Cruz.

We agreed to send someone to take charge of the farm so that it would not arouse suspicions by appearing abandoned, and to urgently go to the Beni zone to purchase a property that meets the minimum requirements. We would like to hear from Manila regarding the matter of the break with Estanislao, or at least to hear if we are authorized to proceed with the men we have. To keep things as they are, Ramón needs to speak with Estanislao. As soon as we buy the farm, we will go there and move everything we have from Santa Cruz (weapons and ammunition).

September 8

We continued the discussion with Pacho on the best way for Mongo to make the trip, on the date of Pacho's return to Manila, and on the best way to resolve the problems posed by the new instructions. We need to reach agreement on a report that will cover the points we discussed, more or less, and expand on those we have come to agreement on.

September 9

We showed Pacho some of the equipment we have acquired: uniforms, boots, canteens, radios, hammocks, machetes, and some weapons. We will also show him the houses we have obtained for contacts, to live in, etc.

September 10

We began preparing the report on our activities up to now.

(TRANSCRIPT)

We have begun taking the steps required to carry out your instructions. The primary thing is to acquire a farm in the indicated zone. We also want to bring you up to date on some of the measures we have been forced to take concerning the work already done along other lines:

1. All our relations for organizing the "dance" have been with the party, that is, with Estanislao.

As explained previously, we had reached an agreement with him to initiate the armed struggle. He interprets this to mean a general uprising that in broad outline would be capable of bringing them to power. This is obviously not our conception of the armed struggle.

We have therefore discussed the need to simultaneously organize the guerrilla struggle in the mountains. Toward that end we obtained from Estanislao a commitment to provide us with twenty of their best men, of which we have ten. We are completely convinced that Mongo can persuade Estanislao to center his efforts on guerrilla warfare. He has stated his willingness to go off to the mountains.

Giving priority to negotiations with the Moisés Guevara group places us in a somewhat difficult situation. Moreover, because of what has already transpired, we do not think it is correct. It would be possible for us to organize a centralized and united command that would include the party's people and those from Guevara's group. To do so would mean not breaking off contact with the party, at least not with the ten men we already have (five of whom have been trained) until you arrive and decide the rest.

Perhaps we are somewhat influenced by our relations with Estanislao's people, but right or wrong, our work has been exclusively with them.

We are aware that this type of public organization — the party — runs the risk of being penetrated and infiltrated, but you can be certain that everything is being done to make a strict selection.

Notwithstanding our lack of contact with Guevara, we have

formed an opinion about him based on his reports and what we know through Sánchez and Francisco. This opinion undoubtedly suffers from inadequate information, something we hope the Frenchman will remedy with his report[4] and through his dealings with Guevara.

Personally we do not think he merits the confidence he apparently has been given. As we see it, he has wavered in small things that should not be overlooked. For example, through Sánchez he sold us a Thompson [submachine gun]. If he is planning to engage in struggle, why is he giving up weapons? He has said one thing to Francisco and another to Sánchez. When we confronted him about this, he tried to make excuses, thereby proving the falsity of his arguments.

We cannot overlook the fact that he has expressed a willingness to fight openly for our line, which is guerrilla warfare. We know his group is made up of workers, miners, and peasants. Twenty men, tested in struggle. We know of their reconnaissance of the possible zone of operations; their tightly disciplined organization; their willingness to join under a single command without raising any disagreements for the moment.

2. The matter of selecting the zone. In our opinion the Beni zone is quite good.

We want to make you aware of what we've done in this regard: We discussed with Estanislao the three following zones: Caranavi, Las Yungas, and Santa Cruz. The first two are in Beni. We decided on the zone in Santa Cruz for the following reasons:

a) It is a tropical zone.

b) It is an area of colonizers, like the other two.[5]

4. The report referred to was a "geopolitical study" Debray was to make of the Alto Beni and Chapare regions. According to Debray, before Che Guevara left for Bolivia, he received the results of this study (containing maps, photographs, diagrams, etc.) both of a topographical and military nature and of a social and political character, with a list of sympathizers and potential collaborators in each region. (Régis Debray, *Che's Guerrilla War* [Penguin, 1975], p. 94–95.)

5. One of the provisions of the agrarian reform that came out of the Bolivian revolutionary upsurge of 1952 was to encourage landless peasants to settle on unclaimed land in sparsely populated regions of the country. The biggest ar-

c) It has large forests and is located near the Cordillera Oriental of the Andes.

d) It is an important zone for the country's economy, due to its large oil wells and its cattle. We could therefore have an economic impact not just nationally but internationally, because Gulf Petroleum has a pipeline to Chile for shipping oil to the United States. The zone of Las Yungas in Alto Beni, which has been selected, is suitable from this point of view. The only difference is in terms of economic activity, since this is the zone that supplies vegetables and grains, etc., to La Paz, and much of the cattle consumed there passes through the Beni plains.

We have already created some of the conditions in the Santa Cruz zone. We have obtained a farm located near Lagunillas and Gutiérrez; this is a region of Chiriguan Indians. As you will note in the attached sketch, it is surrounded by small hills. In addition, we have a house in Santa Cruz where half the weapons are stored. We had begun organizing a supply and information network in collaboration with the party. We left a family in charge of the farm to raise pigs, so no one would be suspicious. Regarding the other matters, we are taking the necessary steps such as moving the weapons, which we will do as soon as a farm in Alto Beni is obtained.

3. We do not understand how our replacement will be able to work, given the instructions to remain apart from the party and from Guevara. Everything we have been able to achieve so far — acquisition of weapons and other equipment, etc. — has been done with their help or through them, and we should not forget our unfamiliarity with the country.

We have no possibility of obtaining the documents. In line with instructions, for reasons of security, we never had any contact with the people who can get them. This leaves us no other option than to use the party's connections.

---

eas of colonization were in Alto Beni, Chapare, and Santa Cruz. While some peasants received resources, loans, and other support, the majority of settlers got little or nothing and farmed at near-subsistence levels.

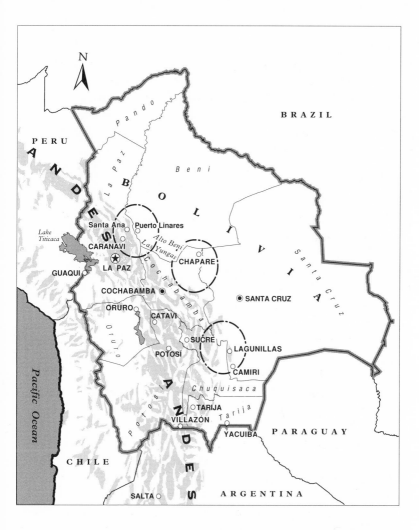

Possible zones of guerrilla operations

4. In our previous report, we asked for instructions on how to resolve the matter of Peru. At the same time, we have informed Sánchez about the change in plans so that he would let Chino know. We repeated our willingness to continue aiding them on a subordinate level to the Bolivian effort. Chino agreed that Sánchez should collaborate with us on the Bolivian plan. At the same time, however, he made clear his determination to continue their efforts. Even though the work was proceeding slowly, he indicated to us, it was being done on a firm basis, and his organization remained determined to engage in armed struggle whatever the cost. We request instructions on whether to tell them that the aid has been temporarily suspended. If, on the other hand, it is to be maintained, let us know how it is to be sent and up to what point.

5. If possible, send us comrades Freddy Maymura and Lorgio Vaca and speed up the training of Inti and Coronado.[6]

6. We need to be sent some addresses in Prague for establishing contacts. The contacts should wait in the airport for those traveling through there, to prevent them from getting their documents entry-stamped.

7. At the recent congress of the Uruguayan [Communist] Party, Comrade Kolle[7] met with members of Brizola's organization,[8] who expressed their decision to engage in armed struggle and requested the party's help in buying weapons and equipment, and for someone to serve as a guide for entering Brazilian territory. They also expressed the view that the party should arrange with us to send two comrades to Cuba — Colonel Arana and Capt. Alfredo Riveiro Damut, an F-86 pilot — to report and discuss aid.

---

6. Freddy Maymura (*Ernesto*), Lorgio Vaca (*Carlos*), Guido Álvaro Peredo (*Inti*), and Benjamín Coronado (*Benjamín*) were members of the Bolivian Communist Party receiving military training in Cuba. All of them subsequently joined the guerrillas.
7. Jorge Kolle, a member of the National Secretariat of the Communist Party of Bolivia.
8. Leonel Brizola is a leader of the bourgeois-nationalist Brazilian Labor Party who had been governor of Rio Grande do Sul in the years before the U.S.-backed military coup in 1964. Following the coup Brizola went into exile in Uruguay, where he sounded out possibilities of organizing a guerrilla movement.

GRANMA

BOHEMIA

Working people in Cuba opened a new chapter January 1, 1959, inaugurating a deepening revolutionary transformation that became the first socialist revolution in the Americas.

Top, Rebel Army fighters celebrate liberation of town in Las Villas, December 1958, days before the regime of U.S. backed dictator Fulgencio Batista crumbles. **Bottom,** Cuban workers take over Texaco oil refinery, June 29, 1960, lowering U.S. flag for last time.

Spurred by the Cuban revolution, a rise in revolutionary struggles occurred throughout Latin America.

Top, peasant unions in Peru demonstrate for land in La Convención valley, early 1960s; sign reads, "Land or death. We will win."
Bottom, working people in Havana respond to a U.S.-organized condemnation of Cuba's revolutionary government at a meeting of the Organization of American States, September 1960. Signs denounce "puppets of the OAS," which one placard calls the "Organization of American Slaves."

UPI / CORBIS-BETTMANN

WIDE WORLD PHOTOS

Top, armed workers patrol streets during insurrection against U.S.-backed regime in the Dominican Republic, May 1965; the uprising was crushed by an invasion of 24,000 U.S. troops. In the photo is Col. Francisco Caamaño (second row at far left, in khaki uniform), leader of the forces resisting the U.S. invasion.
Bottom, demonstrators in Panama attempting to raise Panamanian flag at U.S.-occupied Canal Zone are confronted by U.S. troops, November 1964.

By the mid-1960s, the Vietnamese people's resistance to the escalating U.S. war was at the center of world politics.

Top, U.S. F-5 jet releases bombs over liberated areas in South Vietnam, March 1966. **Bottom,** Vietnamese national liberation fighters.

The deepening war "is provoking repercussions inside the United States," Che wrote in 1966. "The class struggle inside its own territory" is accelerating. **Top,** antiwar demonstration in San Francisco, April 1967. **Bottom,** civil rights protest in Canton, Mississippi, 1966.

In 1952 a powerful revolutionary upsurge shook Bolivia, forcing the nationalization of the largest tin mines, legalization of the trade unions, initiation of a land reform, and enfranchisement of Bolivia's majority indigenous peoples.

Above, thousands rally in La Paz, April 1952.

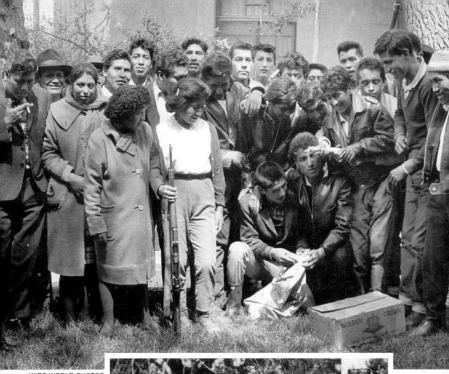

The legacy of the revolutionary upsurge continued to be felt into the 1960s. Miners militias, which had eroded after the 1952 struggles, remained part of the tradition of the trade union movement.

Top, mine workers and supporters receive weapons during a general mobilization in the Catavi-Siglo XX mining area, December 1963. **Bottom,** workers battle police in La Paz, May 1965, during general strike led by miners.

Top, Castro addresses final session of January 1966 Tricontinental conference in Havana. Attended by anti-imperialist fighters from around the world, the conference launched OSPAAAL, the Organization of Solidarity of the Peoples of Asia, Africa, and Latin America (also known as the Tricontinental). Behind Castro are portraits (left to right) of Vietnamese fighter Nguyen Van Troi, Congolese independence leader Patrice Lumumba, and historic leader of the Nicaraguan national liberation struggle Augusto César Sandino, followed by Cuban heroes José Martí and Antonio Maceo.

GRAN

EDITORA POLÍTICA

Above, Che Guevara, 1966, in Pinar del Río province, Cuba, leading training of Cuban volunteers for Bolivia campaign.

If this is approved, we request instructions on how to cover travel costs and on contacts for them in Prague.

8. If possible, send us a barrel for launching FAL grenades, one that can be adapted to a Mauser.[9]

We also want to discuss your decision to travel without our knowing either the possible date or route of your arrival. We think this is an error, because measures can be taken on our part to avoid any possible danger. We could wait for you in any part of the country and provide you with adequate protection. We are even in a position to wait for you in Chile, for which we have the necessary cover.

We have explained to Pacho the possible problems posed by highway travel. Besides the road itself, there are many checkpoints. Furthermore, given the time available, we cannot obtain the necessary documents in Chile that would enable us to move easily from one country to another.

Our plan is for you to travel via Brazil. This means: Frankfurt to São Paulo, and from there to Santa Cruz, where we would wait for you and then go directly to the farm, twelve hours away. There is less security in this airport — practically none. The only place where you would have to pass through some security checks would be in Brazil. We have already told Pacho what this consists of, and we concluded that it has only half the security checks that Chile does. In addition, you would make only one stop in a Latin American country, whereas by the other route you would stop in various countries. We are informing you of this for your reconsideration and decision.

September 11

We are completing the report with some points we overlooked. They are not numbered.

---

9. The Belgian-made FAL grenades were to be fired by blanks from a Mauser bolt-action rifle.

REPORT ON THE ÑANCAHUAZÚ FARM, ITS LOCATION,
STATUS OF WEAPONS AND EQUIPMENT

The Ñancahuazú property is located in the southeast region of
Santa Cruz province, in a mountainous zone of lush vegetation
but little water, although there is plenty on the property.
Ñancahuazú is in a canyon between the Pirirenda mountain range
to the east and the Incaguasi range to the west. This mountain
range extends southward to the Salta mountains in Argentina.
Bordering the farm to the north is the Iripití property (uninhabited),
owned by the same person — Mr. Remberto Villa[10] — who sold
us the farm. He lives at a farm called Terraza near Lagunillas,
about twenty kilometers from Ñancahuazú. In other words, it is
south of the El Pincal farm owned by Ciro Algarañaz, which is
devoted to raising pigs.

The farm is relatively isolated, about 250 kilometers from Santa
Cruz by way of the road to Camiri. It can be reached without going
through Lagunillas — about 25 kilometers from Ñancahuazú — by
taking a detour about six kilometers south of Gutiérrez. The only
property one passes along the way is Aguada Grande, belonging to
Audel León, a young peasant. Ten people live in the house, all of
whom speak Guaraní, the predominant language in the region.
León's house is on a hill, and is about two hundred meters from the
road, so one can pass by without being seen.

Three kilometers from the farm, along the road, is Ciro
Algarañaz's house. This man is the only danger to our work, since
he is the closest neighbor and extremely nosy. During the time of
Paz Estenssoro[11] he held local administrative power in Camiri.
After we purchased the farm, we learned he was telling people
that we were taking advantage of the farm's location to set up a
cocaine processing plant. He is interested in having us buy some

10. Owner of Ñancahuazú farm which was sold to Coco Peredo. Villa was later
    arrested by the army and accussed of collaborating with the guerrillas.
11. Víctor Paz Estenssoro was a leader of the MNR (National Revolutionary
    Movement) and was president of Bolivia 1952–56 and 1960–64. In November
    1964 he was overthrown in a military coup led by generals René Barrientos
    and Alfredo Ovando.

cattle and pigs, which is why he maintains good relations with us. He lives in Camiri, goes there on weekends, and returns on Monday nights, sometimes staying longer.

Apart from this problem, the property meets all the requirements for the job. It is not large at present, but we will create the conditions for this later by building a house farther back so that people cannot see us, since the existing house is at the end of the road. The real problem, though, will be transporting the people, because it will be necessary to deceive Algarañaz.

The trip to Santa Cruz takes twelve hours, and that's a record during springtime. The stretch from Mora to Río Seco is almost impassable. The delay can last two days or more.

The farm is 1,227 hectares, with plenty of timber. On this basis, our legal cover will be raising pigs at first, and then a sawmill.

Important to note is that going north it's possible to cross through the wooded mountainous region all the way to Valle Grande, after which the forest thins out. To the south, one can go all the way to Argentina through natural conditions similar to those on the farm.

The bearer of this message can verbally report on the following questions not contained in the written account:

1. General Esprella.
2. The trainee studying over there.
3. Uruguay matter.
4. Barrels for grenade launchers.
5. Opinion on the forthcoming trip.

September 12

We bid Pacho farewell on his return trip to Manila. We decided that he should buy at least four pairs of boots in Paris and send them to the commercial addresses we gave him. The locally made ones aren't worth a damn. We expected Tania's book, but nothing was delivered.[12]

---

12. A document from Tania was expected.

September 13
Mbili left with Rodolfo to see the farm in the Alto Beni sector.

September 16
Mbili returned from his tour. He says that the timing was bad because the Frenchman was in the zone and it's not advisable for him to see them often.

It is an area of settlers. Sixteen thousand families occupy the whole area (ten hectares per family). Hunters and people looking for cinchona bark[13] go through the forest. There is one man who will sell us his plot (ten hectares) and another who has not made up his mind. The problem is the number of settlers. It's possible to get a permit for logging in the forest reserve, but it will take a number of steps and considerable time. We are trying to get authorization for four hundred hectares.

September 19
We went with Ricardo to give protection to one of our arms buyers. While we waited two blocks from the person who was to make the delivery, we spoke about the turn of events (Mongo's decision to work with [Moisés] Guevara). Our discussion centered on finding the best methods to ensure the success of our actions. In this respect, we discussed the need to invest our resources in the region with care to avoid waste; plan things carefully and calmly, looking at things as a whole; prevent disasters by tying up all loose ends; and organize things well with our neighbors or with neighboring territory, in case Mongo needs to cross into one of these countries.

We should now forget the idea that the struggle in Cuba began with twelve men. Given the current circumstances, the struggle should begin with the largest possible number of forces. We should also bear in mind that the guerrillas' impact on the continent will not be the same as on a narrow island.

13. Cinchona bark contains quinine, used to combat malaria.

The person replacing Mbili should have facial characteristics similar to those of Bolivians, and he will need a good cover.

September 23

Mbili was summoned by Estanislao to discuss some problems. Everything indicates that the meeting was called on account of the Frenchman's activities.[14] Facundo[15] also told us that we have received a message from Manila. He gave us the name and room number of a Cuban staying at the Sucre Hotel.[16] This shows that they are following us.[17]

September 24

(TRANSCRIPT)
MESSAGE NO. 5:

Ariel,

In previous messages we communicated some matters regarding the party that now have to be altered, owing to their stance.

A few days ago we were contacted and summoned to a meeting with Estanislao, in the presence of the four.[18]

At that meeting it was raised with us that our government is establishing contact with the factionalists. This was being done through the Frenchman Debray, who was offering trips to various factional elements. They believe that these are signs of mistrust toward them, which they do not agree with. Furthermore, Debray

---

14. "The frequent comings and goings between La Paz and the Alto Beni, combined with my staying in the area, had alerted the Communist Party and aroused their suspicions." Régis, Debray, *Che's Guerrilla War*, p. 96.
15. Luis Tellería, a central leader of the Bolivian Communist Party.
16. The person was Alberto Fernández (*Pacho*).
17. A reference to the Bolivian Communist Party leadership.
18. Rodolfo Saldaña, Jorge Vázquez Viaña (*Loro, Bigotes*), Coco Peredo, and Julio Méndez (*Ñato*), the four Communist Party members who were assigned by Monje to help prepare the guerrilla front.

has been seen by them in the three regions proposed for guerrilla activities.

They know nothing about Moisés Guevara.

They want this situation to be clarified; they will not put up with any dirty tricks nor will they join with the factionalists in a unified command, since they view them as their enemies in every way.

We said we did not know about the Frenchman's mission, that our government had not informed us of these matters, but that we wanted to take this opportunity to mention some deficiencies we have observed:

1. They have shown no confidence in the guerrilla struggle.

2. They have done nothing on organizational matters. To the contrary, they act as if these are of no importance.

They responded that they have been focusing all their efforts on the general uprising, and that for them the guerrilla effort is secondary.

When we asked them what they had done so far to organize the uprising, they responded that nothing had been done.

We explained that we could not wait here twenty years for them. They proposed sending a representative to Cuba to discuss the matter. Talking with Coco, he told us that Mario had asked him to travel to Cuba to raise the matter of Mario's resignation from leadership in the party to join the guerrilla struggle.

In our previous report we raised the question of our relations with the party, because it is not easy to break commitments that have been made. We await instructions.

During the reconnaissance trip to the farm, we ran into the Frenchman, who tried unsuccessfully to take a photograph of us. We thought he might have taken a picture of the jeep, since he is taking photos of all government vehicles.

The area chosen for the farm, as you already know, is an area of colonization. In the forests you run into a large number of peasants hunting, fishing, or gathering cinchona bark. This signifies a risk that a regular group would be quickly detected. There are concentrations of troops, who are building a road from Caranavi to Santa Ana. These are military work brigades, not regular troops, and their base camp is in Palos.

This whole situation has set us back somewhat, which is why we request permission to obtain four hundred hectares, in compliance with legal requirements, in a zone free of settlers. There we would establish ourselves, dedicating our efforts to agriculture and raising pigs.

After building a house, the farm will be located between Santa Ana and Palos. In addition, we will purchase two plots of twenty hectares that are two kilometers from Belén on the edge of the road. This spot will serve as a jumping-off point to reach the other farm, since it is on the opposite bank of the Beni river, the only waterway (map attached).

At the farm we will leave the jeep guarded and stock up on supplies.

In case your arrival is delayed, it would be helpful for us to travel there to get a more detailed report on the current situation.

(STOP)

September 28

Accompanying Ricardo, we met with Estanislao. We were informed of the questions that will be put to Manila.

Estanislao began by explaining that his commitment to Manila was to help in organizing matters to the south.[19] This included providing twenty men and assigning them to Mbili, in addition to coordinating the matter in Brazil with Brizola. He said that the strategic plan assigned secondary importance to Bolivia, and that the organization and leadership of the Bolivian plan were his responsibility and at the proper time he would request help. He added that these were the commitments made in Manila. He said he had raised the same thing with the Soviets, who told him they were willing to help. Now, he said, we have to take into account the arrival of the Frenchman, who for the second time has been devoting

19. A reference to Argentina.

himself to criticizing the party. Estanislao says that the Frenchman is closely linked to Zamora's party and is offering trips to Cuba on our government's behalf.

Estanislao says that he visited the Caranavi zone, and that he received an order from Cuba to change the location of the farm to the Alto Beni region; from this region it is not possible to extend outward to other countries. He has been able to conclude from this that Bolivia is the centerpiece of the plan, and that he has been kept in the dark about everything.

For this reason Estanislao believes it is his duty to report to the party what is happening. Estanislao added that even though he supports armed struggle, he has had nothing to do with the whole matter. He wants to make it clear, however, that he has proposed to the Secretariat that he resign from the party leadership to protect the organization. He believes the agreements made in Manila are not being honored.

We told him we did not accept his assertions, because they run counter to everything he agreed to earlier. Our country has been kept informed of everything that has gone on. In the first place, we told Comrade Estanislao two months ago that the plans for the south were now secondary, and that the center of activities was here in Bolivia, because the view is that right now this country offers the best conditions. He had agreed with that.

We went on to state that we had told him of the need to abandon the southern zone because the farm was practically inside a military base. For that reason we needed to discuss a better location. Four zones were discussed at that time: Alto Beni, Las Yungas, Cochabamba, and Santa Cruz. It was agreed to send men to scout these out and we proposed the four zones to Manila. A few days ago, one of these was chosen.

Then we said: Estanislao, we cannot understand how you can claim you knew nothing about this, and we do not see where or when we have interfered. If you were not in agreement, you should have raised it two months ago.

He continued to insist they knew nothing of the change in

plans until now, and that we had spoken with him about conditions in a manner that indicated we were thinking of the south. But when Facundo spoke to him about changing zones, then he understood we were talking about Bolivia. We told him this was not so, because we had discussed it with him on many occasions and in the presence of the four, who knew all about these matters.

He admitted that the Bolivia matter was his idea, and that Bolivia was the ideal place, but he would not tolerate things being done behind his back. He was going to participate in the struggle, but he was going to lead it, he said. He insisted that he would not agree to being a puppet in our hands. In his opinion things should be better organized. He was participating in the struggle, but it should be conducted with the entire party. He said he needed to participate more in the leadership and organization of the thing to make assignments that could ensure better organization of the work.

He declared he was ready to join in an armed command together with any organization, but that he was certain Zamora would not join the struggle.

He said he was compelled to hide things from the Secretariat because its members talked too much. In Uruguay, Arismendi[20] mentioned our presence here and Ramón's possible arrival to participate in the operation in the south. Arismendi demanded that the general secretaries of all the parties be kept informed and if not, he would personally take on this task.

We reached agreement that Coco should leave immediately to inform Manila about the situation. He told us that if the PCB leadership decides not to participate in the struggle, we would not be able to count either on him or on the personnel promised or on the support of the four, unless they decide to do so at their own risk. Kolle and Reyes,[21] the other members

20. Rodney Arismendi, general secretary of the Communist Party of Uruguay from 1955 to 1988.
21. Simón Reyes, a member of the Central Committee of the Bolivian Communist Party.

of the Secretariat, came in as we were leaving. They told us that Debray had returned from Cochabamba and had left on Tuesday.

In discussing the situation, we concluded that the Uruguayan matter should be settled before Mongo's arrival, since it was necessary to send someone to Manila. We considered Sánchez but Mbili told me a few days ago that he urgently needed to go. Therefore, we decided to draw up an agenda and to send Mbili. Meanwhile, we will deal with the matter of the farm together with Rodolfo.

September 30

We agreed to prepare a thoroughgoing analysis of the situation and to tell Rodolfo about the state of our relations with the party, to assure his position in the event it is decided to go ahead with the struggle utilizing other people. We explained that, in terms of his position, nothing had been done without the party. We did the same with Coco, who responded that even if the party did not join the struggle he was determined to fight to the death. In Mbili's opinion it's better to take Rodolfo and keep him on the farm without his knowing the matters discussed with Mario; once the matter is decided in Manila, we can then see if he chooses to continue with us or not. I'm opposed to this, because I think a man who participates in this struggle should be informed of the state of things. Nothing should obstruct his work or justify his desertion when he comes up against the hardships of this life. These are the sacrifices victory demands of us.

October 1966

October 2

Rodolfo is on his way to buy the farm. Tuma and I will go later.

October 4

Mbili left for his country to explain the situation. The plane had a minor breakdown and he had to change plans. He did not leave. We had another discussion with Sánchez over the content of the message received last night. After being decoded, it read as follows:

(TRANSCRIPT)

Taco: Starting October 10, you should take the following route, going alone: Everyday, at 9:00 p.m., on foot, starting at the Plaza del Estudiante (the beginning of Prado) go up Mexico Street to Almirante Grau. Renán[1] will meet you along this route. He has orders to contact you only once.

Regarding the message brought by Pacho:

I. We have no guarantees about [Moisés] Guevara. We are only testing his commitments. Don't worry about political relations between Estanislao, Guevara, and us. The important thing is to

---

1. Renán Montero (*Renán*), a liaison with Cuba and a member of the urban network.

guarantee the necessary conditions. Continue relations with Estanislao, avoiding arguments.

The aid requested will be given later.

2. The current farm is good. Get another one, but do not transfer weapons there until you are notified.

3. The proposed supply network should continue to be set up along the lines that Renán will lay out. Don't worry about this.

Carry out instructions to the letter. Documents are not necessary.

Aid to Chino will be channeled from here, maintaining the ties with Sánchez.

Hold off on getting equipment. It should be done with great caution at this stage.

Lorgio Vaca left September 24, on his way there.

Invitation proposals are to be sent January 1. The matter of the Brazilians will be resolved by other means.

Send a telegram signed "Glory to: . . . " acknowledging receipt. Regards to you all. Ramón

(STOP) SEPTEMBER 26, 1966

October 5

Rodolfo arrived and reported that he acquired the farm. He does not think we should go there yet, however, since the property has not been marked off, and our presence could attract the attention of the surveyors, etc. Also, in his opinion, it would be much better to go there on Tuesday, the twelfth (Tuma and me). He also said that after having been in the area for three days, he thinks our stay there will be short because soldiers are patrolling the zone. However, we decided to make a tour of the area, and we will make the decision ourselves whether to move there or to Ñancahuazú. We will leave the question of building houses on the riverbank in Rodolfo's hands.

October 6

Mbili left for his country. We received a message from Manila, which, once decoded, was taken to Mbili at the airport.

(START) MESSAGE NO. 15.

Taco, the route for October 10, Mexico Street, is changed.
Begin this route October 15. Greetings, Ramón.

OCTOBER 6, 1966.

October 8

We spoke with Facundo about the land we applied for and
when we will receive notification authorizing us to take possession of it. He told me the applications were turned down
and that our only alternative was to accept land fifteen kilometers further back; if not, we could accept, as settlers, the
sixteen hectares in the zone we requested. We think that in
order to accept land further inland we would need a legal
permit to trade. This would probably mean we would have to
bring our products to market, but being so far from the river
there are no means of transport. So in order not to attract attention we should insist that the land be right on the river,
since building a road would be more costly than the entire in-
vestment. It would have to be justified first by the sum total of
land to be farmed and secondly by the possibilities for making a profit.

We received the list of supplies purchased, to standardize
things. We have tried to equip thirty men, even though we
cannot do this systematically because Mbili has ordered
equipment for twenty-six men. We are waiting for Ricardo's
arrival to order thirty more knapsacks.

The original list included equipment for fifty men. I don't
know why Ricardo decided to change it without having a
definite idea of the required quantity or type of equipment we
have.

We are buying provisions to store in secret locations. These
will be very useful for us during the first period.

October 10

We were informed that Mario wanted to talk to us about the results of the meeting held with the Central Committee.

Monje told us: "I have been informed that the CC has taken a positive step in unanimously adopting the line of armed struggle as the correct and only road to power. However, I think that much of the support for armed struggle is only verbal and that they are incapable physically of participating in it.

"The discussion focused on the taking of political power in Bolivia. The meeting began with a report on armed struggle as the only way to take power. We explained that the situation is becoming more acute: everything points to a possible coup d'état or crisis in the cabinet, and the regime is getting ready to eliminate the left-wing organizations. Our conception of armed struggle is that of a civil war, a civil war that takes the form of guerrilla warfare. I explained the favorable conditions for guerrilla warfare and that if it can be carried out at all, then this is the country with the best conditions for it. We should not fool ourselves. We face an implacable enemy, an enemy that has at its disposal the vast resources of Yankee imperialism. This makes it impossible for us to take power easily. Therefore, we must believe that our country will create the necessary conditions and develop them rapidly and decisively so that other Latin American countries can begin the struggle. It is possible that many of these countries will attain power before we do. This is our mission, depending on how events unfold."

Mario said that when he finished his statement some of his comrades spoke, asserting they would speak openly because his outline was incomplete. He was keeping the rest to himself, not saying what Cuba's role was to be. "Comrade Mario was not telling everything he knew, in my opinion." Mario said he responded to these questions by asking if anybody had anything else to add, because he had nothing more to say. And he added:

"As far as Cuba's position in this matter, Comrade Fidel told me we can count on his unconditional support both in men, equipment, etc."

After they adopted the line of armed struggle, a question was posed about the party leadership's position, especially Estanislao's. They suggested that Estanislao and the others should be off in the mountains with the rest of the combatants. It was agreed to discuss that later. It was proposed that Reyes be sent to Manila to discuss the question there. But at the suggestion of Ramírez[2] they decided to send Estanislao too because of his greater familiarity with the matter. They will also attend the party congress in Bulgaria.

I explained that I agreed with his reasoning, and that we felt the meeting as he assessed it was positive. But I said I did not think it was necessary for them to go to Manila to carry out a mission that by an earlier decision had already been assigned to Coco. He explained that Coco had no instructions to discuss anything, just to report, since he was unaware of the CC's decision; therefore he was not in a position to negotiate. Also, what was discussed previously was a question Estanislao had posed about his own role and not on behalf of the organization he was representing.

I felt as if my emotions would get the better of me. I felt rage, infuriated by the weaknesses and serious flaws in this man's character. But we had to follow instructions and not get into an argument, so we put the matter aside and continued. We discussed the question of Estanislao's decision to stay in the mountains, and I said that it was correct, but one should not lose sight of what happened to Fabricio Ojeda, Turcios Lima, etc.[3] To this he replied: "Yes, and to a thousand others,

2. Humberto Ramírez, a member of the National Secretariat of the Bolivian Communist Party.
3. Fabricio Ojeda, a Venezuelan guerrilla leader, was captured by the Venezuelan army in June 1966 and murdered in his jail cell a few days later. Luis Augusto Turcios Lima, a leader of the Guatemalan guerrillas, was killed in a car accident on October 2, 1966.

but I don't think that is vital." In any case, I added, the most important thing was that the political leadership be situated in a safe zone where the enemy would not be able to eliminate it easily. And the safest zone is the front. In addition, security measures would have to be undertaken that would allow the party to go underground whenever this becomes necessary.

We should not let ourselves forget, even for a moment, what happened in Santo Domingo, I added.[4] You have already explained to me your conception that the armed struggle is a civil war that takes the form of guerrilla warfare. But if a decision is being considered to launch a general uprising, then we have to look at Santo Domingo. That is the precedent for Yankee intervention in the internal affairs of any country that in their opinion is threatened by "international communism." The decision to intervene in Santo Domingo was taken by themselves alone, since many of the countries that participated in the intervention later on did not have the means for naval landings. But here, any of the neighboring countries can cross the Bolivian frontier by land and it would be a joint intervention by the bordering countries. Given this possibility, we have to be prepared for guerrilla warfare, even after taking power.

October 13

We received a message from Mongo informing us of Mbili's return trip.

(START) MESSAGE NO. 16.

Pombo: Papi arrived without problems. He is leaving on his way back Saturday, October 15. Tumaine and you should stay in La Paz until you receive new orders.

(STOP) OCTOBER 13, 1966.

---

4. In April 1965 a popular uprising in the Dominican Republic was crushed by the invasion of 24,000 U.S. troops.

October 15

We spoke with Facundo again about purchasing equipment and supplies. We asked him to prepare a budget for this because we need to know how the money is being spent. We told him we were interested in an inventory of what we currently have. As of now, we do not know what equipment we have or where it is located.

October 21

Ricardo arrived, very hurt, and talked to me about Ramón's plans and the questions he raised.

Ricardo told me there was no reason for him to have made the trip since Mongo said he was thinking of going to La Paz this Saturday. Mongo said he had made a series of mistakes and that the biggest was sending Ricardo. This hurt Ricardo very deeply since he was there not out of any special interest in Bolivia, but out of personal loyalty to Mongo.

He talked to me about the matter of Tania: she accused him of breaking security rules and getting fresh with her. Mongo will leave for here Saturday, the twenty-second, to meet Renán at the location cited in the message. Then Ricardo is to take Tumaine to Santa Cruz, with six weapons, to pick up Mongo, who will go to the farm by jeep. Afterward Papi will return to La Paz. Then another man and I will go to the farm.

October 22

We spoke with Facundo, who reported that Estanislao told him he was making a trip to Manila to discuss the CC's decisions on the issue of the armed struggle. Estanislao also told him that they want their people to receive military training in Manila to prepare them for positions of command in the event of a general uprising, and that we should be going to the south[5] because we have tried to interfere in the internal affairs of the country. Also, if Mbili had something to discuss with

5. A reference to Argentina.

Estanislao he should have said so, that a meeting could have been organized. Mbili said he had nothing new to discuss, since instructions from Cuba would be sent with Coco when he returns, in accordance with previous decisions.

October 24

Mbili met with Estanislao, who told him he is making a trip to Manila to discuss the Bolivian matter, or better yet, to demand fulfillment of all agreements and commitments made to him, such as our going to the south and their taking charge of matters in Bolivia. At the same time, he blamed Mbili for many of the things that happened here and reminded him that one day history will judge him. Mbili let Estanislao continue his declaration in view of instructions received from Manila about Mongo's intention to enter into contact with all organizations, including Lechín's group,[6] in which Mario's organization has a central role. Mbili believes history will judge them both, and it will decide who was mistaken.

In my opinion Mbili is being very soft on Mario. In front of everyone, he should have held Mario responsible for whatever might happen to us. Due to an error on our part, they are the only ones who know our tactical plans in detail.

Estanislao asked Mbili for 2,000 dollars to pay party salaries. Mbili refused to give it to him, saying he had only 5,000 and will not be left without money, since he is responsible for a number of comrades. Estanislao then claimed he would not ask for a loan but would instead ask for money to cover the young man's travel expenses to Bulgaria.[7] He thus disregarded the earlier agreement that the Bulgarians would pay the fare from Chile to Bulgaria and we would pay it from Bolivia to Chile.

6. Juan Lechín, principal leader of the Bolivian trade union federation, had broken with the Revolutionary Nationalist Movement (MNR) in 1964 and organized the Revolutionary Party of the National Left (PRIN).

7. A reference to Mario Martínez, a Bolivian electrical engineering student who was married to Tania. He had received a scholarship to continue his studies in Bulgaria, which facilitated her work.

Mbili told him that his request amounted to blackmail, and that we would not tolerate being blackmailed by anybody. Seeing his error, Estanislao changed his stance. He then tried to pressure us by mentioning the circumstances of the families of the men he had given us. Then he made an accounting of the 25,000 dollars given to him in Manila, and of the 20,000 dollars given to him in the Soviet Union for the FLIN[8], which they had not delivered, saying they were going to administer the money. He added that they would not allow the families of the men who were with us to go hungry. We agreed to give him 1,000 dollars. He said he thought Fifo[9] would not receive him because of our reports.

Our reports indicate otherwise. Our greatest error has been trusting him and keeping him informed about almost everything.

October 25

Rodolfo was here and we had the opportunity to ask him what he thought of the questions discussed with Estanislao. Rodolfo tried to make excuses for Estanislao, saying he was under considerable pressure within his organization and that makes him vacillate. But as far as they were concerned, we could count on them, that they are ready to keep their word and, furthermore, as party members they will go speak to Estanislao. He declared his annoyance with Estanislao because the latter had promised Rodolfo's wife that she would be sent to the Soviet Union, but later told Rodolfo that if he continued to work with us, this would not be possible.

I reminded Rodolfo that Mbili has promised him that if the families so desired, they can go to Manila with no problem.

8. Frente de Liberación Nacional (National Liberation Front). Launched in April 1964 at a meeting at the Siglo XX mines; one of its main organizers was Rodolfo Saldaña. Closely linked to the Bolivian Communist Party, the FLIN served as the banner under which the Bolivian Communist Party participated in the July 1966 elections.
9. Fidel Castro.

But he responded that Estanislao had already accused him of being a mercenary, and he does not want to give him any grounds to justify that accusation.

October 28
Mbili told us that Renán has arrived and to get Mongo's things together in a small suitcase.

November 1966

November 4

Mbili informed us that Mongo has arrived. He asked us not to say that he told us, because Renán said Mongo does not want us to know. This surprised us because it seemed inconceivable that Mongo would not trust us. Worrying about this, I could not sleep, and neither could Tumaine.

Mbili arrived at around 7:00 a.m. He told us there was a misunderstanding on Renán's part. What Mongo requested was that we not all go together to see him, that we be ready to leave by nightfall. I will go with Bigotes in the second jeep, and Mongo will travel in the first jeep with Pacho and Tumaine.

November 5

Pacho and Tumaine left at 6:30. I said goodbye to Ambuina and María[1] under the pretext of returning to Ecuador. I could not do that with Augusta or Mirna.[2] It was almost 10:00 when we left.

---

1. Ambuina was the owner of the house where Pombo was staying and María was her employee.
2. Augusta and Mirna were neighbors who lived across the way.

November 6

We arrived in Cochabamba at 9:30 a.m., learning that the other vehicle had been through the Alto checkpoint at 8:00.

We continued on, and at about 9:00 p.m. we got to the intersection of the road to Santa Cruz, where we took a short detour using the road to Camiri.

November 7

We reached the banks of the Río Grande at about 4:00 a.m. We still did not know where we were going to cross the river by raft.

After 6:00 a.m. we found the crossing point and joined the other jeep, which was waiting for us. We agreed to cross separately and find a place to spend the night. After searching for the entrance to the road leading to the farm, we stopped in a remote area in the village of Gutiérrez. There, while we ate, Mongo introduced himself to Bigotes, informing him of his decision to come fight in Bolivia because it is the country with the best conditions to serve as a base for guerrilla warfare on the continent. Mongo said that the plans, together with his presence, would prolong the struggle and reduce the chances of a rapid victory. However, we cannot afford the luxury of dreaming about a revolution in Bolivia alone, without at least a revolution in a country on the coast, if not in all of Latin America. If that does not happen, this revolution will be crushed. Ramón told him he had come to stay; the only way he would leave would either be dead or else shooting his way across the border. Mongo wanted to speak with Mario because he thought the latter could be of great help to the revolution. He asked two favors of Bigotes: (1) that he help transport the people who are in transit; (2) that he say nothing to the party about Mongo's presence here, since Mongo knows what that would signify for a party member.

November 8

We cleaned the weapons and went off into the woods. For

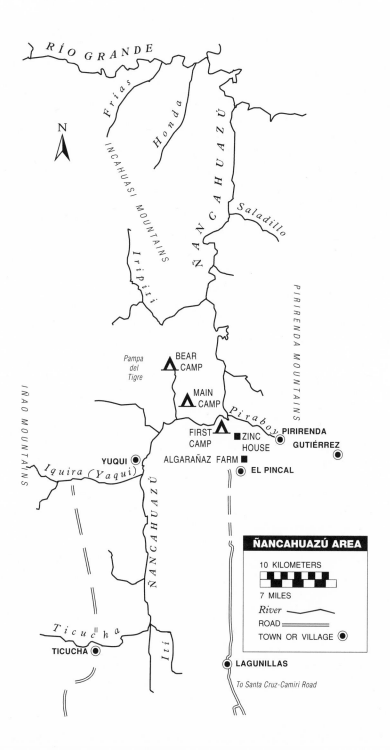

RÍO GRANDE

Frías

Honda

INCAHUASI MOUNTAINS

ÑANCAHUAZÚ

Saladillo

Iripití

N

PIRIRENDA MOUNTAINS

IÑAO MOUNTAINS

Pampa
del
Tigre

BEAR
CAMP

MAIN
CAMP

Piraboy

FIRST
CAMP

ZINC
HOUSE

PIRIRENDA

GUTIÉRREZ

Iquira (Yaqui)

YUQUI

ALGARAÑAZ FARM

EL PINCAL

ÑANCAHUAZÚ

Ticucha

TICUCHA

Itiú

LAGUNILLAS

To Santa Cruz–Camiri Road

ÑANCAHUAZÚ AREA

10 KILOMETERS

7 MILES

River

ROAD

TOWN OR VILLAGE ◉

all intents and purposes, we are now open insurgents.

November 9
Mongo and Tumaine went on a scouting mission and to test the small radios.

November 10
I went out scouting with Pacho. After about four hours we found a place where we can set up camp during the third phase. There is a creek further up and large wooded areas overlooking the ravine. On our return trip we ended up near the house[3] and were seen by Algarañaz's driver.[4] Algarañaz is a man who owns a neighboring farm. As a result of this, Mongo decided we should go into the woods to live. We will build a house of the type that used to be built when I was a child.[5] And so we will go live with the mosquitoes, the marigüis,[6] and other infernal insects.

November 14
We have started to construct a hideaway where we can leave some provisions buried. We spoke with Mongo about the possibility of announcing our presence by attacking an army post. He said no, unless it's a small one, because we cannot run the risk of starting out with a defeat. Instead, we should give the people a chance to gain confidence in us. For that, an ambush is best, where we are assured of victory.

November 15
Mongo spoke to us about the points he will raise with Estanislao:

---

3. The farm along the Ñancahuazú river had a house with a corrugated zinc roof that came to be known as the "zinc house."
4. Tomás Cuéllar.
5. A *bohío*, a thatch-roof hut common in the Cuban countryside before the revolution.
6. A yellow-winged, aggressive mosquito.

1. His interest in Bolivia is not political in nature, inasmuch as he has absolutely no interest in taking power to create a post for himself. Nevertheless, he feels his experience is sufficient to direct military operations and control the finances, because the place money is needed is right here. We can ask China and the Soviet Union for aid, explaining to the Chinese that this would involve no political commitment. We could send [Moisés] Guevara to China with a letter from us to Chou En-lai,[7] and we can also send Mario to the Soviet Union, together with another comrade who will at least let us know how much they have given him.

Mario has to understand that the struggle in Bolivia will be a long one, because the enemy will concentrate all his forces against it. Bolivia will sacrifice for the sake of creating revolutionary conditions in neighboring countries.

We have to create another Vietnam in America, centered in Bolivia.

November 16

Pacho and I went out scouting to look for a site near the creek to set up camp during the third phase (when everyone arrives). But we will have to wait until Mario arrives to begin the talks.

The site is well hidden. The only problem with it is visibility: one can see only about forty meters, which means the enemy will already be on top of us by the time we see them. It's possible we may be able to station an advance squad behind the creek or in the distant hills that could phone or radio ahead and gain us a lot of time.

November 20

San Luis and Pinares arrived.[8] Ricardo stayed behind because the rest of the comrades of the first group have not yet

---

7. The foreign minister of the People's Republic of China.
8. Eliseo Reyes (*Rolando, San Luis*) and Antonio Sánchez (*Marcos, Pinares*). Both had been members of the Central Committee of the Communist Party of Cuba.

arrived in La Paz. Rodolfo came and Mongo asked if he knew with whom he was speaking. He said he did, since Mbili had already told him. Mongo was annoyed, because Mbili had failed to carry out the order that Loro be the one to tell Rodolfo and Coco of Mongo's presence in Bolivia.

November 21
We moved to the new camp on a little hill in front of the house. There we built an observation post.

November 24
Marcos and I went scouting in the hills. He asked me questions and talked about aspects of the struggle in an optimistic way, which pleased me very much. His tone was one of revolutionary frankness. He asked if Ramón is happy with the group, and I told him Ramón thinks that not even Manila could produce a group like this one.

November 27
The rest of the comrades of the first group arrived: Joaquín, Urbano, Braulio, Miguel, and the Bolivian comrades Inti and Ernesto.[9]

We welcomed them and toasted to the success of the armed struggle with a cup of singani (grape liqueur).

November 30
Marcos, Pacho, Miguel, and I went out on a scouting trip heading along the first creek on the left. We discovered a third creek and the possible convergence with the Yaqui river. We returned after two days of hiking without food, arriving at the camp the night of December 1, 1966.

9. Juan Vitalio Acuña (*Joaquín, Vilo*), Leonardo Tamayo (*Urbano*), Israel Reyes (*Braulio*), and Manuel Hernández (*Miguel*) were Cuban fighters; Joaquín had been a member of the Communist Party of Cuba's Central Committee. The two Bolivian combatants were Inti Peredo (*Inti*) and Freddy Maymura (*Ernesto*).

December 1966

December 4

We held a meeting with Ramón, where he spoke to us about discipline and our duty to set an example for the Bolivians, given our guerrilla experience.

Then, he said, in summary:

"Some of the Bolivian comrades have taken courses in the use of weapons and are better trained than many of us, who have been occupied with political duties and have forgotten some of these things.

"It is our privilege to be tested soldiers. We have been under fire before. We have gone through all the very harsh tests of guerrilla life and have overcome them. We are the makers of a victorious revolution. Our moral obligation is therefore much greater, for we must be true communists, full of an immense spirit of sacrifice.

"It's not enough to take every precaution. There are examples in America of guerrilla movements that have been destroyed. In Cuba we received blows that could have destroyed us, surprise attacks like the ones at Alegría de Pío and Alto de Espinosa.[1] We had no experience, we lacked the most basic

---

1. Two battles from the early stages of the Cuban revolutionary war in December 1956 and February 1957, respectively, in which the Rebel forces were taken by surprise. See Ernesto Che Guevara, *Episodes of the Cuban Revolutionary War* (Pathfinder, 1996), pp. 88–92 and 120–27.

knowledge and yet we survived these attacks. The spirit of Fidel [Castro] and his capacity to organize men saved us from defeat. This was an advantage that our comrades in Peru and Argentina lacked. In Venezuela the outcome is still in the balance. It is not a question of either victory or defeat; after the first blow we pass through a formative stage.

"Let us analyze the concrete problems facing the guerrilla force. An open struggle against idleness needs to be waged, and not just during moments of action. We should not fall into slothfulness, neglecting what needs to be done, or doing only what is absolutely necessary. Yesterday, for example, I conducted a little test: a lantern had fallen on the ground and I waited to see who would pick it up. No one did. If you were at home, you would have picked it up, but nobody did. In my battle against idleness I have tried to overcome an attitude of indifference toward things that do not belong to us personally or do not directly concern us. We need to prevent this attitude from taking root among us, because it can destroy the internal cohesion essential for unity in the guerrilla ranks.

"The Manilans will hold leadership positions temporarily in order to begin training the Bolivians and the future cadres in general who will lead the fight for the liberation of the continent. This is the country where the cadres of the Bolivian liberation army and of the sister peoples will be trained, and later on the cadres of the continental army of liberation."

December 20

We held a meeting at which Ramón explained what this struggle represents. He stressed repeatedly that it will not be short, because the insurrectional stage will last ten years or more. We can take power in Bolivia, but unless other countries do the same, we will inevitably be strangled. We are a landlocked country, and a blockade like the one against Cuba would be enough to force the revolution to its knees.

Ramón discussed the organizational plans that were outlined several days ago at a meeting that we — comrades Marcos, Rolando, Miguel, Pacho, and I — did not attend, even though the main item on the agenda was the responsibilities of the political instructors. The duties assigned are the following:

Second in command: Joaquín. Head of operations: Alejandro.[2] Political commissars (the only responsibility assigned to two comrades): Rolando and Inti. Information, collection of data, organization of the troops, etc.: Antonio. Head of all services: Pombo (supplies, medicine, transportation, etc.) with the following under him — head of supplies: Ñato; and head of medical supplies: Moro.[3]

Ramón discussed the responsibilities of each man's position and the absolute duty of every man to obey the orders of each leader in his respective field. He also pointed out that the political instructors are subordinate to the military commander. The political commissar directly oversees, and acts as a catalyst, for the troop's political condition (he is responsible for the men's morale and problems that arise from it, etc.). He must keep the military leader informed at all times. We do not ask that he always be overly strict: on the contrary, all the men should look to him for political guidance and help at difficult moments.

"Those of us from Manila have already been through these things,[4] and we must analyze our experiences so that we don't repeat the negative ones here. This time the situation may arise where the party exists as a political body inside the guerrilla force. But the [Political] Bureau cannot operate; that is, it cannot make decisions on guerrilla matters. Political and military command must be one and the same.

"In a few days Comrade Estanislao will visit us, and I hope

2. Gustavo Machín (*Alejandro*), a Cuban fighter who arrived at the guerrilla camp December 11.
3. Octavio de la Concepción (*Moro, El Médico, Muganga*), a Cuban fighter who arrived at the guerrilla camp December 11.
4. All seventeen of the Cuban volunteers in the unit were veterans of the Cuban revolutionary war with considerable experiences as guerrilla fighters. See the glossary for information on each combatant.

we will be able to come to a decision about the future organization and preparation of this revolutionary struggle. I also hope we receive the total support of the vanguard organization of the working class and of the Bolivian Communist Party.

"It is not necessary for us to choose a name for our movement now, but we will have to select one soon. With regard to our efforts in the future, the Bolivians, who are still few in number, will have to bear the greatest burden, because those of us from Manila cannot be in the forefront at this stage. The Bolivians will therefore have to make a great many sacrifices and will have to display a great capacity for work. The main things we have discussed here — assigning areas of responsibility — do not require further elaboration, because this has already been done and the specific duties of each assignment are simple: those who have been assigned are familiar with them. All leadership positions now being held are temporary, because the leadership cadres for this struggle will emerge from among the Bolivians: their officers and officials, their future economists, administrators, etc."

December 24

We celebrated Christmas eve with much merriment and festivity. We had roast pork, drinks, etc. We got drunk, sang, danced, recited, etc. Ramón recited a poem he wrote. Rubio sang some folk tunes, and Arturo tried to sing, which made us laugh.[5]

December 31

Mario arrived with Mbili, who we had been waiting for since the twenty-fifth. He was accompanied by Tania and Sánchez as well as two more Bolivians who are joining us, Pedro and Walter.[6] We awaited the New Year to celebrate the anniversary of

5. Jesús Suárez Gayol (*Rubio*) and René Martínez Tamayo (*Arturo*) were Cuban fighters who had arrived at the camp December 19 and December 11, respectively.
6. Antonio Jiménez (*Pedro*) and Walter Arancibia (*Walter*) were leaders of the Bolivian Communist Youth at the time.

the Cuban revolution,[7] guide and beacon for all those in Latin America who, like us, are fighting to free their countries from imperialist exploitation. Mario spoke to us, pointing out that we have undertaken a heroic task, as great as that of Pedro Domingo Murillo,[8] and that this has very great significance for him. He said he will return to La Paz and would later join the guerrilla struggle, with the same faith that all the peoples of the Americas have placed in it. He let it be assumed that he had decided to fight.

His statement disturbed me, because we already knew that he and Ramón were unable to reach an agreement as to who would lead the struggle. He maintains that as party secretary he cannot submit to Ramón's orders on political or military questions, even though Estanislao as an individual would be proud to do so. Mario put forward three conditions: political and military leadership; that the pro-China line be rejected; and he also proposed that he tour the countries of the continent to obtain support for the armed struggle from fraternal parties, and to get the Venezuelans to pardon Douglas Bravo.[9]

Then Ramón spoke, explaining the significance of the date being celebrated in Cuba and giving a brief account of the triumph of the Cuban revolution.

---

7. January 1, 1959, marked the victory of the Cuban revolution.
8. Bolivian patriot who led an uprising against Spanish rule in 1809. He was captured and executed by royalist troops the following year.
9. Douglas Bravo was a member of the Central Committee of the Venezuelan Communist Party and the central leader of the FLN/FALN (National Liberation Front/Armed Forces of National Liberation), which had carried out guerrilla actions since its founding in February 1963. In 1965 the CP drew back from its support to the FALN, and tried to use its control over the FLN to strangle the guerrilla movement. Bravo resisted these moves and was expelled from the CP's Central Committee in 1966. He was expelled from the party itself in April 1967.

   A second guerrilla front in the El Bachiller region was led by the MIR (Movement of the Revolutionary Left), commanded by Américo Martín.

January 1967

January 1

Monje left in the morning, and in the afternoon Ramón gathered everyone together and reported on the meeting with Mario. He said he could not understand Monje's stance. He did not know whether to characterize it as egocentrism, or ambition, or political or personal cowardice. Monje said that as the leader of the party he could not accept Ramón as his leader, even though personally he would be very proud to do so. He said he would go to La Paz and resign his leadership position. He would alert the party of what he intends to do, so it is not taken unawares or destroyed, and will then rejoin the guerrillas as a rank-and-file member within ten days at the most.

He raised three conditions for the party to join the struggle:

1. The exclusion of the pro-Chinese group.

2. They would hold political and military leadership.

3. Conducting a tour of the continent with the aim of holding discussions with the fraternal parties on adopting the line of armed struggle. He would also raise with the Venezuelan party that they pardon Douglas Bravo.

"On point 1," Ramón continued, "our view was to create a single command that would include all the organizations willing to fight. Nevertheless, I accepted his proposal.

"With respect to point 2, I explained that I could not accept the position of adviser. I told him I believed that I was more qualified than he was, both militarily and politically, since I have had the advantage of going through a revolutionary process in which I acquired the necessary experience, and that false modesty served no purpose. I explained that I did not aspire to lead the revolutionary struggle in Bolivia but to collaborate in the continent-wide struggle. He had to realize that I could not stand by and calmly allow mistakes to be made, that the political and military leadership had to be one and the same. I told him I could protect his reputation in the eyes of public opinion by appointing him the nominal leader, but this would not be a Marxist method.

"Let us assume that we turned over the leadership to you and we went on to Argentina, Ramón continued. If Fidel were to come give us his collaboration there, we would turn over leadership to him and place ourselves unconditionally under his command. We would do so in recognition of his experience, his qualities, and because he has been our teacher.

"Furthermore, I added, as revolutionaries, we cannot allow the guerrilla struggle to be used as an instrument of political blackmail, as happened in Venezuela, Colombia, etc., rather than as a vehicle for taking power.

"With respect to point 3, I expressed my view that it would be impossible to get the parties to change their line, because it would signify negating their very existence. Nevertheless we accepted this proposal."

Mario then held a meeting with the Bolivians in which he told them that the party is not going to join the armed struggle. He told them they must go back to the city. If not, they would be expelled from the party and payments to their families would be stopped inasmuch as they had leadership standing.

Mario reported that the party had made a commitment to give the Manilans four men. So the following comrades were authorized to remain with the guerrilla force: Ñato, Coco,

Loro, and Rodolfo. He had a big argument with Carlos,[1] who did not understand this stance.

January 6
A meeting was held of the group assigned to positions of responsibility. Ramón analyzed some of the weaknesses of the work carried out so far. He criticized Comrade Marcos for the way he treats the Bolivians and explained why Marcos has not been named second in command even though he was head of the group at the outset in San Andrés.[2] Second in command now is Joaquín.

January 10
Joaquín, Inti, Marcos, Miguel, Benigno,[3] and Braulio went out on a scouting mission to find the Frías river and the Pampa del Tigre and to see if these areas can be used to get to the Río Grande, the zone where we hope to establish contact with the peasants.

January 11
A monotonous day.

January 13
Joaquín, Marcos, and the others returned. They think they have found the Frías river. After their report, the arguments begin. Ramón said that if the river we found empties into the Ñancahuazú instead of the Río Grande, it cannot be the Frías, unless the map is wrong.

---

1. Lorgio Vaca (*Carlos*), a member of the Bolivian Communist Party who had joined the combatants on December 11.
2. The site of the training center for the Cuban internationalists preparing for Bolivia, July to September 1966. It is located near Viñales, in Pinar del Río province.
3. Dariel Alarcón (*Benigno*), a Cuban fighter who had arrived at the camp on December 11.

January 15

We held a meeting in which Ramón announced his intention to schedule the departure after the arrival of Comrade [Moisés] Guevara, who is expected to join us before the twenty-fifth.

January 16

A *gondola* day.[4] This is the name Tuma has given to our activity of moving supplies and equipment from the farm to the camp.

January 18

Today is my third wedding anniversary (leather anniversary). I think of my wife and son with great affection on this date. A thousand kisses for Harry and Cristi[5] (a million kisses).

January 29

[Moisés] Guevara arrived, accompanied by Loyo.[6] He is ready to join us, but needs two weeks to recruit a few men, in other words, until after carnival time. Loyo has been made financial secretary on the national level.

January 31

A meeting was held to explain and outline the objectives of the planned march:

1. The need to get adapted to the vicissitudes of guerrilla life, such as hunger, thirst, lack of sleep, exhausting marches — factors that are equally if not more important than combat itself in terms of molding the future revolutionary soldier.

---

4. *Gondola* is a Bolivian term for bus.
5. Cristina Campuzano, Pombo's wife at the time.
6. Loyola Guzmán. A leader of the Bolivian Communist Youth who was a central person in the urban support network and head of finances for the guerrilla movement.

2. Establishing a base of peasant support. More precisely, exploring possible zones where we can begin establishing the peasant base of the ELNB.[7]

3. To get familiar with and expand the territory explored by our forces as possible zones of operation.

7. National Liberation Army of Bolivia. This did not become the official name of the movement until March 25.

February 1967

February 1

We left on a twenty-five-day exploration mission. After suffering intense pains from drinking too much water, we came to a stream where we made camp.

February 2

We passed by Marcos's small house but did not reach the creek.

February 3

Even though a torrential rain was falling when we awoke, we climbed through steep terrain until we came to a creek that at first we thought might be the Frías river. Marcos was waiting for us with a campfire and coffee. We cooked and set in for the night.

February 4

We set out early along the riverbank of the Ñancahuazú. After hiking for about six hours, we made camp.

February 5

Early, at about 11:00 a.m., we received a radio message from the forward detachment telling us they had procured some domesticated animals. They were ordered to take precautions

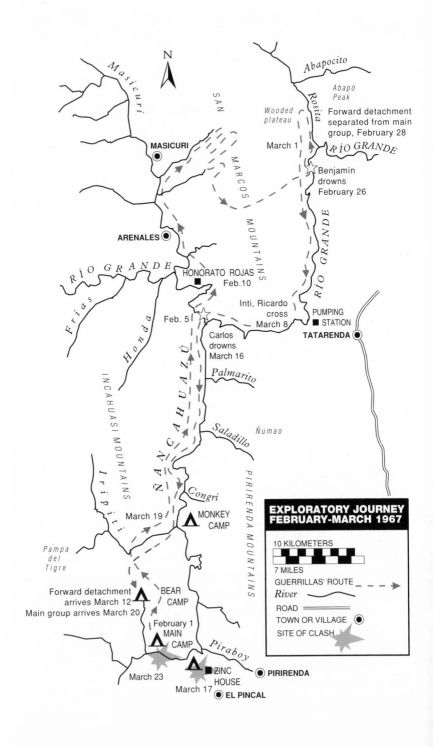

N

Masicuri

SAN

Abapocito

Abapó Peak

MASICURI

Wooded plateau

Forward detachment separated from main group, February 28

March 1

Rosita

RÍO GRANDE

Benjamín drowns February 26

ARENALES

MARCOS MOUNTAINS

RÍO GRANDE

HONORATO ROJAS
Feb. 10

Inti, Ricardo cross
March 8

PUMPING STATION

TATARENDA

RÍO GRANDE

Frias

Feb. 5

Carlos drowns March 16

Honda

Palmarito

INCAHUASI MOUNTAINS

ÑANCAHUAZÚ

Saladillo

Ñumao

Iripiti

PIRIRENDA MOUNTAINS

Congrí

March 19

MONKEY CAMP

Pampa del Tigre

Forward detachment arrives March 12
Main group arrives March 20

BEAR CAMP

February 1 MAIN CAMP

March 23

ZINC HOUSE

Piraboy

PIRIRENDA

March 17

EL PINCAL

EXPLORATORY JOURNEY FEBRUARY–MARCH 1967

10 KILOMETERS

7 MILES

GUERRILLAS' ROUTE - - - →

River

ROAD ═══

TOWN OR VILLAGE ●

SITE OF CLASH ★

and to continue on. They reached a river that, judging by its size, must be the Río Grande. The tracks there were from two horses.

February 6

We organized scouting expeditions and celebrated their return with two dinners. The exploratory mission led by Joaquín revealed that we cannot cross to the other side of the river even though there appears to be a ford. He said he walked for eight kilometers. The scouting mission led by Marcos revealed: (1) that the path leads nowhere; and (2) he found a place where we can make the crossing.

February 7

We started to cross the river at 1:00 p.m. by columns: forward detachment, center group, rear guard. After Marcos and his men crossed, the raft was dragged off by the current so that the center group was split up — half with the forward detachment and half with the rear guard. Tomorrow we will continue the crossing. Another raft was built.

February 8

At daybreak, the rest of the center group that was unable to cross yesterday (Muganga, Rolando, Chino, and I) started to cross, as did the rear guard. By about 8:00 a.m. all the men had crossed. We went through a brief period of thirst when we had to turn back because our path was blocked and then had to climb up a hill without any water whatsoever, since the river water was very dirty. When we climbed down toward the valley we found a small pond with some pigs wallowing in it. We camped in the valley.

February 9

Ramón, Inti, Alejandro, Chinchu, Tuma, and I continued toward the river. We came to a cornfield with baby corn. Inti and Chinchu went on to scout the area and found a path and some peasants. They sent for the rest of the men. The house belongs to a peasant named Honorato.[1] We bought corn and pigs and stayed where we had slept the night before.

February 10
We stayed to take advantage of the peasant's offer.

February 11
We spent the night across the way from some houses on the road that runs between Honorato's house and the home of a peasant named Montaño. We took the necessary precautions so that the peasants on the other side of the road would not see us. The creek water is very cold, so we named it Cold Creek.

February 12
We reached Montaño's house, but he wasn't there. According to his son, he has been gone for a month. The son is about twenty years old and had never seen a hammock, which filled him with admiration. His great discovery, however, was the *guayo* to shell corn, which we made from a can. He asked us to give it to him.

February 13
Miguel and Marcos left on a scouting mission to keep looking for a passageway or find a road.

February 14
We continued clearing a path to the next house, which must belong to a rich cattle rancher or someone like that, because he has fifty head of cattle.

February 15
We reached the house we were looking for, but instead of

1. Honorato Rojas, a peasant from the Masicuri region. Months later he was to lead a section of the guerrillas into an army ambush.

finding the cattle rancher we discovered that his brother, Miguel Pérez, lives there. Naturally we are a little afraid he might inform on us, because his niece is the girlfriend of an army lieutenant. It turns out that his brother, who is the owner of the land, exploits him. He seems to be well-disposed toward us.

February 16
The river yielded large quantities of fish. We know that the army is in Masicuri, but they are military work brigades who repair roads and do not have many weapons.

February 17
It started to rain and lasted sixteen hours, so we camped again in the same place.

February 18
We had a meeting with Ramón. Because of the army's presence in Masicuri, and the fact that it would not be to our advantage to attack, he announced that we would head toward the Rosita river. We have to cross the entire mountainous region of Masicuri to get there. After we reach the mouth of the Rosita we will return to Ñancahuazú via the Río Grande.

February 19
We made preparations to cross the mountains. We camped about a hundred meters from the summit.

Marcos and Tuma were sent to scout the area, and they discovered that the mountains end in cliffs, which makes it impossible to descend to the other side.

February 20
We found ourselves forced to take an animal path that descends through a ravine to a creek, where we made camp. A few days earlier we had to cross the stream near its mouth.

February 21

We got up early and crossed over a small ravine, reaching a creek at 10:30. Two men scouted the zone: Marcos went upstream looking for a path, and Joaquín went downstream. The latter found a field of baby corn. Marcos's expedition was unable to continue because the creek has steep drops that are like cliffs.

February 22

The march continued. When we reached the long creek, Marcos and I went on a scouting mission to find a place where we could cross.

The creek was too long, however, and after a day's hike we were unable to reach its origin. We killed an *urina*[2] along the way. When we returned to our starting point, Rubio and Pedro were waiting for us. The rest of the men continued the march to Boy's Creek.

February 23

We reached Boy's Creek very early. We had spontaneously christened it with the name of the place near our campsite when we were in the mountains. We decided to continue going upstream after Marcos guaranteed we would be able to cross in that area. We had some trouble walking through the creekbed because we encountered four deep pools of water that blocked the way. We were able to cross by making a bridge from some long pieces of wood. I slipped on one of them and fell into the water, which is very deep and cold.

February 24

After passing through some very dangerous places, we were able to leave the creek and climb a ravine up to the ridge. We found a pool of water in a ravine. Marcos and Braulio went out to scout the area.

2. A deerlike animal common to the region.

February 25

Marcos, Braulio, and Tuma were sent out to find an area where we can descend. At 11:00 a.m. we reached the site where Marcos was waiting for us. He pointed out where he thinks the Río Grande joins with the Rosita and the Masicuri. We began our descent down a steep cliff with an almost vertical drop. The fewest number of times anyone fell down was ten. We hiked along the edge of a ravine until 6:00 p.m. We were unable to find water, so we could not cook, and orders were given to cut back on the use of water.

February 26

After walking for six hours we came to a creek where we found some *totai* plants[3] and prepared a salad of hearts of palm. Marcos and Urbano went out to scout. They think they have found the river, but it would be very difficult to continue along the creek because it ends in a marsh. We need to find another route. We had a new experience: Moro made a soup out of snails. It's edible, but a little bitter.

February 27

Marcos, Miguel, Braulio, and Tuma went out to do scouting. Pacho was sent to maintain radio communication using the walkie-talkie. Pacho returned in the afternoon, saying that Marcos ordered him to go back. Later he confided to Ramón that Marcos had threatened to kill him and had struck him with the handle of a machete.

Ramón summoned Inti and Rolando and told them what had happened. He said this was the last straw and that a revolutionary army cannot tolerate abuse of any kind. We had to put a halt to it. Pacho lied about having been struck.

February 28

Ramón met with Marcos and Pacho. All the comrades were

---

3. A type of palm.

notified that a meeting would be held, so that everyone could see that the Manilans who came to help are nothing but a bunch of softies.

The meeting:

"Everybody knows what the goal of this march is," Ramón began. "But for us it has been a big surprise to witness the fact that comrades already tested are the first ones to present problems. We are in the process of getting the Bolivian comrades used to the trials and difficulties of guerrilla life, which in our view is the hardest part of the struggle. We want them to get used to hunger, thirst, constant marches, the solitude of the forest, etc. We are discovering that it is not only the Bolivians who are having problems, but comrades who could be classified as veterans since they have found themselves in these situations many times. This should provide us a lesson for the future: Men who once gave their heart and soul for a cause have gotten used to life in an office; they have become bureaucrats, accustomed to giving orders, having everything solved in the office, having everything come to them already worked out.

"This is the case with comrades Marcos and Pacho, who are unable to adapt to this life. I would not like to think that the reason for their constant problems with the other comrades is that they do not have the courage to say they want to leave.

"Comrade Marcos has commanded large units, and this is a typical case. We must acknowledge that Marcos was a great combatant in the insurrectional struggle in Cuba and deserves our consideration. Comrade Pacho is a comrade who has been in combat but needs to go through the school of guerrilla training, which is why as a guerrilla he is incomplete. If we have any more problems with Pacho he will be punished and sent back to Manila, because he lied about the way things happened."

At 2:00 p.m. Comrade Benjamín fell into the river when he made a sudden movement. He was dragged off by the current and drowned. Rolando jumped in but was not able to get him out.

This struggle has begun with a sad incident similar to what happened in the Congo with the drowning of Comrade Mituodidi, the chief of staff. [4]

---

4. During the Cuban internationalist mission in the Congo, Leonard Mituodidi, chief of staff of the Congolese guerrilla army, drowned in Lake Tanganyika on June 7, 1965. He was traveling by boat and jumped into the water to save some villagers who had fallen in because of the high waves. Despite all efforts, he could not be saved. With his death, Guevara said, they lost the man who had begun to instill some organization at the guerrilla base in Kalimba.

March 1967

March 1
We reached the Rosita river. Our food ran out. Only the center group has some beans and two boxes of oatmeal, which were distributed among the forward and rear detachments. We ate some very bad soup made from bamboo.

March 2
We built a raft and part of the forward detachment crossed, except for Miguel. The current carried the raft away. Earlier Urbano and Rolando left to hunt and brought back a bird of prey and a dead fish they found. Miguel, Inti, and Loro went up the Rosita river. A torrential rainstorm began. Once again we are separated into two groups.

March 3
It continues to rain. We attempted to make radio contact with the forward detachment but with no success. We stationed a sentry in case someone appeared along the riverbank, but nothing happened.

March 4
The rain stopped at 10:00 a.m. We followed the path to the place where it crosses the one leading directly to the hills. We took the new path for eight to nine kilometers until we lost it.

We made camp, intending to return along the trail we were following in order to reach the paths we created.

March 5
In the afternoon we arrived at the creek from which we set out toward the Rosita river several days ago.

March 6
Miguel and Urbano went out to cut a trail, and the rest of us spent the day looking for hearts of palm. We have eaten nothing in the last few days except a few small birds that we caught and hearts of palm. We are going to build up a reserve for two or three days.

March 7
Joaquín and Braulio went out to help cut the trail. Braulio fainted and was able to walk only with difficulty.

March 8
We made camp some four or five kilometers from where we were, still on the banks of the Río Grande.

March 9
After passing through dangerously steep areas, we came to the turbine that pumps water for the village of Tatarenda. Ricardo and Inti crossed the river pretending to be members of a hunting expedition that ran out of food. They have taken longer than planned, which has made Ramón impatient.

March 10
Since we had no news of what had happened, we began building a raft to make an expedition across the river and see what was going on. Our plan, after all the men had crossed, was to take over a house. As we prepared for the crossing, we stationed Miguel and two other comrades to give us cover. Their orders were to open fire at the first sign of any suspi-

cious movement along the other bank.

At 9:00 a.m. Miguel reported that a raft was crossing from the other side. To our delight it turned out to be our men returning with food (rice, coffee, sugar, pork, etc.). They told us that Marcos had passed through there claiming to be a Mexican engineer.[1] Inti almost drowned when he got a cramp. Ricardo saved him.

March 11

We continued the march in search of the mouth of the Ñancahuazú, and did the same the next day.

March 13

We made camp after crossing the most difficult and dangerous terrain we have encountered thus far in the entire trip. Ramón said that Miguel has shown great strength in clearing a path, and did so in just one day.

It started to rain again. I was hoping to hear the speech by El Caballo.[2] I talked with Mbili about several things. A few days ago Ramón had asked me to spend some time with him, as he was worried about Mbili's attitude. Mbili mentioned that things are going badly in the city. I told him Ramón had asked me to speak with him, that Ramón is worried because he appears withdrawn.

March 15

We arrived at the banks of the Ñancahuazú. It was decided to dispatch Urbano to the main camp with a message to send

---

1. The forward detachment led by Marcos had become separated from the unit on February 28, during a crossing of the Río Grande. The two groups remained apart for the remaining weeks of the expedition. The forward detachment had been through the village of Tatarenda on March 4, and their appearance there eventually became known to the army.
2. A reference to Fidel Castro (literally "The Horse"). Castro's speech of March 13, 1967, can be found in *Selected Speeches of Fidel Castro* (New York: Pathfinder, 1992), under the title, "Those Who Are Not Revolutionary Fighters Cannot Be Called Communists."

us some food, but the river rose precipitously and prevented us from crossing it. Since Urbano does not know how to swim, Rolando was sent in his place.

March 16
The men of the center group crossed the river on the raft that we built a month and a half ago, but the strong current swept away the raft and the rear guard found it impossible to cross. Tuma and I tried to find Rubio and Ernesto, who should have passed this way, but we did not locate them.

March 17
We received word that Joaquín and his men have appeared and that, to our sorrow, Comrade Carlos drowned when his raft overturned. Carlos was one of our most valuable men; he was from Santa Cruz. In addition to this irreplaceable loss, we also lost three weapons and seven knapsacks. Many comrades were left practically naked because they lost their clothing.

March 18
We headed toward the camp after replenishing our strength a bit because yesterday we had to slaughter the filly.

We hunted an urina. After waiting three hours for the men who remained behind, we had to make great efforts to reach the place where we camped the last time. I had a heated discussion with Urbano in which Ramón intervened. Urbano had refused to cook, and I insisted on it since I am responsible for organizing these activities.

March 19
We set out with the aim of reaching the small stream that we take to the Ñancahuazú camp, and then we continued to the spot where we made the first camp at the beginning. Ramón expressed suspicions that something had happened because a plane flew over the river, apparently on a reconnaissance mission. In addition, we should have met up with

some of the men who had been sent to the main camp. Those
in back of us killed another urina. Ramón suggested I carry
some of the things Alejandro was carrying, including the radio, and he was relieved of these items. It was hard for me,
and I had to make great efforts to keep up with those in the
lead. The truth is I'm only able to stay among the first rank
because of Ramón's example: he's sick, but always first, which
impresses me greatly; secondly because men who I consider
weaker than me do it; and thirdly because I don't think anyone should let themselves be defeated by difficulties. I fell in
the river and Urbano had to help me up.

When we reached the creek, we met one of our comrades
who was looking for us, saying he had come with Benigno.
This comrade is the Peruvian doctor.[3] Benigno brought a report
from Marcos explaining what is going on in the main camp:
Two of the men brought by [Moisés] Guevara have deserted.
The army (six soldiers) conducted a search of the house. Loro
had a confrontation with the army and killed a soldier. Coco
went to Lagunillas to bring back a group of Guevara's people.
Among the people who arrived were Danton, Chino and his
comrades, Carlos, Tania, and Guevara and his comrades.[4]

We cooked some *charqui*[5] and ate it with meat, coffee, etc.
We spent the night there.

3. Restituto José Cabrera (*Negro*), a Peruvian fighter who had recently joined the
   guerrillas.
4. While the main guerrilla body was off on the exploratory march, a number of
   individuals had arrived at the main camp. These included French writer Régis
   Debray (*Danton, Frenchman*); Juan Pablo Chang (*Chino*) and two other Peruvian fighters; the Argentine artist Ciro Bustos (known as *Carlos*—not to be
   confused with the Bolivian combatant who drowned on March 17); and
   Moisés Guevara and eleven of his men. Several other Bolivian recruits belonging to the Communist Party also arrived.
      On March 11 Vicente Rocabado (*Orlando*) and Pastor Barrera (*Daniel*), two
   of the new recruits from Moisés Guevara's group, deserted. Three days later
   they were captured and provided detailed information to the army on the
   Ñancahuazú camp and Che Guevara's presence. This led to a raid on the farm
   March 17, in which Loro shot a soldier, and to continual air surveillance.
5. Meat that is salted and sun-dried (jerky).

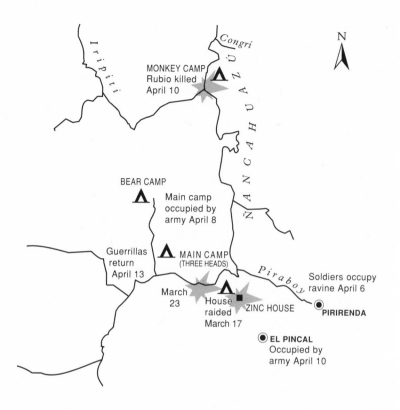

N

Iripiti

Congrí

MONKEY CAMP
Rubio killed
April 10

Ñ
A
N
C
A
H
U
A
Z
Ú

BEAR CAMP

Main camp
occupied by
army April 8

Guerrillas
return
April 13

MAIN CAMP
(THREE HEADS)

Piraboy

Soldiers occupy
ravine April 6

March
23

House
raided
March 17

ZINC HOUSE

PIRIRENDA

EL PINCAL
Occupied by
army April 10

**ZONE OF COMBAT
MARCH 17–APRIL 10, 1967**

10 KILOMETERS

7 MILES

SITE OF CLASH

River

ROAD

TOWN OR VILLAGE ◉

March 20

Ramón directed Benigno and Negro to leave early in the morning with a report for Marcos and instructions for the defense of the camp. They should arrive during the day. For our part we will try to reach the camp we had stayed at the first day of the march, which has been named Bear Camp in honor of a small bear hunted by the Frenchman, according to what Benigno told us.

At approximately 10:00 a.m. we set out toward the camp. Shortly after noon we met Pacho on the road to Marcos's little house and he gave us a message. He repeated what Benigno told us, adding that Salustio[6] had been captured and that the visitors had arrived at the first camp, now called Bear Camp. He also reported on the route he took during his return. We hoped to get to the little house before 4:00 p.m. and if so, we intended to continue on to the camp. We arrived at 6:30 p.m. and were met by Danton and Carlos, who were on sentry duty even though they are visitors.

Later on we met up with Rolando, who had been sent by Marcos to find a suitable place to hide supplies and equipment since the caves have been abandoned.[7] Ramón was angered by these and other measures that had been taken. We were met by Tania and Moisés.

March 21

In the morning Alejandro and the men of the center group left on Ramón's orders. This leaves Tumaine, Urbano, and me with instructions to prepare an ambush further ahead along the river's path. The men of the rear guard left in the afternoon. Discussions began with Danton, Carlos, and Tania. The latter was criticized for disobeying instructions not to go to

6. Salustio Choque (*Salustio*), a member of Moisés Guevara's group who had arrived at the guerrillas' camp during the exploratory journey. He had been sent out as a messenger.
7. The guerrillas had built a series of caves at the site of the main camp, in which they stored food, weapons, medicine, documents, and other items.

the farm. Ramón had given her orders to keep herself at a distance from the organizational activities, with the aim of protecting her identity. Due to Monje's decision, things were up in the air about what had been arranged with him, so she felt compelled to come out into the mountains.

March 22

We set out toward camp, leaving Ñato, Chapaco,[8] and several sick comrades who had brought the supplies.

All the food has been lost. The rifles were left in the cave. When we reached Three Heads — the name by which Ñato christened the main camp — the comrades were waiting for us with bread, coffee, etc.

Ramón ordered a patrol sent out, and Alejandro assigned Antonio and Miguel. When they returned at night and reported on how the patrol was conducted, there was a sharp debate between Antonio and Ramón because they had not taken all the proper security measures. They had crossed roads without taking any precautions. Later, when this was pointed out to them, they said that if the army had been there the troops would have opened fire, so they crossed the road with few precautions. This became the focus of a heated debate with Antonio, which reached a point where Ramón had to intervene and explain that they did not realize they had left tracks.

March 23

An army patrol fell into our ambush, and we captured 16 Mausers, a 30-mm. machine gun, 3 60-mm. mortars, 3 Uzis, 2 radios, and other field equipment. We inflicted the following casualties: 7 dead and 14 prisoners, among them 5 wounded. Two horses were recovered belonging to Algarañaz, which had been taken by the army. There were about 150 soldiers.

On our side eight comrades participated. Rolando was in

8. Jaime Arana (*Chapaco*), a Bolivian fighter who joined the guerrillas earlier in March.

charge of the ambush, and Ramón later ordered others of us to be added. The encounter developed as follows:

Just as Rolando was reviewing positions, noises were heard in the water. A group of soldiers appeared along the bend in the creek, which has a steep cliff along one side.

They waited until a larger group entered and Rolando, as the one in charge, opened fire, taking the soldiers by surprise. Many of them took up combat positions. The few who offered resistance were killed or wounded; the remainder ran away and did not fight. For this reason we were not able to capture the food they were carrying.

Ramón ordered Marcos to head out along the first path of operations with the mission of cutting off the army's retreat from the rear if it advanced along the riverbed trying to get to the camp. He sent Braulio with the rear guard along the second path of operations with the mission of preventing them from getting out of this canyon, which is a trap. Meanwhile, we of the center group were to attack them from the positions prepared for the camp's defense.

March 24

The prisoners were set free. We shared the little we had with them. The soldiers asked that Major Plata[9] be executed because he has mistreated them. We gave them three days to recover their dead and explained to them that hostilities would be resumed after that.

Some planes flew over the site of the ambush. A man was seen.[10]

March 25

All is quiet. A discussion was held and we approved the

9. Hernán Plata Ríos.
10. That same day Tania's jeep was seized in a garage in Camiri, where she had left it to go to the guerrilla camp. Tania's identity, which had not been discovered until then, was revealed through statements given by the deserters Vicente Rocabado and Pastor Barrera, followed by a search of her house.

discharge of Paco, Pepe, Chingolo, and Eusebio. We have learned that the members of the youth organization who are here have been expelled.[11] Study classes are resumed. At a meeting we decided to adopt the name National Liberation Army of Bolivia.[12]

March 27

No change. We study.

A meeting was held of the general staff in which Ramón reported on the replacement of Marcos as head of the forward detachment and the assignment of Miguel to this task. This was done after a long discussion between Ramón and Marcos. Our future plans were set.

Che drafted Communiqué no. 1 of the ELN.

TO THE BOLIVIAN PEOPLE
COMMUNIQUÉ NO. 1

Revolutionary truth vs. reactionary lies

The military thugs who have usurped power, murdered workers, and laid the groundwork for surrendering our resources to U.S. imperialism are now mocking the people with a comic farce. As the hour of truth approaches and the people rise up in arms, responding to the armed usurpers with armed struggle, the round of lies continues.

On the morning of March 23, forces of the Fourth Division, based in Camiri and numbering approximately 35 men, under the command of Major Hernán Plata Ríos, entered guerrilla territory

---

11. On February 5, Antonio Jiménez (*Pedro*), Aniceto Reinaga (*Aniceto*), and Loyola Guzmán were removed from the Executive Committee and Political Bureau of the Bolivian Communist Youth (JCB) for "indiscipline, abandonment of the organization's work, and disagreement with the line of the JCB."
12. Ejército de Liberación Nacional de Bolivia (ELN).

along the Ñacahuaso river.[13] The entire group fell into an ambush
set by our forces. As a result of the action, 25 weapons of all
types fell into our hands, including 3 60-mm. mortars with a
supply of shells, and an ample supply of ammunition and
equipment. Enemy losses were 7 killed, including a lieutenant,
and 14 prisoners, 5 of whom were wounded in the clash. These
were given the best medical treatment at our disposal.

All the prisoners were set free following an explanation of our
movement's aims.

The list of enemy casualties is:

Dead: Pedro Romero, Rubén Amenazaga, Juan Alvarado,
Cecilio Márquez, Amador Almasán, Santiago Gallardo, and the
informer and army guide, named Vargas.

Prisoners: Major Hernán Plata Ríos, Capt. Eugenio Silva,
soldiers Edgar Torrico Panoso, Lido Machicado Toledo, Gabriel
Durán Escobar, Armando Martínez Sánchez, Felipe Bravo Siles,
Juan Ramón Martínez, Leoncio Espinosa Posada, Miguel Rivero,
Eleuterio Sánchez, Adalberto Martínez, Eduardo Rivera, and
Guido Terceros. The last five of these were wounded.

In making public the details of the first battle of the war, we
hereby establish what our norm will be: the revolutionary truth.
Our deeds demonstrated the integrity of our words. We regret the
innocent blood shed by the soldiers who fell. Yet peaceful
bridges — as the clowns in braided uniform claimed they were
constructing — are not built with mortars and machine guns. They
are attempting to paint us far and wide as common murderers.
There has never been, nor will there ever be, a single peasant with
cause to complain of our treatment and of our manner of
obtaining supplies — with the exception of those who betray their
class and volunteer their services as guides or informants.

Hostilities have begun. In future communiqués we will clearly set
forth our revolutionary positions. Today we issue a call to workers,

13. There are many spellings used for the Ñancahuazú river in Bolivia, including
on maps. The spelling here is reproduced as it appears in the original text of
Guevara's document.

peasants, and intellectuals. We call upon all who believe that the time has now come to respond to violence with violence; to rescue a country being sold piece by piece to the U.S. monopolies; and to raise the standard of living of our people, who with each passing day suffer more and more the scourge of hunger.

THE NATIONAL LIBERATION ARMY [ELN] OF BOLIVIA

April 1967

April 1

All possible measures were taken to guarantee success in case the army advanced with superior forces.

Tuma gave the alarm from the observation post; he had seen three soldiers who apparently also saw him, since they ran away. It was decided to send the center group to take up its positions. Nothing happened. Ramón decided to send the forward detachment and the rear guard (commanded by Rolando) to the camp by the little house to see how things are there. They are to round up some cows and hide themselves in the Piraboy ravine to set up an ambush along the road from the farm to the Lagunillas highway.

We slaughtered the horse because it was necessary to leave meat for Joaquín and Alejandro, who are sick and must remain in a camp upriver that was quickly prepared for them. Muganga, Polo, Eustaquio, and Serapio stay to keep them company.[1]

---

1. Muganga was the Cuban combatant Octavio de la Concepción (*Moro, El Médico*). Apolinar Aquino (*Polo*) was a Bolivian fighter who joined the guerrillas December 19. Lucio Edilberto Galván (*Eustaquio*) was a member of the Peruvian ELN who arrived with Chino at the camp in February. Serapio Aquino (*Serapio*) was a Bolivian combatant.

April 2

At an early hour we started to transport everything that needs to be left for the sick men.

Departure plans were changed. The center group will join the rest of the troop along the narrow trail to the mountains, because we think it is better to travel along the river road.

April 3

We left at 3:00 a.m. and arrived at the farm at 9:00 a.m. without any problems.

We tried to make contact with our people. In the afternoon we reached the place where they camped. They have slaughtered one of our cows and gathered a large quantity of corn.

April 4

We set out for Pirirenda, and from there we will continue on toward Gutiérrez with the hope of obtaining supplies for the sick and for ourselves, as well as finding a way for Danton and Carlos to get out. Before reaching Piraboy we found signs of an army ambush, abandoned two days earlier. During the night we entered the settlement. The first house we saw was empty; its owner has abandoned it. We found some army equipment, which we took. A meal was prepared out of what we found in the other houses. We tried to find out if there are troops in Gutiérrez. Due to our carelessness one of the farmhands escaped from the house, which forced us to suspend operations. We began to pull back to the foot of the ravine. We were able to learn that the army was headed toward Ñancahuazú along the ridge. We left on a forced march to reach the river's mouth, where an ambush was set up.

April 5

We reached the waterfall, where the rear guard set up an ambush under Rolando's command. We learned that an army unit is camped approximately one kilometer away. Soldiers from there came to the waterfall to bathe, etc. It was

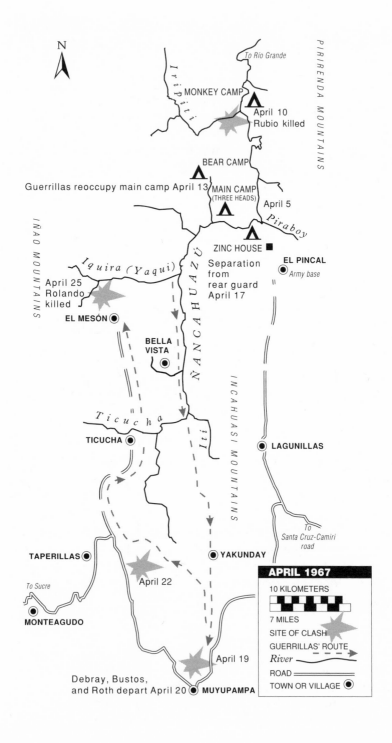

N

To Río Grande

Iripiti

PIRIRENDA MOUNTAINS

MONKEY CAMP

April 10
Rubio killed

BEAR CAMP

Guerrillas reoccupy main camp April 13

MAIN CAMP
(THREE HEADS)

April 5

Piraboy

ZINC HOUSE

EL PINCAL
Army base

IÑAO MOUNTAINS

Iquira (Yaqui)

Separation
from
rear guard
April 17

April 25
Rolando
killed

EL MESÓN

BELLA
VISTA

NANCAHUAZÚ

Iti

INCAHUASI MOUNTAINS

Ticucha

TICUCHA

LAGUNILLAS

To
Santa Cruz-Camiri
road

TAPERILLAS

To Sucre

YAKUNDAY

April 22

MONTEAGUDO

April 19

Debray, Bustos,
and Roth depart April 20 ● MUYUPAMPA

APRIL 1967

10 KILOMETERS

7 MILES

SITE OF CLASH

GUERRILLAS' ROUTE

River

ROAD

TOWN OR VILLAGE ●

decided to cross the Ñancahuazú before dawn, and we left
at 3:00 a.m.

April 6

At the indicated hour we proceeded to cross the river. We
stayed there until the light of dawn allowed us to continue
with our plans. We know that the army has set up camp at the
foot of the ravine.

We continued on and got lost. We decided to return to the
Ñancahuazú river during the night. We ran into some herdsmen who were taking cattle to the army. We took their cattle
and paid them.

We set up camp at Monkey Creek.

April 7

We set up an ambush and began to look for a place that
would serve as an observation post. The ambush was under
the command of Rolando and consisted of the rear guard and
some men from the forward detachment.

April 8

Urbano, El Médico, and Julio[2] left to find the sick men or,
more precisely, to see if they are able to walk so they could be
sent to join us. Urbano and Julio returned with Polo and a
message from Joaquín. The soldiers have taken the campsite.

April 9

We started to clear two paths toward Pirirenda and from
there to the highway, with the aim of preparing an ambush
against the army.

April 10

An army patrol fell into the ambush as it advanced. It appears
that they expected to find us in the area, since they were advanc-

---

2.   Mario Gutiérrez (*Julio*), a Bolivian combatant who joined the guerrillas March 10.

ing with great caution. We suffered our first death in action: we lost Rubio, a good man both as an organizer and as a future military cadre. This was his first battle. We answered their shots with an intense round of fire, and the soldiers who were not cut down went fleeing. In the afternoon the army returned to recover their dead and, inexplicably for us, advanced without much caution. Once again they fell into the ambush, which Ramón had ordered reinforced with men from the center group and the forward detachment. They consisted of 120 men under the command of Major Sánchez,[3] who was taken prisoner by Coco. This officer refused to order the rest of his troops to surrender.

April 11
The column headed out toward the intersection that leads to the campsite. Several of us, including Urbano, [Moisés] Guevara, and me, stayed behind to bury Rubio. The prisoners were set free, and Major Sánchez was given our first communiqué.

En route to Three Heads we met up with the sick comrades who had been sent to a hiding place and had stayed by that creek in case of an encounter with the army. Muganga reported that they are well.

The rear guard was left behind to continue the march two days after our departure. Alejandro stayed with them.

The forward detachment left for the camp, followed by us.

April 13
In the afternoon we reached the camp, where the forward detachment was waiting for us. An ambush was prepared. To our surprise they have not discovered the caves.

April 14
We proceed to take inventory of the provisions. Everything is here except twenty-two cans of milk that are missing from storage depot no. 1.

3. Rubén Sánchez Valdivia.

We concluded that someone passing by committed the
theft, since it did not make sense that the army would have
done so and not taken the weapons.

Che prepared the second message. Danton will take it when
he leaves.[4]

TO THE BOLIVIAN PEOPLE
COMMUNIQUÉ NO. 2

Revolutionary truth vs. reactionary lies

On the morning of April 10, 1967, an enemy patrol led by Lt.
Luis Saavedra Arombal and composed in its majority of soldiers
of the CITE,[5] fell into an ambush. Killed in the encounter were the
above officer and soldiers Ángel Flores and Zenón Prada
Mendieta; wounded was the guide Ignacio Husarima of the
Boquerón Regiment; taken prisoner were 5 soldiers and a
noncommissioned officer. Four soldiers were able to escape,
bringing word of the clash to the company headed by Major
Sánchez Castro. The latter went to the aid of his comrades,
reinforced by 60 men from a nearby unit. These forces fell into
another ambush, costing the life of Lt. Hugo Ayala,
noncommissioned officer Raúl Camejo, and soldiers José
Vijabriel, Marcelo Maldonado, Jaime Sanabria, and two others
not identified by us.

Wounded in the action were soldiers Armando Quiroga,
Alberto Carvajal, Fredy Alove, Justo Cervantes, and Bernabé
Mandejara, who were taken prisoner together with the company
commander, Major Rubén Sánchez Castro, and 16 other

4. According to Debray, Che told him that the plans for future operations consisted of returning to the north, taking the village of Samaipata, and establishing a base in Santa Cruz. He asked Debray to conduct an urgent study of the
   socioeconomic conditions of the peasantry of the department of Santa Cruz.
   Debray was also asked to take the two ELN communiqués and get them published. (*Che's Guerrilla War*, p. 91.)
5. Special Troops Training Center.

soldiers. In line with the norms of the ELN, the wounded were treated with the few means at our disposal. The prisoners were all set free following an explanation of the objectives of our revolutionary struggle.

The enemy army's losses are summed up as follows: 10 dead, among them 2 lieutenants; and 30 prisoners that included Major Sánchez Castro, 6 of whom were wounded. The weapons captured include a 60-mm. mortar, automatic weapons, rifles, M-1 carbines, and semiautomatic weapons. Ammunition for all these weapons was also captured.

On our side we must record with regret the loss of one man. The disparity in casualties is comprehensible if it is recalled that the time and place of all the battles that have taken place have been chosen by us; and that the Bolivian army brass is sending inexperienced soldiers, little more than children, to the slaughter. At the same time, while issuing official statements from La Paz and later pretending to grieve at demagogic funeral ceremonies, they hide who the real culprits are for the bloodshed in Bolivia.

Now they are shedding their mask and beginning to call for U.S. "advisers." This is how the war in Vietnam began, a war that is drowning that heroic people in blood and endangering world peace. We do not know how many "advisers" will be sent against us (we will know how to confront them), but we warn the people about the dangers of this act initiated by the military sellouts.

We call upon the young recruits to follow these instructions: When a battle begins, throw your weapon aside and put your hands on your head, remaining silently where you are at the moment when shooting starts. Never advance at the head of a column marching into combat zones; let the officers who incite you to battle occupy this position of extreme danger. Against those occupying the forward position, we will always shoot to kill. As much as it hurts us to shed the innocent blood of recruits, this is an unavoidable necessity of war.

NATIONAL LIBERATION ARMY [ELN] OF BOLIVIA

April 15

Ramón spoke with us about our future actions. These are: clearing the enemy off the highways and roads through ambushes; the need to win the support of the peasants in order to organize our rural base, etc. He pointed out the great truth that theft is incompatible with socialism, and it is also incompatible with the guiding principles of this guerrilla unit. Therefore, anyone caught committing this crime will be punished, including with the death penalty.

April 16

In the afternoon we reached the settlement called Bella Vista, which is at the junction of the Iquiri river and the Ñancahuazú river. Alejandro and Tania, who are sick, were left behind at the Iquiri river so they can join us later. Our aim is to reach the Sucre-to-Santa Cruz highway in the area around Muyupampa or Monteagudo, with the idea of getting Danton and Carlos out and obtaining food supplies.

April 17

Another peasant got away from us. We spent the day waiting in case the army advances. Carlos talked to me about his concern in having left his wife without a source of income, and I advised him to speak with Ramón.

April 18

We waited for the arrival of Alejandro and Tania, who were left with El Médico (Negro) at the Iquiri river to look after the comrades who are sick. When they arrive we will leave. It was decided that the rear guard should stay behind in the area with the sick, (Joaquín and Moisés are also ill), and wait for our return, which should be within three days at the most.[6] In case we do not return by that time, they should return to the

---

6. The separation with the rear guard led by Joaquín, meant to last three days, turned out to be permanent.

Iquiri and wait for us there. We marched all night. At dawn we stopped in a cane field to wait for daylight. Our people rested and slept.

We captured a peasant who came by on horseback and who was the brother of the one who escaped, the son of Carlos Rodas.

April 19

We made camp near the house of a Guaraní peasant[7] where we stayed until nightfall. In the meantime we cooked. At dawn, during a torrential rain, we came to the house of a peasant[8] who had very pretty daughters. He is hostile toward us. We captured an Englishman who told us he is a freelance journalist.[9] Measures were taken to prevent him from seeing Urbano, Tuma, or me,[10] and to avoid his speaking with Cubans if at all possible. We therefore sent him with the forward detachment; later on, Inti talked with him and did an interrogation.

April 20

On the road to Muyupampa we met a peasant named Nemesio Caraballo who acted very friendly and offered us coffee, which we did not accept. Once on the road, at Danton's suggestion, we let him speak with the English journalist, whom he offered to release with the proposal that he help the journalist get an interview with the leader of the guerrillas, with photos and everything, and in exchange the Englishman would help them leave.

The journalist accepted and was given an interview with Inti. We returned his camera and gave him some documents.

7. Nemesio Caraballo.
8. His last name was Padilla.
9. George Andrew Roth, an Anglo-Chilean journalist believed by the combatants to have been a CIA agent. Guided to the guerrillas by some children from Lagunillas, Roth reported to them, falsely, that a diary by Braulio had been found at the main camp, providing information to the army.
10. All three were Black.

The attempt to enter Muyupampa failed because a peasant sounded the alarm and the population was mobilized. The village had been alerted by two peasants and a member of the DIC.[11] They were intimidated by Coco, who told them dryly, "Give me those guns," and pulled them out of their hands.

Carlos and Danton requested permission to stay behind and try to get out accompanied by Roth. We told them to do whatever they thought best, and they decided to stay behind. Ñato reported that Danton remained behind because of Carlos. We advised them not to enter the village, but to go around it.

We withdrew from the highway as fast as we could. In the morning we again came to Nemesio's house, but he was not there. Some neighbors told us he went to Camiri. (We were a little suspicious.)

We made camp here. Around noon we were warned that a vehicle with a white flag was approaching. We took some precautions. It was the subprefect of the village, the priest, and the doctor.[12] They came to ask us to leave because the army was standing firm and they didn't want any bloodshed. We agreed on condition that they brought us some medicine and food we needed. At around 4:00 p.m., they sent a plane against us that bombed the house where we had been staying. A piece of shrapnel from a bomb wounded Ricardo slightly.

We learned that our visitors — Debray, Carlos, and the Englishman — have been taken prisoner.

April 21
At dawn we arrived at the house of a peasant named Roso Carrasco. He is a man who knows the area very well. He treated us well and explained in detail the routes we could take and offered us what he had.

At nightfall we reached the intersection of the Muyupampa-to-Monteagudo road, at a place called Taperillas. The peasants

11. The Department of Criminal Investigation, the police force.
12. Justino Corcuí, Leo Shwarz, and Mario Cuéllar, respectively.

welcomed us and we went down to the street where Rodas lives. We were told that a man who had been born in the village returned recently and appears to be an informer.

April 22

We captured a group of men who told us they were following our tracks. They had a Mauser rifle. We stopped a small truck full of merchandise, and later stopped another truck. We purchased various things.

After nightfall, as Ricardo and Urbano headed toward the ambush, they discovered the army coming down a hill. They opened fire. Confused, the army retreated. Later on a general exchange of fire began. Fernando[13] issued orders for us to leave in stages. We took a pickup truck and several horses. There was confusion caused by the loss of 2,000 dollars of the money that I carry in a bag. Urbano, Inti, and I came back to look for it. The forward detachment was ordered to dig in to wait for Loro to return, since he has gotten lost.[14]

April 24

At 6:00 a.m. we arrived at the priest's plantation where we found large fields of corn, *jocos*,[15] beans, and a lot of marijuana. Fernando ordered us to move the camp further back, that is, onto the banks of the creek. Benigno and Aniceto[16] left to search for Joaquín. Coco went with Camba to scout and, if necessary, to prepare the trail that goes to the Río Grande to allow the passage of animals.

---

13. Known first as *Ramón,* Che changed his pseudonym to *Fernando* on April 22. He made the change, at Rolando's suggestion, after learning from Roth that the army knew the leader of the guerrillas was named Ramón.
14. Separated from the unit, Loro (*Bigotes*) was wounded and captured two weeks later. Kept incommunicado, he was subjected to severe torture before being murdered. His body was tossed from a helicopter into the jungle.
15. A type of hard-shelled squash.
16. Aniceto Reinaga (*Aniceto*), a Bolivian combatant who had joined the guerrillas by January 1967.

April 25

We moved the camp to avoid being discovered and set up an observation post on the hill at the other side of the creek. This position seemed to us a poor one since, in case of combat, it could be difficult for the person on lookout to go across. Fernando gave Rolando instructions to change the position.

From the observation point, a column was seen advancing. Fernando ordered us to take up positions not anticipated beforehand, forcing us to fight in places not well suited for an ambush. Possibilities for observing the enemy's movement were not good, and there was inadequate camouflage. We were practically out in the open, and we tried to fix the problems.

The army was advancing along the middle of the road with all necessary precautions. (They came with three dogs, the guide and two soldiers walking about fifteen or twenty meters ahead of the rest of the troop.) At this position were Fernando, Miguel, and Urbano.

The soldiers took positions and open combat began. The firing came from their side, since we could not see the positions they held.

With his characteristic courage, Rolando placed himself in the most difficult position: at the end of a curve facing the road. When the fighting began he faced a 30-mm. machine gun that wounded him in the thighbone. Chapaco and Tuma went to get him (six of our men were missing).

We tried to evacuate him with the help of Urbano, Antonio, Inti, Chinchu, and me.[17] After this loss I was assigned to take charge of the ambush.

Speaking about the loss of Rolando, Fernando said, We have lost one of our most valuable cadres, both as a political and a military leader, because he was already a proven fighter. For me personally it has been a great loss, because in addition to all those qualities he was a man trained under our leadership.

17. Despite efforts to save him, Rolando bled to death.

We withdrew along a trail the army had recently created that led to Ñancahuazú.

April 27

We continued our march toward a more suitable and safer place. Benigno and Urbano were sent ahead to scout. We rested and ate what was left of the urina. We received word that it is impossible to continue through this area because the hills end up in cliffs.

April 28

It was decided to follow an old trail that leads to the Río Grande and from there to Valle Grande, and then head toward the Iquiri. We made camp in a place where there are oranges (very bitter) and some water.

April 29

After marching for several hours we realized that we were heading west and were lost.

We made camp and began work on a trail while preparing an ambush under my command. Coco and Camba returned with news that they have found a trail that they believe leads to the hills.

April 30

We set out to cross the hills by following the trail. We abandoned it, however, once we realized that it does not go in the direction we need to go. We made camp on a small ridge.

May 1967

May 1
In the morning we came to a hillcrest, where we heard the noise of a waterfall. We decided to climb down since we have not had water since last evening. At 11:00 a.m. we drank a little tea with milk. We listened to the speech by Commander Almeida.[1]

May 2
We camped on a ridge at the source of a small creek.

We returned south with the aim of finding the creek that will take us to the Iquiri. We marched along the plain.

May 3
We have food for only four days at light rations (soup and canned meat). We stopped at night on the slope of a mountain range whose name we do not know.

May 4
In the afternoon we came to a stream that runs north. In the morning we sent out two groups of scouts to determine its course:

---

1. Juan Almeida, a central leader of the Cuban revolution. His speech to a May Day rally in Havana was broadcast over Radio Havana.

(1) Coco and Aniceto went downstream; and (2) Benigno and Pablito[2] headed upstream. Their job was to try to clear a path toward the plain that is on our right.

Night fell at 6:00 p.m. Some believe the stream to be the Frías river; others think it is the Iquiri or the Congrí.[3]

May 5

On the radio we heard of the arrest of Loro, who was captured by a peasant. In the afternoon we came to an abandoned hut that Benigno recognized as one of those built during his reconnaissance. We are therefore at the Congrí Creek, perhaps no more than a day's forced march from Three Heads and a half day from Bear Camp.

The radio also reported that Debray's mother arrived in Bolivia. He is being tried by a military tribunal that is pressuring the congress to approve the death penalty, which would be used against Debray.

May 6

We reached Marcos's little house. There we spent the night and ate the last of our reserves of canned meat (two cans.) We hope to find some cans of milk, coffee, and sugar with which we will prepare breakfast when we arrive at Bear Camp. We heard news of the events in Cochabamba.[4]

---

2. Francisco Huanca (*Pablito, Pablo*), a Bolivian combatant who arrived at the guerrilla camp in February.

3. The Congrí Creek was named as such by the combatants for the amount of *congrí* (a Cuban dish of rice and black beans) served there in March, as they returned from the exploratory journey.

4. ELN Communiqué no. 1 was published in Cochabamba's *Prensa Libre* on May 1, 1967, making the ELN's existence and political perspectives known throughout the country. The document had been leaked from the military offices in Cochabamba after the army had seized copies from Major Sánchez and from Debray. The director of the newspaper, Carlos Beccar Gómez, was later arrested.

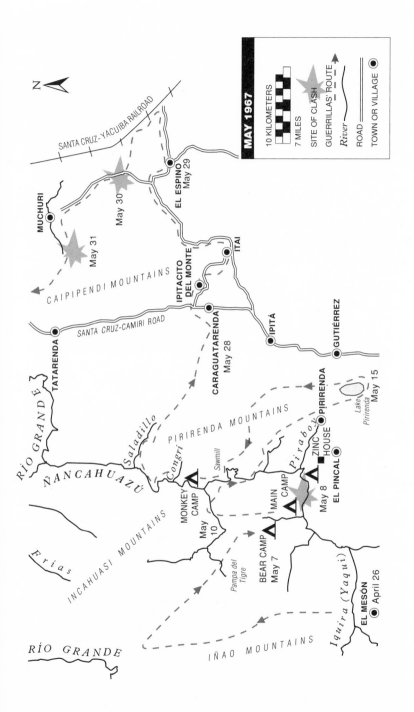

N

MAY 1967

10 KILOMETERS

7 MILES

SITE OF CLASH

GUERRILLAS' ROUTE

River

ROAD

TOWN OR VILLAGE

SANTA CRUZ–YACUIBA RAILROAD

MUCHURI

May 31

May 30

EL ESPINO
May 29

CAIPIPENDI MOUNTAINS

IPITACITO
DEL MONTE

ITAI

IPITÁ

GUTIÉRREZ

SANTA CRUZ–CAMIRI ROAD

TATARENDA

CARAGUATARENDA
May 28

Saladillo

PIRIRENDA MOUNTAINS

Congri

Sawmill

Piraboy

PIRIRENDA

Lake
Pirirenda
May 15

ZINC
HOUSE

EL PINCAL

May 8

RÍO GRANDE

ÑANCAHUAZÚ

MONKEY
CAMP

May 10

MAIN
CAMP

BEAR CAMP
May 7

Frías

INCAHUASI MOUNTAINS

Pampa del
Tigre

Iquira (Yaqui)

EL MESÓN
April 26

RÍO GRANDE

IÑAO MOUNTAINS

May 7

On arriving at Bear Camp we found some coffee as we had expected, an indication that Joaquín has not been here.

We continued toward the [main] camp. Five men are sent as a scouting group to the farm. The army has set up its camp there.

May 8

We planted an ambush and captured two men with very little food on them. We made the mistake of opening fire and wounding them, though not seriously.

At 2:00 p.m. I assumed command of the ambush and we captured two men without having to fire on them. During the night a group of 28 soldiers fell into the ambush: 6 were taken prisoner, 3 killed, and 1 wounded. We also captured 10 rifles. The rest of them escaped. Fifteen hundred rounds of ammunition were captured.

May 9

We pulled back. Early in the morning we reached the top of the ridge where we rested up. We headed toward the Pirirenda lake by a new route. We ate a little charqui and gathered the remnants of the last cow we slaughtered. The army attacked the camp with aircraft and artillery.

May 10

Today I am twenty-seven years old. I've been hungry for the last two days. The only thing I have eaten is lard soup, which is all we have left.

May 11

While going along the stream leading to the Pirirenda, after crossing a small rise, we were informed that a wild pig had been killed, with which we relieved our hunger somewhat. At 2:00 p.m. we resumed our march and camped not too far from the ridge, from which one can now see the lake.

May 12

We are now in Pirirenda. We are camped near a field of crops from which we took some jocos and calabash. Two groups of scouts were sent toward the road to find the house.[5] Food was prepared.

Ramón read from the diary taken from one of the prisoners (Lieutenant Laredo). In it there is information about the lack of combat morale among the soldiers, citing cases where the troops broke ranks and began screaming when they learned of the presence of guerrillas in their sector. The diary noted that the town of Pirirenda was evacuated and that during the four days when the people were away, their livestock were eaten by the soldiers.[6]

Our men moved toward the house. I remain in the camp with Willy, Arturo, and Darío.[7]

We have enough food for some ten days (corn and rice.) We plan to rest here for about five days and then launch an attack on the highway leading to Gutiérrez.

May 13

We are resting here and have started to make fritters since we have a corn mill and there is baby corn here.

TO THE BOLIVIAN PEOPLE
COMMUNIQUÉ NO. 3

Revolutionary truth vs. reactionary lies

On May 8, in the guerrilla zone of Ñacaguasu, troops from a mixed company under the command of Second Lieutenant Henry Laredo were ambushed. Those killed in the action include the

---

5. The house of the peasant Chicho Otero.
6. Along with the diary of Lt. Henry Laredo, who was killed in the battle of May 8, was a letter from his wife where she asked for "the scalp of a guerrilla to decorate our living room."
7. Simón Cuba (*Willy*) and David Adriazola (*Darío*) were Bolivian fighters who joined the guerrillas in February.

above-named officer, in addition to Román Arroyo Flores and Luis Peláez, students from the training school for noncommissioned officers.

The following soldiers were taken prisoner: José Camacho Rojas, Bolívar Regiment; Néstor Cuentas, Bolívar Regiment; Waldo Veizaga, noncommissioned officers school; Hugo Soto Lora, noncommissioned officers school; Max Torres León, noncommissioned officers school; Roger Rojas Toledo, Braun Regiment; Javier Mayan Corella, Braun Regiment; Néstor Sánchez Cuéllar, Braun Regiment.

The last two were wounded in a prior action after failing to heed a command to halt. As always, the prisoners were set free after receiving an explanation of the aims and scope of our struggle. Also captured were 7 M-1 carbines and 4 Mausers. Our forces suffered no casualties.

The repressive army has issued frequent statements announcing guerrilla deaths, mixing elements of truth about their own acknowledged losses with fantasy about ours. Growing desperate in their impotence, they resort to lies. Or else they brutalize journalists who, because of their political views, are natural adversaries of the regime, blaming them for all their problems.

Let it be known that the ELN of Bolivia is the only force responsible for the armed struggle, where it stands at the head of its people, and that the struggle will not end until final victory is achieved. At that time we will know how to punish those responsible for crimes committed in the course of the war; this is apart from any reprisals that our army's command feels are appropriate to counter acts of vandalism by the repressive forces.

ELN OF BOLIVIA

May 14
Mother's Day, a day that has great meaning for me since I wish with all my heart to be with my beloved mother.[8]

8. Engracia Tamayo.

We had a meeting with Fernando in which he discussed the fact that he is very, very hurt by the thefts of food that have occurred in the past few days. This is something that completely demoralizes the troops.

He was very hurt to have to report the cases of Benigno and Urbano. (Benigno, according to El Médico, ate a can of meat.) Later Tuma told me that this is true and that he also ate some. Several comrades stated that Urbano was innocent of the charge that he took the dried meat at Monkey Creek. All we have to eat is lard soup.

We received word that the army has arrived at the house of the peasant where we were a few days ago.

May 15
We moved the camp very early in an effort to be closer to the shore of the lake, which is very beautiful. While some of our men were looking for beans the army began advancing on us with ground forces and aircraft. During the action we climbed a peak and stayed there to observe. We came to a well-stocked house, where we ate a little roast chicken and rice. We left there at dawn, about 4:00 a.m. Fernando became very sick and we had to give him injections to control it. For this reason we made a stretcher and carried him to a small mountain. At 7:00 p.m. we put him in a cart that we found during one of our scouting missions.

May 17
We made camp in a sawmill where we were two or three days ago. We found some things to eat and a little water in bottles, (white flour, corn, bacon, sugar, *mote*,[9] etc.)

A while ago Loro had told us of the existence of this sawmill and of a path that leads to Ñancahuazú and that comes out some nine kilometers below our farm.

9. A dish made of boiled kernels of corn.

May 18

We found a place with water at the foot of the mountain. We plan to rest for five days and set up an ambush along the road. Fernando extracted one of Camba's teeth. We heard news of fighting along the Masicuri river.

May 19

We moved to the house at the creek or lake. The owner is Benito Manfredi.

May 20

I was sent to take charge of the ambush. It was not in a suitable location, so I proposed to move it to another spot, which Fernando approved. We prepare to move to another place.

May 21

A quiet day at the camp. Fernando assigned me to be cook's helper. Fernando has taken charge of the cooking for five days.

May 22

The attendant at the sawmill arrived. He, his son, and a mill hand were stopped at our ambush site.[10] We made preparations to leave tomorrow during the night because we think we have been seen and spied on. After talking with us they offered to collaborate, and we decide to run the risk of a betrayal by them.

May 23

The man was sent to get us a large quantity of provisions (food and medicine.) His son stayed with us as hostage. We gave him until 11:00 p.m. to return. After that time passed, and having waited three hours more without his returning, we left along the road that goes to the Ñancahuazú river.

---

10. Guzmán Robles, Moisés Robles, and Vicente Tapia, respectively.

May 24

We reached the river at 7:00 p.m. We walked in the water so as not to leave tracks. We spent the night in the old camp of the previous trip.

May 25

In the morning we reached the Saladillo river, using this stream as our path to reach the farm of the grandfather[11] of the boy we are holding as prisoner. We spend the night in a place which the local people call La Cumbre.

May 26

We came to the farm of grandfather Bruno. We ate a few sweet limes and, at night, pork and yucca. We headed out to the cabin of two peasants that others say is a one-hour walk from here. From them we learned that the army is stationed in the little village of Ipitá, with about thirty men.

May 27

We captured an old man and a farmhand as they tried to return after following our tracks. Bruno says that he tried to bring the supplies and was arrested. The army took the merchandise and the money he had.

Debray has been denied habeas corpus on the grounds that he is under military jurisdiction.[12]

May 28

In the morning we crossed the Camiri-to-Santa Cruz highway, capturing the settlement of Caraguatarenda. We were discovered by a peasant woman who got away because of indecision on the part of Pablito and Pacho, who did not stop her since she was a woman. Subsequently Fernando ordered

11. Bruno, Moisés Robles's great-uncle.
12. At a press conference on May 20, 1967, Barrientos refused to recognize Debray's status as a journalist and announced that he would ask the congress to reinstate the death penalty, which had been abolished on January 26, 1967.

us to take the village, which was done rapidly. The peasants
who have served us as guides were let go. We stocked up on
food and at 6:00 p.m. continued along the road to Ipitacito,
where we bought some food. We went to a plantation to buy
cheese. They apologized for having sold it all and gave us
some of theirs. Fernando was recognized by a teacher.[13] Later
on we bought a little bread.

13. Elfi Tapia.

PART TWO

May 1967
March 1968

Pombo's diary of the Bolivian campaign from May 29, 1967, until February 1968, when he and the other Cuban survivors crossed the border from Bolivia into Chile, was confiscated from him by the Chilean authorities. Salvador Allende, president of the Chilean senate at the time, later turned over photocopies to the Cuban government.

After his return to Cuba, Harry Villegas conducted a series of seminars at the La Cabaña military fortress in Havana. Basing himself on his notes and personal experiences, he presented a detailed account of the events of the guerrilla struggle in Bolivia. Part two of the book is a summary of these presentations.

Published here for the first time ever is the story of how the combatants commanded by Pombo broke through the encirclement that the Bolivian army and CIA had drawn around them after Guevara's murder.

FROM EL ESPINO TO THE RÍO GRANDE

With the peasant guide Gregorio Vargas

We set out again for El Espino on May 29, but were delayed because the truck we were traveling in got stuck. It took us several hours of work to dig it out, but soon afterward the motor burned out and we had to abandon it for good. Our forward detachment, which was riding in the jeep, had meanwhile taken over a farm in the settlement of El Espino. Concerned about the delay, they set out to meet us. They made a total of four trips to transport us all to our new location. We had breakfast and cooked a stew of turkey, congrí, and pork. Later we seized another truck and set up two ambushes, with Miguel and Antonio in charge.

There was great confusion about what route to take. Finally it was decided to head toward the farm at Muchiri, located between El Espino and Limón, because there was water there. Once again, the truck we were traveling in got stuck, and this time all our efforts to dig it out were in vain. The forward detachment went ahead in the jeep and the rest of the comrades continued on foot.

At dawn [May 30] we reached the railroad tracks and found out that the information we had on which route to take was incorrect. We took the necessary measure of setting up ambushes, and the forward detachment discovered a route that took them through an area that had been marked off in squares by Yacimientos Petrolíferos.[1] Antonio told us that he had seen a boy walking with a dog, and that the boy had run away when Antonio ordered him to halt; Antonio did not shoot at him because he was an innocent passerby. Che ordered Antonio to set up an ambush fifty meters from the path behind a tree trunk at the center; later the ambush was reinforced with Ñato and his Mauser rifle with its attachment for firing FAL antitank grenades.

When Antonio heard the noise of the railroad cars on the tracks, he had Raúl come tell us to send reinforcements. But Raúl took such a long time, on account of his injured leg, that we heard the shots before he arrived. We inflicted three enemy casualties when they fell into our ambush as they tried to advance.

We lifted the ambushes and resumed the march.

The forward detachment carried out three scouting expeditions altogether, looking for water. All of them were in vain.

Miguel had set out in the jeep to look for new roads, but the vehicle kept stopping because of lack of water. Che ordered us all to urinate into the radiator, which solved the problem. We continued on, and late that night we roasted three turkeys.

We moved forward in stages, with our group and the forward detachment taking turns riding in the jeep and walking. When we had gone about four or five kilometers, we met a hunter on one of the side paths. He seemed very suspicious to us. His name was Gregorio Vargas, and he had come on his bicycle to set his traps. He explained to us how to get to the main road and how far it was to the river, and he told us about a pool of water we had already passed. A search was organized for the precious liquid, and everybody except Fernando drank up their reserve supply.

---

1. Yacimientos Petrolíferos Fiscales Bolivianos (YPFB — Bolivian State Petroleum Reserves), the state oil company.

One group went to the spring with Gregorio as their guide. Just as they were arriving, Gregorio heard the motors of army trucks off in the distance and sounded the alarm They came back, and one group under the command of Papi was rapidly sent to set up an ambush. Ñato got nervous, and instead of loading blanks he loaded lead bullets and shot the grenade. Miraculously, he was not hurt, but the barrel was destroyed.

The army troops, as soon as they heard the explosion, emptied out of the trucks and fanned out in the woods, where they repelled our attack.

After walking about fifteen more kilometers, we came to another lagoon. We rested, ate, and moved on. After several more hours of walking, we heard an army communiqué over the radio admitting that two soldiers had been killed and three wounded on May 30, although they identified the encounter as taking place in another area.

We continued along our route, and as we followed the railroad tracks we began to see the lights of the town of Abapó. We quickly made a detour in search of the farm belonging to Gregorio's boss. Gregorio put on Miguel's clothes and different sandals so that he would not be recognized if someone saw him or his footprints.

Totally exhausted, we rested until dawn.

Seven kilometers further on we reached the farm. Benigno and Urbano captured a pig.

Later Che ordered Inti and me to go meet up with the forward detachment. As a security measure, we left Camba, who we no longer had much confidence in,[1] on the other side of the Camiri-to-Lagunillas highway. Julio stayed behind, too. The rest of us crossed the highway and organized a meal fifty meters or more past the highway in a little thicket. The creek water was extremely bitter.

---

1. The members of the guerrilla general staff had noted certain weaknesses that Camba had exhibited in combat. They believed this was due to his lack of prior military training.

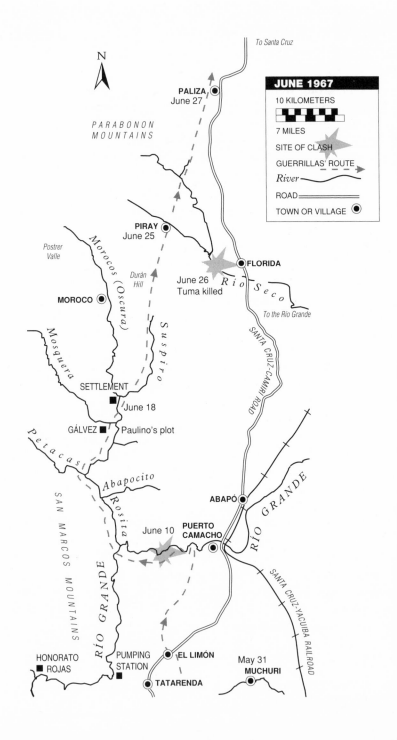

N

To Santa Cruz

PALIZA
June 27

PARABONON
MOUNTAINS

PIRAY
June 25

Postrer
Valle

Morocos (Oscura)

Durán
Hill

Suspiro

June 26
Tuma killed

FLORIDA

Río Seco

To the Río Grande

MOROCO

Mosquera

SANTA CRUZ-CAMIRI ROAD

SETTLEMENT
June 18

GÁLVEZ   Paulino's plot

Petacas

Abapocito

Rosita

SAN MARCOS MOUNTAINS

RÍO GRANDE

ABAPÓ

June 10   **PUERTO**
CAMACHO

RÍO GRANDE

SANTA CRUZ-YACUIBA RAILROAD

HONORATO
ROJAS

PUMPING
STATION   **EL LIMÓN**

May 31
MUCHURI

TATARENDA

Later Che showed up with some prisoners, including one person who said his stepfather Simoni was the owner of the farm, and also a cattle herder named Braulio Robles and his son. We used their horses to transport the pig we had cut up, bringing it to the creek. Then we set the prisoners free, paying each of them 10 Bolivian pesos.[1] After the meal, 100 pesos was given to Gregorio, who we had kept hidden.

At 6:30 [June 3] we set off on the road that bordered the pipeline. We turned left and continued for about four kilometers, at which point we set up camp. Che sent out a scouting party to look for a good place to set up an ambush. At 1:00 p.m. we took our positions: Che and Ricardo in the middle with people from the center group; Miguel with the forward detachment on the left flank; and me on the right flank with three comrades. Due to the nature of the terrain, Che gave us the following instructions:

As soon as the vehicles arriving from the left came into Ricardo's firing range, Miguel was to open fire on them to prevent their retreat. If they came from the right, they would enter Che's range, and he was to open fire on them, after my group had given him the signal with a yellow rag, which would indicate whether the vehicles contained soldiers. If more than two trucks came, my group's mission was to take care of the third truck, to prevent it from either advancing into the ambush or retreating.

Between 1:00 and 5:00 p.m., two civilian vehicles went by and then at 5:30 an army truck passed by. I gave the signal indicating there were soldiers in the truck. Che did not open fire. Afterward he criticized me for having given the signal, saying that it would have been a crime to kill two helpless men, wrapped in blankets and possibly sleeping. I explained that I had done so because I thought there were four men, not two.

At 6:00 p.m. he gave the order to lift the ambush and continue along the path in search of a creek where we could cook

1. The exchange rate at the time was 11.88 Bolivian pesos to the U.S. dollar.

a meal. As we moved on, we heard trucks go by and a voice asking, "Are we close yet, Gregorio?" Someone answered, "No, it's a little farther." We thought it was the same Gregorio who had been our guide.

In search of Joaquín's group

We advanced along the sides of the creek and followed a footpath that took us to a place a little off from the main road, where we considered setting up another ambush. We continued along the footpath in search of the Río Grande and the mouth of the Rosita. Che thought we might find Joaquín's group in this area, since Joaquín knew that Che's idea was to use this route to get to Samaipata, which had been chosen as a zone of operations.

We spent the night in a ravine of a little valley. A cold front from the south blew over, which made us wet and uncomfortable with its fine drizzle. At the same time, however, it helped us by partially filling the little ditches with water, enabling us to cook. We prepared oatmeal, and tea with milk.

We were only able to walk a short distance. The hands and feet of the machete team got numb from the wetness and cold. We crossed a little hill and camped, lighting a fire in order to dry our hammocks. Our remaining water was put aside for breakfast.

Che sent the point of the forward detachment on a scouting mission, and we moved over to the bank of the Río Grande, where we made coffee. Then he sent Coco, Julio, and Aniceto out to explore the area, telling them that if they found any house, they should occupy it. This is what they did, and at eight o'clock that night we set out again. The night was extremely dark, and we were constantly tripping and falling. Finally we arrived at the house they had taken, where we got ready to slaughter a goat. But the comrades asked Che if they could kill a pig, and this was done.

The house was located some three kilometers from Puerto Camacho. After spending the whole night cooking the pig and some *locro*,[1] we set out in the morning. As guide, we took with us the son of the house's owner, who was a cattle herder.

We walked through bramble patches along the sand embankment, and camped at a farm with jocos, corn, plantains, and other crops.

On June 8 we heard news reports on the state of siege and the threat of a miners' strike to oppose a 50 percent cut in wages.

At dawn we moved our encampment forward in order to avoid search parties. Ñato, Benigno, Urbano, and León tried to create a path, which turned out to be impossible because it ended in completely smooth and vertical cliffs. The only way to cross the river was on a raft or by circling around, but the latter option was very difficult because of the distance involved.

We began building a raft, while we set up an ambush in a place that served as a good lookout post. Our attempt to cross the river failed because the water was so cold that it made our muscles numb. Ñato tried it, and we had to drag him out of the water.

Pacho, Coco, Ñato, and Aniceto left with the assignment of returning to the house we had just left and bringing a boat back to the river. On the way, they ran into an army unit that was moving along the opposite bank. We heard the gunfire, and then Aniceto and Ñato arrived and told us about the encounter. Pacho and Coco had stayed behind fighting so that the others could withdraw.

We moved the ambush up to a place that was better situated, and we began to construct a path of operations.

Pacho had fired ten shots and thought he had caused some enemy casualties. We kept the ambush up, amid a calm day. Benigno and Urbano continued along the path.

---

1. A dish of the eastern region of Bolivia prepared with meat, potatoes, rice, and root vegetables.

We moved out early [June 12] and camped in a ravine with a pool of water in it, making tea. The radio was broadcasting news of Saturday's encounter, reporting one killed and one wounded. Pacho's bullets had not been fired in vain. In addition, we were surprised to hear a report on our composition: 17 Cubans, 3 Peruvians, 14 Brazilians, and 3 Argentines. The first two figures were exactly right; the others were false.

We passed through a deep warm cave that beckoned us to stay. But we moved on and after hiking across muddy ground we reached the creek emptying into the Río Grande, some three kilometers from the mouth of the Rosita. Che sent Coco and Aniceto to explore the area, but they did not reach the river's mouth because a hill was in the way. Had they gone over it, they would have had to return in the dark. We gave our peasant guide Nicolás 150 pesos and let him go.

FROM THE RÍO GRANDE AND THE ROSITA TO FLORIDA

We crossed the river; the water was very cold. Chino and Antonio were the last to cross and the current almost swept them away.

We walked quite a distance, and at 3:00 p.m. [June 17] we stopped at the mouth of a creek that was not on our map. Ricardo ran off, fired a few shots, and killed a *hochi*,[1] which meant we had meat, even if only for soup.

We continued our march, crossing three more creeks, although the Abapocito was the only one on the map. At the

___
1. A type of rodent found in eastern Bolivia.

end of a small woods we stopped for the night. In the meantime Ricardo and Inti did reconnaissance upriver.

Paulino Baigorría

At 8:30 [June 19] we left, and after a long walk we arrived at
a farm while it was still morning. We quickly organized the
cooking and the collection of foodstuffs, so that we could
continue on toward some houses that were indicated on the
map. Pablito and Benigno went on a scouting expedition.
They came upon a farm and captured a peasant who was in
the back. After waiting a few moments, they captured some
more peasants who were approaching the place.

We decided to head over to the farmland that belonged to
the boys we had taken prisoner.[1] This farm was located at the
mouth of the road coming from Abapó. There we had to hang
our hammocks because there were so many chiggers. One of
the boys, Paulino, said he wanted to join our ranks.[2]

Under a sun that could split rocks, we left for a small village
nearby. When we arrived we camped at the house of Paulino's
stepfather; there we bought pigs, jocos, and corn. Then we
went to the house that belonged to the mayor of the village, a
peasant named Calixto, who refused to sell us the big load of
beans he had. Finally we forced him to sell us two quintals
[200 lbs.].

As it was getting dark, three men arrived at our encampment without having been detected by our guards, for which
Aniceto and Chapaco were punished. Calixto assured us the
men were buyers of pigs.

1. According to Guevara their houses were ten or fifteen kilometers north of the junc-
    tion of the Mosquera and the Oscura, on the latter river (*Bolivian Diary,* p. 214).
2. Paulino Baigorría, a young Bolivian peasant, functioned as guide for the
    guerrillas and asked to become a member. While conducting a mission as
    guerrilla messenger in the city, he was captured, held incommunicado, and
    tortured.

With Benigno and Moro in charge, we made congrí and fried pork, cooked on a spit.

A very poor job was done of interrogating the three visitors. The weapons they were carrying were not even taken away.

Paulino (our recruit) was the boyfriend of the mayor's daughter. Through her he learned that one of the visitors was an army officer who on other occasions had passed through the area taking livestock by force, and that furthermore, he was one of those who had named Calixto as mayor. When Che found out these details, he brought the intruders together and said that if the officer did not identify himself right away, all three would be shot. The officer[1] stepped forward crying and begged us not to kill him. At first Che considered shooting them. Then he said it would be better not to do so, because it should be the enemy, not us, that started the repression.

We got our things ready to continue our march the next day [June 21] and agreed to leave at 3:00 p.m. Among other things, we bought fourteen hens.

We kept watch on the prisoners until we had gotten two leagues[2] away from our old encampment. We took away their clothing, shoes, and animals before letting them go. The mule we confiscated was given to Che, who was sick.

Paulino stayed with us pretending to be a prisoner in order not to arouse suspicions. He had agreed to go to the city [Cochabamba] with four communiqués, two messages, and a letter to Inti's wife, Matilde Lara. He was the first peasant who joined us. He was twenty years old and suffered from tuberculosis. It was decided to send him as a messenger after analyzing the situation — the guerrilla unit was divided into two groups, neither of which had sufficient combat strength.

1. Esquivel, a second lieutenant in the carabineros.
2. One league is roughly 3.5 miles (5.5 kilometers).

TO THE BOLIVIAN PEOPLE
COMMUNIQUÉ NO. 4

Revolutionary truth vs. reactionary lies

In recent dispatches, the army has acknowledged some of its losses suffered in clashes between advance detachments. At the same time, as usual, they attribute to us a large number of dead that are never exhibited. Although we have not received reports from all of our patrols, we can state with assurance that our losses are very small; and in the recent actions acknowledged by the army, we did not suffer any.

Inti Peredo is a member of our army's general command, where he holds the post of political commissar and commanded several of the recent actions. He is in good health and has been untouched by enemy bullets. The falsehood about his death is a tangible example of the absurd lies being spread by the army in their impotency in fighting our forces.

Regarding announcements about the supposed presence of combatants from other Latin American countries, for reasons of military secrecy we will give no figures. In line with our watchword — revolutionary truth — we will simply state that citizens of any country who accept our minimum program, the liberation of Bolivia, are accepted into the revolutionary ranks with equal rights and responsibilities to those of the Bolivian combatants, who naturally constitute the vast majority of our movement. Every man who fights for the freedom of our country arms in hand deserves — and receives — the honorable title of Bolivian, independently of where he may have been born. This is how we interpret genuine revolutionary internationalism.

ELN OF BOLIVIA

Entirely isolated from the urban organization, we were only able to receive messages from Cuba, not transmit them. For the guerrilla column to grow, it was necessary to make contact with the city, since the inhospitable conditions and isolation of the rural areas of Bolivia made direct recruitment there almost impossible.

We camped at the mouth of a creek.

We left early and walked along the river until noon, when we moved away from it and climbed a hill. We made camp atop the ridge about 3:00 p.m. We resumed the march, but we had not even walked an hour when it began to rain, which made Paulino, acting as guide, lose the trail. The forward detachment located it again before nightfall, but it was late and they still had to cut a passageway so the animals could get through. We made camp.

We climbed up to where the passage had been cut. After walking for two hours, we got to a bare hillside from which we could see the Río Grande. The landscape was beautiful, and we all took pictures of each other. Che's was taken on horseback.

We descended a very steep hill, following the tracks of some cattle herders. We rested at a creek near Durán Hill.

We continued along the path forged by the herdsmen who were ahead of us, as we learned when we reached the place they had camped the night before. The fire had not yet gone out. We tried to catch up with them but were not able to because a huge fire blocked our crossing. We believed it had been set on purpose. Later a plane flew over the area; we did not know whether it was because of the fire or for some other reason. We arrived at Piray.

We continued ahead until we got to the house of Paulino's sister, but we decided to move on to another house that was closer to the road to Florida, belonging to Paniagua's daughter. There we bought a cow, and a group was organized under Coco's command to go to the village of Florida and purchase supplies.

We came back with some sugar and with news about the existence of troops in the area.

The day passed normally. We cooked, looked for sugarcane,

and assigned Camba to make bread. To carry out this task, he was authorized by Che to leave his position in the ambush that had been set up by the forward detachment under Miguel's command.

THE BATTLE OF JUNE 26

The death of Tuma

At 4:30 I was ordered to go with Antonio, Tuma, Arturo, and Ñato to relieve those on the ambush. When we got there we heard gunfire, threw ourselves to the ground, and advanced to the positions. The gunfire ended quickly, and we were able to reach Benigno's location. He pointed out to us four bodies lying on the sand. Miguel was in the middle of the ambush, and since there was no retreat path, we had to go right up to where he was, exposing ourselves to the enemy's view. The army had spread out and taken positions on the other side of the river. They did not fire on us as we crossed, however, apparently because they were waiting for reinforcements. We told Miguel that we were there to relieve him, but we thought we should send a messenger to Che to explain the situation. He agreed and proposed that I cover him while he tried to recover two rifles that could be seen in the middle of the river. I refused, since we did not know whether the enemy had a clear view of the river.

Later Che arrived and we went over to him. He assigned me to take charge of the other flank together with Miguel. Miguel notified us that the troops were fanning out, since we could hear the noise they were making breaking branches. We asked Che for reinforcements, and he sent us Pacho and Antonio.

After we had positioned these two comrades, we heard trucks arrive, and soon there was generalized gunfire. We had been caught in an area completely without tree cover. Pacho was able to get into a little ditch and return fire. I threw myself on the ground and got off a few shots, but I was lying on slanted ground, giving the enemy an advantage. Pacho signaled me to try to get to the ditch. I turned around and felt a blow to my leg. I shouted to Pacho to open fire because I had been wounded. Covered by Pacho and Antonio, I was able to move over to the woods. There I bumped into Miguel, who told me Che had given the order to retreat.

At the end of the path we saw El Médico, who told us Tuma had been wounded in the stomach just as he was shouting, "Muganga, watch out. This is fucked up." He was put on a horse.

Tuma's wound was very bad. He was operated on in the house of the peasant Fenelón Coca, but it was useless. His liver was protruding through his wound and he died. With this loss, I felt like part of my life was gone. Tuma was more than a combatant to me. He was my companion, my brother, my friend, and the delight of the whole group with his joyful personality. We lost a comrade of the Sierra Maestra, of the invasion, of the Las Villas campaign,[1] of the Congo, and of Bolivia. In addition, we had been together through the experience of the first stage of the construction of socialism.

Tuma was put on a horse, tied down, and Urbano took charge of moving him.

We buried him in a shallow grave, because the ground was extremely hard and we did not have the necessary tools to dig in it.

1. The "invasion" refers to the Rebel Army's westward march from the Sierra Maestra in eastern Cuba to the central province of Las Villas. It was conducted between August and October 1958 by the columns led by Guevara and Camilo Cienfuegos. From then until January 1, the two columns captured virtually all major towns and cities in Las Villas, sealing the fate of the Batista dictatorship. See *Episodes of the Cuban Revolutionary War*, pp. 323–40 and 360–98.

EDITORA POLÍTICA

EDITORA POLÍTICA

Members of the preparations team based in La Paz, 1966.

Top, left to right, Pombo, Papi (also known as Mbili and Ricardo), and Tuma. **Bottom,** Sánchez (Julio Dagnino Pacheco) and Pombo.

EDITORA POLÍTICA

EDITORA POLÍTICA

Top, Fidel Castro reviews Che Guevara's false papers prior to his departure for Bolivia, October 1966; Guevara is in disguise. **Bottom,** Pombo during visit to La Paz zoo, 1966.

Top, Guevara, in disguise, taking his own photograph at the Hotel Copacabana in La Paz, November 3, 1966. **Below,** Guevara, in sports jacket (lower left), buying newspaper outside La Paz train station.

En route from La Paz to the encampment at the Ñancahuazú in early November 1966.

Top, Guevara, standing by jeep; behind wheel is Pacho. **Bottom,** Tuma (left) and Papi.

Top, Moro, walking in the Ñancahuazú river.
Bottom, the "zinc house" at the Ñancahuazú farm.

Pombo served as a member of the general staff of the military command, in charge of supplies, medicine, and transportation.

Facing page, top, left to right, Rolando, Antonio, Pombo, Marcos. **Below,** Pombo next to one of guerrillas' supply caves. **This page, top,** Pombo, Pacho, Serapio. **Bottom,** Pombo (front) with Urbano. Photos were taken during the early stages of the campaign.

This page, top, Joaquin, Ernesto, and Rolando prepare a holiday meal for New Year's Eve, 1966. **Bottom,** left to right, Inti, Pombo (in beret, facing away), Urbano, Rolando, Alejandro, Tuma, Arturo, Moro.

Facing page, Miguel (left) and Inti (right) scout the Ñancahuazú area during the first months of the campaign.

Che Guevara (at right in both photos) meeting with Bolivian Communist Party general secretary Mario Monje, December 31, 1966, at the Ñancahuazú camp.

Top, Che Guevara (left) and Loyola Guzmán, a leader of the urban support network, January 26, 1967. Also that day, **bottom,** Che met with miners leader Moisés Guevara, who agreed to join the guerrilla front, together with a dozen others from his group; Moisés Guevara appears at right, with Antonio.

Facing page, top, left to right, Urbano (partially obscured), Miguel, Che, Marcos, Chino, Pacho, Pombo, Inti, Coco, December 2, 1966. Bottom, left, Tania taking photo during her visit to Ñancahuazú camp, December 31, 1966–January 1, 1967; at right is Alejandro. Above, Guevara holding discussion, March 1967. At left, with glasses is Chino. At right, Régis Debray. Below, Guevara next to the Ñancahuazú river.

In response to intelligence reports that Guevara was leading revolutionary front in Bolivia, Washington stepped up joint operations with the dictatorship, sending in U.S. military and intelligence forces, trainers, weapons, and supplies.

This page, top, CIA agent Eduardo González climbing into army jeep at Valle Grande, October 9, 1967, the day of Guevara's murder. **Bottom,** U.S. Army Maj. Robert Shelton, at U.S.-organized counterinsurgency training camp near Santa Cruz, September 1967. **Facing page, top,** Bolivian army mortar unit in the zone of operations, July 1967. **Bottom,** Bolivian dictator René Barrientos at press conference, September 22, 1967, confirming Guevara's presence in the country.

BRIAN MOSER

BRIAN M●

Guevara was captured October 8, 1967, and murdered the following day on orders of Barrientos, following consultation with Washington.

Top, Bolivian troops in Valle Grande carrying Guevara's body, October 9. **Bottom,** the schoolhouse at La Higuera where Guevara was executed.

During the battle we had taken two prisoners, two new spies. One was a carabinero lieutenant named Walter Landívar, and the other a carabinero. Che gave them a lecture and let them go. We had earlier taken away all of their belongings, and set them free in their underwear. Che later criticized us for this, which he said was an affront to their human dignity that nobody had the right to commit.

We left with nine horses that belonged to Celso Roca. At dawn we heard prolonged gunfire. We thought it might be the army approaching, or that they were shooting by mistake at the prisoners we had freed.

ON THE ROAD TO PALIZA,
TOWARD THE LOS AJOS RIVER

At about two o'clock we set off in the direction of Paliza. On the way we met a peasant who was looking over some tracks. When we asked him what he was doing, he answered that his wife had told him a large group of people had passed by, and he was checking to see if it were true.

We arrived at seven o'clock that night [June 27]. Pacho was taking care of me like a brother. We obtained a guide to lead us to Don Lucas's house. We advanced to an abandoned house, where we stopped while Benigno milked some cows that we found there. Meanwhile, Che was furious about Chinchu and Moro's delay.

That day the radio broadcast news of the outcome of the recent battle and announced that the army had suffered three killed and two wounded in the area of the Mosquera river. It appeared that one of the soldiers was only pretending to be dead, because by our count there had been four.

Che's analysis and instructions

We continued our advance the next morning. [June 29] When we got to the junction we halted while Che organized a meeting to analyze the results of the battle. On balance, he said, from the army's point of view we had been the victors. But from our standpoint we suffered a defeat, because the casualties the enemy suffered could be replaced while ours could not. We were being slowly whittled down, he said, and it was therefore essential to find Joaquín or make contact with the city forces. He added that the whittling down was not only in quantity but also in quality, because death was taking our best men.

Che gave an assessment of Rubio, mentioning his spirit of sacrifice, the responsibilities he had left in order to come to Bolivia and be part of the struggle, and his assignments during the Cuban revolution, in which he had proven his organizational ability. Che also pointed out that Rubio had been selected, at Rolando's side, to be second-in-command of the front we were planning to open in Chapare.

When he spoke of Rolando, Che began by highlighting his leadership ability. Che said he considered Rolando the most rounded cadre of the entire guerrilla force, both politically and militarily. His death was something Che felt very deeply. He said he was proud to have had Rolando at his side and to have helped train him.

Before moving on to Tuma, Che explained that he was not going to speak right then about the very valuable Bolivian comrades who had died. He said he wanted those of us who were present to understand the fraternal ties that bound him to the Cubans who had fallen, as a result of the amount of time he had spent with them. But without a doubt, he continued, in the future the same strong ties would unite all of us — Cubans and Bolivians — as the Latin Americans we all were.

He also said he was coming to love this country as if it were his own. Pointing to the mountains, he said he was beginning to love them like the Sierra Maestra. Still, his wish was that if he had to die, it would be in Argentina.

When he began talking of Tuma, Che spoke with great feeling. He recalled the years they had spent together. He spoke of the invasion and of the peacetime that followed the triumph of the Cuban revolution. He said that Tuma's death represented a terrible personal blow because he was almost like a son. "We have lost the first of those who began this mission with us much more than a year ago."

He analyzed in general terms the manner in which the ambushes had been set up. He pointed to the fact that there was no serious preparation of the fixed positions or of the hidden paths that would make an effective operation possible. He promised to give us talks and instructions on guerrilla tactics.

He indicated that we needed to draw lessons from the heroic people of Vietnam and adapt their experiences to our own conditions. Above all, he said, we should not lose sight of the most essential features of their tactics. He said we had been applying certain principles empirically, such as being aggressive, and it was undeniable that we had been extremely bold and audacious. But this should never lead us to neglect being careful or to forget about organizing our ambushes carefully. The Vietnamese, he pointed out, had developed the method of defeating large forces with smaller ones and had managed to hold at bay the most powerful army of oppression, that of imperialism. He explained that we had to consistently apply a policy of economy of life, without losing our aggressiveness. We had to be conscious of making maximum use of explosives, which were used frequently and effectively in Cuba and which we had not used at all in Bolivia. Che pointed out that antipersonnel mines and booby traps could be used to cause enemy casualties, that they generated fear in the enemy's ranks and undermined their morale. For this reason, these weapons were an element of psychological warfare as well as armed struggle.

"We have not been able to take advantage of these things

because we thought we could solve everything with our courage. But this is not just a war of guts, but of guts plus intelligence, and the most intelligent side will win," Che concluded.

We heard the news about the struggle in the mines.[1]

TO THE MINERS OF BOLIVIA
COMMUNIQUÉ NO. 5

Comrades:

Proletarian blood has once more been shed in our mines. Over many centuries, the blood of enslaved miners has alternately been sucked dry, and then shed whenever built-up injustice has led to explosions of protest. This repetitive cycle has continued without variation for hundreds of years.

In recent times, the pattern was broken temporarily, and the insurrectionary workers were the decisive factor in the victory of April 9.[2] This event gave rise to hopes that a new day would dawn, and that the workers would finally become masters of their own destiny. But the workings of world imperialism have revealed, for those with eyes to see, that when it comes to social revolution

1. On the night of June 23–24, in an attempt to crush a broadening struggle against the dictatorship led by Bolivia's tin miners, the army opened fire on miners' housing at the Siglo XX mines. The confrontation had been building for weeks. On June 6 an assembly of miners at Huanuni declared its solidarity with the guerrilla struggle. The government decreed a state of siege in the country. On June 15 the industrial unions declared a state of emergency, and on June 23 miners and students signed a mutual defense pact. The workers declared the mining district "free territory" and decided to donate medicines and one day's pay to the guerrillas. On June 24, in the middle of the San Juan Eve holiday and as workers from around the country gathered at the Siglo XX mines for a meeting to plan nationwide resistance, the armed forces occupied the main tin mines and massacred residents, who were sleeping. The result was 87 dead in Siglo XX, including women and children. One of those killed was Rosendo García, secretary-general of the miners union at Siglo XX, who was organizing support for the guerrilla struggle.
2. April 9, 1952, was the date of the insurrection that toppled the Bolivian military government and installed a new regime led by the Revolutionary Nationalist Movement (MNR). The Bolivian trade unions, led by the miners, played a central role in the uprising.

there are no halfway solutions. Either all the power is seized, or the advances won with so much sacrifice and so much blood will be lost.

The armed militias of the mining proletariat were the only serious force at the beginning. Then militias were formed of other sectors of the working class, of declassed elements, and of peasants. The members of these groups were unable to see their fundamental commonality of interests, and, under the demagogy of the antipopular forces, fell into conflict. Finally, the professional army reappeared as a wolf in sheep's clothing. Small and insignificant at the beginning, this army was transformed into the armed tool against the proletariat, as well as the most reliable accomplice of imperialism. For this reason, the imperialists gave their approval to the military coup.

We are now recovering from a defeat caused by a repetition of tactical errors on the part of the working class. We are patiently preparing the country for a deep-going social revolution that will transform the system from top to bottom.

We must not repeat false tactics that are heroic but futile, and would lead the proletariat into a bloodbath and deplete its ranks, depriving us of its most combative elements.

Over long months of struggle, the guerrillas have shaken the country. They have inflicted a large number of casualties on the army and have brought about its demoralization, suffering virtually no losses of its own. Yet this same army, in a confrontation lasting several hours, ended up master of the day, strutting like peacocks over the bodies of workers. The difference between victory and defeat lies in the choice of correct or erroneous tactics.

Comrade miner: pay no further heed to the false apostles of mass struggle, those who interpret this as the people marching forward, in compact formation, against the oppressors' guns. Let us learn from reality! Against machine guns, bare chests, however heroic, are of no avail. Against modern instruments of destruction, barricades, however well constructed, are of no avail. In underdeveloped countries with a large peasant base and a vast territory, mass struggle should revolve around the action of a small, mobile vanguard — the guerrillas — firmly based among the people. This guerrilla force will increasingly acquire strength at the expense of the enemy army, and will act as catalyst for the masses' revolutionary fervor, until a revolutionary situation is created. At that time, state power will be toppled in a single well-aimed and well-timed blow.

Listen well: We are not calling for total inactivity; we simply recommend that forces not be expended in actions that do not guarantee success. The working masses should continuously bring their pressure to bear against the government, since this is a class struggle whose fronts are without limits. Wherever he may be, a worker has the obligation to fight with all his strength against the common enemy.

Comrade miner: the guerrillas of the ELN await you with open arms, and invite you to join the workers of the subsoil already fighting at our side. Here we will rebuild the worker-peasant alliance that was broken by the demagogy of the antipopular forces. Here we will convert defeat into victory, and transform the lament of proletarian widows into a hymn of victory. We await you.

ELN

We arrived at Don Lucas's farm in the rain and positioned ourselves in one of the adjacent houses. The old man seemed very cooperative, even though one of his daughters gave him a hard time for offering to help us.

We took two peasants prisoner, and the old man volunteered to accompany us.

In the morning [July 1] we set out in the direction of Barchelón. During a break we detained a very talkative peasant named Andrés Coca.

Along the way my horse threw me several times. At last we camped at the house of a certain Yépez. He had three children, only one of whom knew how to read.[1]

1. The peasant was Andrés Yépez. His children were Juan, Hipólito, and Renán Yépez.

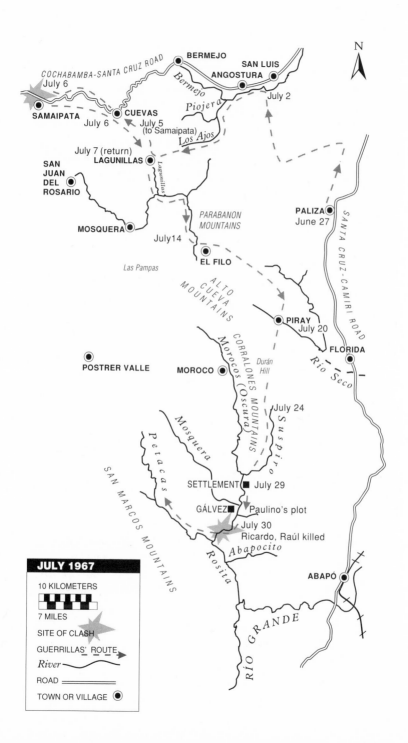

N

BERMEJO

SAN LUIS

ANGOSTURA

July 2

COCHABAMBA-SANTA CRUZ ROAD

July 6

Bermejo

Piojera

SAMAIPATA

CUEVAS

July 6

July 5
(to Samaipata)

Los Ajos

July 7 (return)

LAGUNILLAS

SAN
JUAN
DEL
ROSARIO

Lagunillas

PALIZA
June 27

*PARABANON
MOUNTAINS*

S
A
N
T
A

C
R
U
Z
-
C
A
M
I
R
I

R
O
A
D

MOSQUERA

July 14

EL FILO

Las Pampas

A
L
T
O
CUEVA
MOUNTAINS

PIRAY
July 20

FLORIDA

POSTRER VALLE

MOROCO

*Durán
Hill*

Río Seco

CORRALONES MOUNTAINS (Oscuras)

Morocos

July 24

*S
u
s
p
i
r
o*

Mosquera

Petacas

SETTLEMENT ■ July 29

GÁLVEZ ■

Paulino's plot

July 30
Ricardo, Raúl killed

Abapocito

ABAPÓ

SAN
MARCOS
MOUNTAINS

Rosita

*RÍO
GRANDE*

JULY 1967

10 KILOMETERS

7 MILES

SITE OF CLASH

GUERRILLAS' ROUTE ➤

River ∼∼∼

ROAD ═══

TOWN OR VILLAGE ◉

We arrived early at the home of Don Nicomedes Arteaga, where we ate plenty of oranges. They sold us *ponchados* (home-made cigars).

We went down to the Piojera river in search of the main house and we ate there. Che took photographs of the peasants.

We spent the next day there too [July 3], because Che was quite sick and had not been able to sleep all night. In order to convince Che to stay, El Médico told him it was necessary for me to rest because my leg would never heal properly if it was always hanging down on horseback.

A plane passed over the settlement, flying low, and this started the rumor that there would be bombing during the night. The residents left their houses and went to sleep in the coffee fields.

We left very early; almost all the comrades had stomach troubles.

Che's asthma was getting worse. Looking through my pack again, we found a small flask of asthma medicine. There was just a little bit left at the bottom, not enough to use in an inhaler, but enough to extract and apply through an injection.

On the road from Los Ajos we met up with the eldest of the Yépez brothers,[1] who told us that the army was in the narrow pass and that he had also seen soldiers pass through on the way to El Filo. We continued, and arrived at the Junction in the afternoon. We camped there at Manuel Carrillo's house.

The peasants were all frightened and fled. There was nothing unusual in this; it happened every time we arrived at a village. We walked up to the house of a peasant named Ramón. His mother-in-law did not want us to stay there, but he convinced her by saying that his dealings with us were strictly business.

We set off toward Peña Colorada and stopped to rest on the Alto del Palermo in order to regroup. There was a fierce wind that almost blew us over. From there we could see the high-

1. Renán Yépez.

way. As we continued on, we came to a well-stocked grocery store, where we purchased cigars, caramels, milk, and sardines. We did not buy any more to avoid excess weight. At night we reached the highway, and Che sent Antonio to a house where an old woman lived to ask permission to cook in her house. But she refused to open the door. Then the owner of a grocery store also refused to sell to us, so we had to force her to do so.

Our plan was to stop a vehicle on the highway and use it to get to the town of Samaipata, where we would raid the pharmacy and the hospital. This action would enable us to get various types of medicine, and especially those Che needed for his asthma, which was getting worse by the minute because of the lack of anti-asthma medication.

He had calculated the amount of medicine he would need to control his asthma attacks during a year of combat. But on Che's own instructions, these had been left in the caves of the camp that the army had occupied. He only carried small quantities of it, which he had divided among several of our knapsacks. Because of the continuous attacks he had suffered, it was already used up.

ATTACK ON SAMAIPATA

The attack on the town of Samaipata, the capital of Florida province, was proposed by all the members of the guerrilla column as the only possible way to acquire the medicine Che needed. He was completely against it, because he felt it was his own fault there was no medicine and that it was not right for other comrades to risk their lives to get it. A lot of discussion was needed to convince him; he finally agreed when we explained that medicines were also critically needed for the rest of the guerrillas.

Papi, Coco, Pacho, Aniceto, Julio, and Chino were chosen for this mission. It was July 6.

A number of vehicles were stopped on the highway. One of them tried to escape; we shouted for it to stop several times and finally Inti shot out its tire.

A pickup truck was used to transport our people to the town. They went to the bus stop, where they bought some cold drinks and they invited those present to share. Two carabineros arrived; and they were disarmed and invited to share the refreshments. Supplies, clothing, and other things were purchased. A resident asked Pacho if he were Argentine, and with a South American accent he said yes, but that he was from La Paz, trying to throw them off. (From that moment on, we called him "the Argentine from La Paz.")

They were still there drinking refreshments when Lt. Juan Vacaflor arrived; he was also detained and given something to drink. Faced with this situation, the comrades decided on a surprise attack. They took up assigned positions, leaving Chino along with Julio and Aniceto watching over the prisoners, the telephone, and other things. The lieutenant was led to the jail, where he was forced to give the password so the door would be opened. As it was being opened, Ricardo and Pacho pushed through and entered shooting. Behind them, Coco, and the lieutenant with him, surprised the troops, not giving the soldiers enough time to throw themselves out of their beds and repel the attack. Only one of them, who must have been awake, was able to throw himself to the floor. He hid behind some tanks of fluid and shot at Pacho. Ricardo saw what was happening and pushed Pacho aside so the bullet missed him. Pacho, responding quickly, threw a grenade that killed the soldier. This was the only casualty of the encounter.

From a military and political point of view, the action was a success. We had taken a provincial capital, an event that would have national and international repercussions.

Nine soldiers had been captured, as well as five Mausers, a BZ, field equipment, and a map that had our entire route traced on it. This map even foresaw where we would come out and our incursion into Samaipata.

At the time, we were very surprised that with such precise intelligence they had not taken the security measures that were called for. On the basis of information received later, we decided that this was because they thought it was more important to prevent us from establishing a base in El Filo, from which we could carry out our guerrilla operation. They thought that if this zone fell into our hands it would be impossible to dislodge us. They decided to occupy the villages, roads, and high ground before we got there, in order to make it difficult for us to stay.

The prisoners taken in the action were set free during the walk back and relieved of their belongings about a kilometer outside the town of Samaipata. In terms of medicine, we obtained some of what we needed but nothing for asthma.[1] Che ordered an immediate retreat to the grocery store. When we got there we made coffee with milk.

The shoes were distributed in the order of people's length of time in the guerrilla unit.

Afterward we marched up to a nearby house, that of Ramón, where we had not met any hostility on our previous visit. When we got there, the peasant went out to the crossroads to check if there were any traces of the army. "All quiet." (That was their way of saying nobody was there.) Che was quite ill; he used what was left of the vial of talamonal, adding some distilled water to it, trying in this way to bring the fierce asthma attack under control. This peasant told us about the presence of soldiers in Los Ajos and San Juan.

---

1. According to army major Arnaldo Saucedo Parada, when the army learned that Guevara needed asthma medicine, they sought to ensure that no supplies were available. Arnaldo Saucedo Parada, *No disparan . . . soy el Che* (Santa Cruz, Bolivia: Editorial Oriente, 1987), p. 41.

FROM SAMAIPATA TO THE OUTSKIRTS
OF EL FILO

We walked from that house to the river without making any contact with the soldiers. Everything indicated they had not been there. Che thought that the peasant had lied about the army's presence in order to get us to leave, so that he could avoid having to deal with the guerrillas.

We continued toward the Piray, where we camped in a nearby cave.

We resumed the march without any fixed course, because we had lost the road to El Filo. We camped in a shack.

The march began again and we walked until we reached a fork in the road, where the forward detachment was waiting for us. We decided to go right, and came to a shack; there we could see in the distance some cultivated land we thought might be El Filo. But the road did not go through; it ended at an outcropping of rock.

The radio was reporting a battle in El Dorado. We tried to locate it on the map — according to the information on the radio it was near our area, between Samaipata and the Río Grande — but it did not exist. We did, however, find a place with this name between Ñancahuazú and Muyupampa. We set up camp.

It was raining hard, and we got separated from the forward detachment.

Chinchu killed a calf. Ñato and Aniceto went to help him but they got lost. León left to look for them and he found them. We all worked on carrying the meat back to camp.

As we rested, waiting for news from Miguel about the route that the forward detachment was opening up, we heard over the radio about a battle in Iquiri. It was probable that Joaquín was there waiting for us. This confirmed the possibility that Benigno's encounter was with Joaquín and not with the army,[1] because if the enemy had come up the creek it would have run into Joaquín. They spoke of one guerrilla killed.[2]

In the morning [July 13] we reached the creek after going down a steep hill where the forward detachment was camped. In the afternoon we came to an abandoned farm, where there were oranges, limes, and tracks made by pigs. We followed the tracks and found the house of a peasant named Aurelio Mancilla, who gave us information about the army. Everything indicated that they were waiting for us on the road, but in getting lost we had fallen behind. An advance guard was placed inside the house of the mayor, who had fled, and later we found out that a woman had informed the enemy of our presence in the area. The mayor's brother-in-law was taken prisoner.

It rained the whole night. Nevertheless we cooked pork, corn, and jocos.

At noon on July 14, after dividing up some oranges, we began our march. As guides we took Aurelio and Pablo, the mayor's brother-in-law. We were headed toward Pampa, and from there to the stone house on the road to Florida, which was the contact point with Paulino.

Shortly before arriving at Pampa, we could see in the distance two men on horseback. We sent Papi to warn Miguel, because the forward detachment was passing through a depression and was unable to see them.

They turned out to be one young soldier and the peasant Anselmo, who was carrying corn and wheat flour for the army. The soldier was bringing a message from his commanding officer to the second lieutenant at El Filo. Che decided to change our route and take the old trail to Florida. We camped there with the detainees and our guide.

We set off. Aurelio had told us about very difficult stretches that were almost impossible to get across. They were bad, but

1. A reference to a possible encounter by Benigno and Aniceto with the army on April 25. See Guevara's *Bolivian Diary,* pp. 183, 191.
2. Serapio Aquino (*Serapio*), a member of Joaquín's column, was killed July 9 at the Iquira river.

better than expected. Along the trail he pointed out some cows that belonged to the mayor, who was also the owner of all those lands and the exploiter of the peasants. Aurelio suggested we take one of the cows to eat in the afternoon; we took three. Later Che ordered us to let one go and we killed the other. We spent the night cooking and grilling.

We started the next day by clearing brush to make it possible for the animals to get through, after which we advanced very slowly because of exhaustion and the terrible condition of the path. Part of the forward detachment continued ahead and we slept separated from each other because the loaded horses could not get through.

We advanced very little because the road was so uneven. Our guide had led us to believe there was an orange grove nearby, but when we got there we found the orchards completely barren. We camped on the side of Durán Hill.

At dawn [July 18] we left along the path Miguel had opened and we got to the intersection of the road to the Piray. There we rested, and Coco, Pacho, and Pablito went out to see whether Paulino had left the things he was responsible for in a cave as planned. The prisoners were set free. We gave Aurelio a coat and some matches, and we gave him money without letting the young soldier see what we were doing.

Later we reached the place we had camped the month before, near the Piray. During the night Coco arrived and told us that the rifle we had left behind was still in the same place. He said there was no sign of Paulino but many signs of the army. This worried us because we had already detected signs of the army in the encampment, too.

Che's analysis of the political situation

Che spoke to us after hearing the latest news. He analyzed the political crisis that the Barrientos government was suffering. Our leader continued his analysis, pointing out that the danger was not that Ovando[1] or some other big general would come to power, but rather that some pseudorevolutionary like Lechín, who had some prestige, would do so.

It was during these days that Che would write in his war diary: "It is a pity we do not have a hundred more men at this moment." He was convinced that if we had them, the Bolivian government would have collapsed completely, considering the amount of pressure we had been able to put on it even with a small number of fighters.

We continued on and arrived at the two houses we had visited previously. We met one of the sons of Benjamín Paniagua and Paulino's brother-in-law. We found out that the army was looking for Paulino as a guerrilla collaborator. His whereabouts were unknown. We also found out that the tracks we had detected belonged to a contingent of a hundred men who passed by after us, heading toward Florida.

Che sent Coco, Camba, León, and Julio to explore and to buy supplies in Florida. They came back with a man named Pedro Melgar, who told us that all the men in the little village of Moroco, including the mayor Calixto, had been taken prisoner and sent to La Paz because they were accused of being guerrilla contacts. He added that the day we had retreated the army did not advance until the morning, going only as far as Tejería, without trying to pursue us. Furthermore, the mayor had told him that a group of guerrillas had passed through, among them a woman. From this man, we learned that Tuma's body, eaten by animals, had been found four days after we retreated.

From Melgar's information, Che thought that the group under Joaquín's command might possibly be moving in our direction; we assumed that the woman was Tania. The same day the radio announced that the dead guerrilla taken to

---

1. Alfredo Ovando, one of the leaders of the November 1964 coup d'état, was commander in chief of the armed forces under Barrientos. He served as president of Bolivia 1965–66 and 1969–70.

Santa Cruz for identification was the miners leader Moisés Guevara.[1]

We remained in the area, about three hundred meters from the river. Later, after night fell, we bought a pig and some *chancaca*[2] in Tejería.

We proceeded ahead in the morning, [July 22] leaving the road to Moroco and taking the one by the lagoon in order to mislead everyone about the direction we were going. Later, we came upon two peasants. Despite our warning to them to say absolutely nothing about our presence in the area, this partially ruined our plan to throw our pursuers off the scent.

Miguel lost the path and we were lost for quite a while until we reached a creek, where we decided to spend the night.

The radio announced that Bustos's wife had confirmed that her husband had held a meeting with Che in La Paz to discuss political questions, according to what he had told her.

We believed, in short, that Bustos had talked too much and become a turncoat, because the radio also reported that on arriving in La Paz, Bustos had been told to go to a farm in Camiri and though he did not refuse, he was reluctant because he felt he had been "deceived."[3]

Days of exploration

Che sent out scouting expeditions to find out where the two paths led before making a decision. The result was that one went to the Piray river near where it flowed into the Florida; the other bordered the chain of hills and possibly came out at the Rosita. The sound of vehicles was heard.

1. A false identification; the guerrilla killed was Serapio.
2. Brown sugar and water cooked in a pan.
3. After his capture Bustos adopted the stance of having been "taken in" by the guerrillas, giving a detailed account of his discussions with Guevara and providing sketches of guerrilla fighters for Bolivian authorities. In November 1967 he and Debray were sentenced to 30 years' imprisonment; they were amnestied in 1970.

At midday we arrived at a shack and waited for reports from the scouting parties that had been sent out, one under Miguel's command and the other under Benigno's. We decided to go down to the creek and continue explorations the following day.

At dawn [July 25] a new scouting party set out led by Coco. They climbed up to the ridge, together with Benigno's party.

Miguel thought the creek was the Suspiro and that it therefore went directly to the Rosita, even though this route would require us to cut a path with machetes.

The radio reported two clashes, one in Taperas on the way to Muyupampa, and the other in San Juan del Potrero, to our north, on the way to Samaipata. In other words, these were two encounters at opposite extremes of the area.[1] On July 26, 1967, we began cutting a trail. Benigno, Urbano, and Camba were chosen for this task, even though it was almost worthless to assign Camba, since by this time his morale had weakened considerably. He did not even want to work, much less fight.

July 26, 1967

Che held a meeting and spoke about the significance of this date for us and about the Cuban revolution, emphasizing its importance in the development of the Latin American revolution. He stated that the national liberation movements in Latin America and even the reform policies that imperialism was trying to carry out through the so-called Alliance for Progress,[2] as well as the whole process of phony democratization that was occurring on the continent, were all conse-

---

1. This was deliberate misinformation by the army command, which knew that the guerrillas listened to radio reports.
2. The Alliance for Progress, announced by Washington in 1961 in hopes of countering the example of the Cuban revolution, allocated $20 billion in loans to Latin American governments over a ten-year period, and millions more in gratuities to line the pockets of willing political allies.

quences of the existence of the Cuban revolution and of its example. We had to draw the lessons of the Cuban revolution, emulating its positive achievements and studying its negative aspects in order to avoid them. He told us that the Cuban revolution was the beginning of the genuine and definitive revolution of the peoples of Latin America. He was convinced that however difficult it might seem, the continental character of the struggle would by necessity bring the peoples closer together and unite them. This dialectical process of integration, he said, would lead to the formation of one great Latin American community without borders, either territorial or in ideas — a great socialist America.

We were getting ready to leave in the morning, after listening to the news, when Willy arrived all out of breath, telling us he had seen the army.

THE BATTLE OF JULY 27

Che strengthened the rear guard composed of Antonio, Arturo, Chapaco, and Willy by adding Ricardo, Inti, Chino, León, and Eustaquio. Antonio was chosen to command the operation.

The troops came into sight as they climbed a small rising. There were eight soldiers, who signaled and fired three mortar shells. Then they called out to a certain Melgar,[1] and someone came forward as if to climb down into a ravine. Two others followed him; they entered a little thicket and came out again. The other one who had stayed behind watching the road joined up with them. They advanced with few precau-

1. Antonio Melgar, a Bolivian army courier who died in that battle.

tions. The others remained behind, which meant that not all of them were inside the ambush when the shooting started. Four soldiers fell, but in accordance with our methods, we counted them as three dead and one wounded.

Che ordered us to retreat along a very steep and difficult path, which the horses could not get through. They kept falling, so we had to make our way on foot. Most of the path was through shallow water.

An advance party composed of Pacho, Coco, Raúl, and Aniceto set off with the mission of reaching the mouth of the creek. If this turned out to be the Suspiro river, they were to set up an ambush there to cover our arrival. The forward detachment got so far ahead that we ended up spending the night in separate places.

On the afternoon of the next day we reached the mouth of the creek, where we rested for a good while. Che explained the necessity of crossing past the farm of Paulino's stepfather that day, so the army would not be able to set up an operation on the lower road and cut off our advance.

When we resumed the march, Che ordered me to take a message to Miguel, telling him to choose a good spot to set up camp. He selected a place situated between two paths, on the edge of one of them and on the bank of the river. When we got there, Che called Miguel over and explained that the site was no good because if the army passed by we would be forced to fight.

Later a meeting was held in which Chino spoke about his country's independence day, July 28, 1821.[1] He compared that struggle with the present one. Before ending, he expressed his pride at being able to fight alongside a man like Ernesto Guevara.

Che explained that in light of the poor location of our camp, wake-up time would be at 4:30 a.m. so that we could set off at 5:00 to get to Paulino's farm.

---

1. The day Peru declared its independence from Spain.

THE BATTLE OF JULY 30

The death of Ricardo and Raúl

In the early morning, while Moro was on guard and was making coffee, he saw a light. He notified Che and Miguel, who were awake beside him. They warned me to get out of the light. The enemy's advance party shouted "Trinidad Regiment," confusing us with an army encampment. Hearing this, Moro opened fire. His M-2 jammed, but Miguel covered him with fire from his Garand. Che ordered us to set up a line of defense. Benigno threw a grenade at a group of soldiers hidden in a small ditch. The grenade exploded in the water without reaching its objective, but it terrified the soldiers and they took off running. We began our retreat in good time, but the delay in getting the horses, plus the confidence we all felt because of the army's ineffectiveness, slowed us down. The sun came up before we had crossed the farm. Chino was bringing one of the horses, and its load fell off (beans). Rather than gathering it up quickly, he waited until the rear guard arrived. Muganga, for his part, decided to try on some new boots he had confiscated. During the gunfire, one of the horses that was loaded with equipment we had captured (a mortar, rifles, clothing, etc.) took off for good.

This delay enabled the enemy's forward detachment (25 men) to alert the body of the army forces (about 120 troops in all), and they began to pursue us. We crossed three fords, and as we crossed the fourth one under fire, Che's horse slipped and fell. Julio, Coco, Miguel, and Che immediately set up a line of defense to prevent the enemy from being able to shoot freely. The troops were practically on top of us before they were forced to take cover.

Julio also slipped and fell into the water as he was crossing a stone slab. The soldiers began shouting "We got one, we got one," thinking they had hit their mark.

We reached the house and spoke to one of Paulino's sisters. She told us that Paulino had been taken prisoner and was in Samaipata, and she confirmed that all the men of the village had been arrested and brought to La Paz. Meanwhile, the army took a shortcut trying to cut off our retreat. Che placed Benigno with Pablito at the first farm in order to continue the march.

Our group crossed the river on the run, because the army was almost in control of the river and the crossroads. Part of the forward detachment — Pacho, Aniceto, and Raúl — were covering the Abapó road. The rear guard, reinforced by Chinchu, retreated without being able to cross the river, because the army had the ford under heavy fire. Aniceto and Chinchu tried to get across, but the latter was wounded in the attempt. Covered by a curtain of gunfire, Pacho and Raúl took off to rescue Chinchu. Raúl died in the attempt, shot in the face as he tried to reach them. Pacho attempted to carry Chinchu, but he was hit by a shot in the buttocks, grazing his testicles. He took cover behind Raúl's lifeless body and was able to silence a machine gun. There was a momentary pause in the gunfire, which Arturo and some other comrades used to carry off Chinchu.

For our part, we had reached a more advantageous spot where the army was forced to advance along a single path, and there we organized our resistance. Che, Inti, Chino, Moro, and I had established a line of defense when Camba arrived with the news that Chinchu had been gravely wounded.

Che sent Urbano, Ñato, and León to help, and to look for Miguel and Eustaquio. Camba later returned with news that Miguel had been taken by surprise by the army. We retreated downriver to the place where Coco was standing watch.

Urbano — who had been assigned to assist in the withdrawal of the wounded — got Benigno and Pablito, who were located in the ford, to help him. This enabled the army to advance and catch Miguel by surprise. With the help of Benigno and Pablito, however, Antonio's group was located and the wounded were carried off. Benigno cut our retreat path by machete, and Urbano gave first aid to Chinchu, binding up his wounds with his undershirt. About ten o'clock that night Ricardo (Chinchu) died. We buried him in a well-hidden place.

It was dawn already when we resumed our march, without leaving any tracks. During the morning we reached the creek, where Miguel was waiting. He had mixed up the instructions Che had given him and had left tracks behind him.

Che stopped there to draw a balance sheet of the ambush that had turned out so badly for us. We had lost two men, in addition to one wounded. We had also lost a tape recorder with messages received from Cuba, Debray's book *Revolution in the Revolution?* with Che's handwritten notes, a book by Trotsky on the Russian revolution, Ricardo's diary, and all our reserves of medicine. The necessity for the latter had already been deeply felt, since we had needed plasma to try to save Ricardo's life, and in the end he died without it. The plasma had been in Willy's knapsack, which was one of the eleven knapsacks lost.

Che listed the principal errors we had committed that had produced these results. Even though the army had taken more casualties, he explained, its losses were insignificant given the relationship of forces. The reports that had been broadcast, which were not very clear, spoke of 4 dead and 4 wounded; another broadcast from Chile reported 3 dead and 6 wounded. Since our forces had no possibility of being replenished at that moment, our losses were tremendous, and even more so when the caliber of the combatants was taken into account.

He spoke about those who had fallen: Raúl and Chinchu. He said very little about Raúl because he did not know him well. Concerning Chinchu, he spoke in general terms, reviewing the important role he had played in the insurrectional stage in the Congo, where for all practical purposes he was Che's right-hand man. Che finished by making some critical remarks about the attitude Chinchu had exhibited in the Bolivian struggle. Of those of us here who had participated in the Congo, Chinchu was the second to die.

For me it was a hard blow. We had gone through difficult moments together, during which human beings acquire strong feelings of affection and attachment. Together we had been through the first stage of organizing the struggle; together we learned all the norms required to withstand underground life in the city. He was a demanding comrade, both toward himself and toward others. He left behind his mother, three children, and his wife.

NEAR THE ROSITA RIVER

New encampments

Afterward, we began to construct the defense of our encampment. The location could not have been better; it was the kind of place from which a whole battalion could be knocked off. Our idea was to stay there unnoticed. In the event the army came up the creek looking for us, we were to let them pass by, and then hit them hard when they tried to get out.

Miguel and Camba left to begin clearing a path, but they did not make any progress. The countryside was a thorny mess. We killed a horse in order to have something to eat.

Benigno and Pablito made some progress with the path. It took them two hours to get back to camp.

Che's asthma was getting worse, to the point where it seemed like he might have to be given an enema to relieve the attacks if it were not possible to contain them with the remaining anesthesia injections. Moro told me he thought this would be very dangerous and that he was afraid of what could happen, but that he had prepared an injection of calcium, which, if the situation got serious, would neutralize the effects of the talamonal.

The scouting parties discovered a creek that we thought might lead to the Río Grande. Che ordered Miguel to follow it and try to reach a clearing visible in the distance, to determine whether what we saw were farms. The results were negative.

We moved our camp to a spot less than an hour away, which was actually as far as the path had been cleared. Miguel and Aniceto followed the creek downstream to see what they could find. Two teams went out to cut the trail: Benigno and Camba, and Urbano and I. We made very little headway.

That night we had a meeting to commemorate August 6, the day Bolivia's independence is celebrated.[1]

Miguel did not come back that night. This was contrary to Che's orders that he return before nightfall, causing us to lift camp very early the next morning. We took the corresponding security precautions. One group, led by Antonio, followed the creek upstream, and the other, under Benigno's command, followed the creek downstream. Che's orders were that they should proceed with extreme caution and try to get to where the creek flowed into the river.

About noon Benigno returned with Miguel. What happened was that nightfall came upon him and, since it was too late to come back, he was forced to spend the night where he was.

Another creek was found, which we moved to in the morning.

Moro talked to me about signs of apparent demoralization in the group, and later he spoke with Che about it. The points raised were more or less as follows: León said he had been deceived; he said that when he was assigned to look after the

---

1. Bolivia won its independence in 1825.

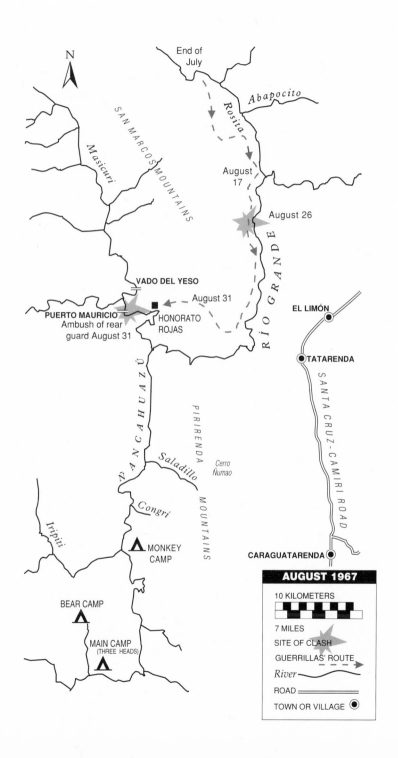

N

End of
July

Abapocito

Rosita

SAN MARCOS MOUNTAINS

Masicuri

August
17

August 26

VADO DEL YESO

August 31

PUERTO MAURICIO
Ambush of rear
guard August 31

**HONORATO
ROJAS**

RÍO GRANDE

EL LIMÓN

TATARENDA

SANTA CRUZ - CAMIRI ROAD

N̄ANCAHUAZÜ

PIRIRENDA

Saladillo

Congri

*Cerro
Ñumao*

Iripiti

▲ MONKEY
CAMP

MOUNTAINS

BEAR CAMP
▲

MAIN CAMP
(THREE HEADS)
▲

CARAGUATARENDA

AUGUST 1967

10 KILOMETERS

7 MILES

SITE OF CLASH

GUERRILLAS' ROUTE

River

ROAD

TOWN OR VILLAGE ⦿

farm, the party had promised him they would give his wife 200 pesos, but they had not given her anything. In terms of Camba, it was not even worth talking about his attitude. Willy wanted to go visit his family. Also, Che had lost control and inflicted a gash on his little mare.

That night [August 8] a meeting was held, at which Che could hardly stand up. He began with a self-criticism because of the state of mind that had led him to gash his mare. "We have reached a moment when great decisions are called for. This type of struggle provides us the opportunity to become revolutionaries, the highest level of the human species. At the same time, it enables us to emerge fully as men. Those who are unable to achieve either of these two states should say so and abandon the struggle."

Che said he would talk to each of the combatants privately so that no one would be afraid to explain his decision. Those who wanted to abandon the struggle could leave as soon as security conditions permitted. He explained his decision to send a group off in search of medicine, because it was clear that his own weakened state was having a bad effect on the combat morale of the guerrilla column.

In order to do this, he outlined the following plan: Benigno, Julio, Ñato, Coco, Aniceto, Pablito, Darío, and Camba would leave. The first day Camba would return to report back; the second day Pablito and Darío would do the same. The remaining five would go as far as the house belonging to Vargas, the peasant who had died in Ñancahuazú.[1] After they got there, Coco and Aniceto would return to us, and the other three — Ñato, Benigno, and Julio — would continue on to the Three Heads camp to get the medicines we had hidden there.

In the morning, the path clearers left to continue their work, and an ambush was set up under my responsibility. I was be-

---

1. Epifanio Vargas, a peasant, was killed in the ambush of March 23 while being forced to act as army guide.

ginning to take part in operations, since I could walk even though my legs were not completely recovered.

The next day [August 10] Camba returned with news that the group had not found water, and that Pablito and Darío would come back when they found it. If not, they would continue until they reached the river. Antonio and Chapaco caught an urina, which improved Che's physical condition because he was allergic to horsemeat and it caused him serious harm. When it was proposed that he eat the urina, he did not want to, because he said he should not have special privileges. It was only after great insistence by us that he agreed.

Pablito and Darío arrived in the afternoon with a message from Benigno saying that it would take them about three days more to reach Vargas's house. The camp was moved to a new creek found during the exploratory journey, one that had the characteristic of disappearing and then reappearing at midnight.

On August 12 we heard on the radio news of a clash in Monteagudo. They mentioned the body of an "antisocial element" (a guerrilla) named Antonio Fernández. After looking through our files, we found that the closest match was Antonio Jiménez (Pedro), from Tarata.[1]

Coco and Aniceto arrived to report the presence of soldiers in Vargas's house.

Three days later we heard a radio report of an encounter in the region of Monteagudo, Muyupampa, in which two prisoners were taken. Everything indicated that Joaquín's group was in a tight spot, given the short interval between clashes. The radio reported a battle in Chuhuayaco without any army casualties.[2] (These two locations are very far apart from each other.)

---

1. Antonio Jiménez (*Pedro*) was killed on August 9 in the Inão hills.
2. The report was disinformation by the army.

EN ROUTE TO THE ROSITA RIVER

We headed for a puddle of stagnant water that we assumed was close to the river. It had its effect: we came down with diarrhea.

Later an airplane appeared and circled over the river. Che ordered us to collect our things so as to leave in the morning on a forced march. We would try to reach the river and from there proceed to where the Rosita joined the Río Grande. Anticipating that the army would advance along this river, we had to get out before they came.

Later an advance party was picked to leave at daybreak to go down along the Rosita and cautiously explore downriver. Those who were sick would march with me, and the rear guard would follow. The rear guard would in turn relieve the forward detachment at their ambush post, and we would continue on like that until we reached the end of the river.

Seizure of the caves

The most important news received between August 14 and 17 was the radio announcement that the enemy had found the caves — which our comrades were heading for. An exact description was given of everything. It was clear that someone had talked.[1]

Che was extremely worried about the fate of the comrades who had gone in search of the medicine.

1. Eusebio and Chingolo, two of the expelled guerrillas accompanying Joaquín's column, deserted in late July and were taken prisoner several days later. On August 4 Chingolo led the army to the guerrillas' supply caves at the Ñancahuazú. The caves contained stockpiles of arms, ammunition, and equipment, as well as documents, photographs, and other items useful to the Bolivian regime. Government forces proceeded to hunt down and arrest members of the ELN's urban support network and collaborators.

The next day [August 18] Camba decided to openly raise his desire to desert the guerrilla column. He alleged he was not in good physical shape and did not think the struggle had any prospects.

We reached the creek in the afternoon. A scouting party was sent out consisting of Miguel, Coco, Inti, and Aniceto in search of a place to cross the river, to avoid the hills.

Arturo and Urbano, who were on guard duty, shot an *anta* (a kind of tapir). It was the first one we had seen, even though they were plentiful in the area. This provided some relief and made possible Che's idea of saving the animals to the last moment. We needed to conserve the animals, first because they were our reserve food supply, and secondly because it was the only way for Che to get around. He could not walk a step.

Our situation was getting worse. Moro had been suffering from back pain (lumbago) since the day before and had no appetite. Pacho had recovered.

The next day [August 21] was calm and the work of cutting the path continued. We stayed where we were. Five monkeys were caught. Moro's health continued to decline.

Che had to have another abscess on his foot lanced, and he took pills to counter his asthma.

My foot was getting better.

We were moving ahead, expecting to reach the end of the path, when Moro's animal fell down in a ravine. We spent a long time getting it out. Che scolded the path clearers because he felt their work was poorly done. The white horse got stuck in a bog and we had to abandon it. It was not much of a loss, since it had harness sores and a stomach tumor. Even so, Che admonished us for not having made use of the meat that could still be salvaged.

We captured two peasants who claimed to be hunters. They told us that the army was in Vargas's house, which we were already quite near. Later we learned that the soldiers went out in small groups to wander around and fish. We also learned that there were garrisons in Ipitá, Caraguatarenda, Tatarenda, and Ñumao.

The information we got from the peasants showed that the army was setting up ambushes in all the places we knew, to force us to operate in unfamiliar territory.

We went fishing with the dynamite that the hunters had brought with them.

We got up at dawn [August 24] in order not to be seen if the army came to fish.

From the ravine the forward detachment informed us of obstacles preventing the animals from getting through. Che had the rear guard set up an ambush, reinforced by people from the center group and the forward detachment. He assigned Miguel, Urbano, Camba, and Darío, along with one of the alleged hunters (Hugo Guzmán), to a scouting expedition. Later we saw three civilians who fired off some shots. It appeared to be a signal, since the soldiers arrived to fish right afterwards.

For dinner we had a soup made from *suchi* (a type of vulture) and a rotten cat that Miguel had caught, cooked with anta bones.

The next day was tense. We were expecting the army to arrive, approaching along the opposite bank. They stopped for a long time opposite our position, and then went off to a bend in the river to fish.

Guerrilla actions

In the afternoon, Che summoned Antonio and gave him instructions to attack one way or another. He said that if it was a small group, Antonio should let them fish and take them prisoner to get information on the location of the troops. Our objective was to get to Honorato Rojas's farm, and then go up the Río Grande, looking for the Acero or the Frías river. From there we would continue on to the Muyupampa region, where we thought Joaquín's group was operating.

The planning of the attack turned out badly. Unlike previous days, the army arrived with caution. They divided into two groups; one remained behind at the bend of the river, and the other advanced with many security measures along the bank of the river up to the ford. They passed in front of my position, which was next to Pacho's, and we did not open fire. The instructions were that Antonio would be the one to begin firing, since he was on the right flank and was in charge of the ambush.

Two young soldiers arrived at the ford and began to undress. When the first of them put his foot in the water, Antonio opened fire too soon, and missed. The rest of us concentrated our fire on the group of soldiers. They threw down their rifles and took off running. They got away unhurt. Pacho and I fired on those at the bend in the river. Inti, Coco, and Pablito suggested to Che (who had just arrived at our positions) that they go down to the other side of the river to recover the rifles. Che agreed. Eustaquio, who apparently was distracted, did not realize that it was our own men going down the river and opened fire on them. Inti was almost wounded. Che was furious and grabbed Antonio by the shirt. Antonio said, "Damn it, Fernando, nobody has ever done that to me." Che let him go and apologized. Later there was a meeting to analyze who was responsible for the failure.

A retreat was ordered, and Che put the group of our sick under my command. Moro remained behind with the rear guard, about two hundred meters from our camp, to sleep. He was so sick that he could not keep walking.

We continued our march, with almost everyone out of water. I gave the little bit I had left to Moro.

We started to eat little reeds to quench our thirst somewhat, even though the liquid inside is bitter.

Despite all this, we all got a very happy surprise when Benigno, Ñato, and Julio showed up. We had considered that we might never see them again, or at best, they might catch up with us at Honorato's house.

We found out from the comrades that there were troops stationed in Ñumao and Vargas, and that army units were patrolling the road from Vargas to Ipitá, some stretches in vehicles and some stretches on foot. When the comrades had reached Ñancahuazú, they observed fresh signs of troops, and there was practically a highway built. The army had built good roads at the Congrí Creek. There were three very slippery routes up the hill. Further in, at the site where we had established Bear Camp at the beginning, there was now an antiguerrilla encampment.

Che explained to us that this was a good psychological move by the army, because their troops were being trained in camps that had supposedly been taken in battle from the enemy, and this boosted the army's fighting morale.

On the basis of what the comrades had seen, they calculated there were more than 350 soldiers in the area. On their way back they had gone to the grandfather's farm,[1] and as they were leaving they heard our gunfire. They set up camp nearby so they could later locate and follow our tracks. Benigno was virtually positive that Joaquín's people had been in the area shortly before.

We were out of water to quench Moro's thirst. He had finished off the three bottles Che was carrying.

Several comrades set to work looking for a cactus called *caracoré*, a parasitic plant that has a natural water reserve inside.

We found some in the afternoon and organized to slaughter the little mare that Che had looked after with such affection. We filled three bottles with cactus water for Moro.

The next day [August 29] we suffered tremendous thirst. Miguel and Chino began to drink their own urine, and as a result came down with diarrhea and cramps.

---

1. This was the farm visited on May 26. It belonged to the great-uncle of Moisés Robles, a peasant guide of the guerrillas.

We received a message from Cuba that we could not copy well.

The rear guard, reinforced with elements from the center group, stayed in the spot where the comrades who had gone looking for water had to pass by on their way back.

At noon [August 30] we reached a high spot from which we could make out the confluence of the Masicuri and the Río Grande. We thought it was only a day's march away, but the path clearers were exhausted. Miguel asked permission to go down into a ravine, but by the time the authorization came, Benigno, Urbano, and Julio had already started down. At 4:00 p.m. we heard a voice cry out, "Water!" Urbano brought me up some canteens full of water. It was a blessing, since we were dying of thirst. Che stayed on top watching his troop of animals that could not make it down the ravine. Ñato, León, and Inti stayed with him; later water and food were taken up to them. We had spent three days without water.

We decided to spend the day there, and a scouting party set off downriver to look for a place the animals could get through. The scouts, Aniceto and León, came back with news that they had found a place.

The mules were able to get down, but the horse fell into a ditch. In point of fact, as hungry as we were, we wished the horse had died, forgetting that Che needed to ride it.

IN THE VADO DEL YESO

We advanced slowly. Julio returned from scouting saying that the Río Grande was less than an hour away.

At about 6:00 p.m. we came to the ravine that led down toward the farm of Honorato Rojas.[1] At 7:00 we arrived at the junction of the road, and we sent scouts to the house. We did not find anyone at home, but there were traces indicating that people had left there a short time before. The fire was still burning. We ate flour and killed two goats for fricassee. All this took place on September 1, 1967.

In the early morning of September 2, we left an ambush at the house composed of Miguel, Coco, Pablo, and Benigno, and the rest of us withdrew along the side of the creek. After 10:00 Chino, Eustaquio, and I took over the ambush. The instructions were that one person would keep watch while the other two rested. If the army came, the alarm would be sounded by imitating a dog barking. I kept watch for three hours and then turned it over to Chino for one hour. At about 1:00 a.m., I heard his voice saying "A soldier!" and then shots. It turned out it was the soldier, realizing he had been discovered, who opened fire on Chino. For his part, Chino did not have his rifle in his hands, and went around in circles looking for it, since he was half blind and could not see it. I joined in and opened fire at the shadows of the solider and the peasant, who were already lost around the bend. I managed to kill their horse.

Che was upset and had a lot to say about it; the outburst toward me was simple, while the one at Chino really stung.

Miguel had captured several peasants (their last names were Santos, Veizaga, and Burgos). We let them go after buying a little bull from them. Before leaving, they told us that Honorato Rojas was in Valle Grande, recovering from a tiger bite.

On that day — September 2 — foreign radio reported the demise of a group of guerrillas commanded by the Cuban Joaquín with ten killed. (It is important to keep this detail in

1. A peasant the guerrillas had met on February 10. Just twenty-four hours before, on August 31, Rojas led the rear guard group commanded by Joaquín into an ambush at the Puerto Mauricio ford on the Río Grande.

mind, owing to its importance in the subsequent course of events).

On the morning of September 3, Coco headed a group composed of Benigno, Inti, León, Pablito, and Julio that went to the house to obtain food supplies. They captured two peasants who said they had not seen the army and that their first news about the guerrillas in several months had come from some peasants who passed by fleeing the day before.

Arriving at the large landowner's house, the man in charge did not want to give information, so he was threatened. A group of soldiers then appeared; hearing the argument, they had come to see what was going on. They immediately started running toward the woods to cut off our comrades' retreat. Nevertheless, with shouts and shots our people managed to break out of the semi-encirclement.

That day the radio was broadcasting news of the detention of José Castillo as the only survivor of the group of ten men. They placed the combat at the Vado del Yeso, Masicuri.[1]

Everything seemed to indicate that the news we had been hearing since September 2 was false.

The Vado del Yeso on the Masicuri river was indicated as the site of the battle. How was this possible, if we were there and had not heard a single shot? How was it possible that they had annihilated the entire group? If we were guiding ourselves by guerrilla tactics, that was practically impossible. Furthermore, the survivor they were announcing was José Castillo (Paco), who belonged to the rejects.[2] In other words,

1. The ambush did not take place at the Vado de Yeso (Yeso ford) on the Masicuri river, but at the Puerto Mauricio ford on the Río Grande. The announcement of a different location in the military dispatches was the result of contradictions and rivalries between the commanders of the Eighth and the Fourth Divisions of the Bolivian army. The Eighth Division, which conducted the ambush, was carrying out its operations in the territory under the jurisdiction of the Fourth Division. They tried to cover up the fact by lying about the location of the massacre.

2. These were the four members of the guerrilla unit — José Castillo (*Paco, Paquito*), Julio Velazco (*Pepe*), Hugo Choque (*Chingolo*), and Eusebio Tapia (*Eusebio*) — who were expelled on March 25.

he was someone who had wanted to abandon the struggle and was kept prisoner by Joaquín's group. There was also the possibility that he might have escaped.

But it was true. The rear guard group — separated from us due to an unforeseen series of events — headed by the heroic commander Vilo Acuña, had been annihilated. Over time, the answers to many of our questions have been pieced together. Basing ourselves on some journalist accounts — and especially the account by Paquito, the only survivor of the treacherous ambush — we now have a Dantesque picture of that massacre, made possible by a vile betrayal.

OUR REAR GUARD: JOAQUÍN'S COLUMN

Our rear guard was commanded by Joaquín and composed of Braulio, Marcos, Pedro, Walter, Ernesto, Polo, Víctor, and the expelled individuals Pepe, Eusebio, Chingolo, and Paco. Negro stayed to treat the sick; he, together with Tania, Alejandro, Serapio, and Moisés had originally belonged to the center group. Altogether there were seventeen comrades waiting for Che's return.[1]

The day after our departure [on April 17], the rear guard relocated to the other side of the river, approximately five hundred meters away, at the bottom of the bank. They camped there for five days and then moved to another place about four hundred meters from the previous location. They stayed at this camp longer than at the first one. They stocked up on food from nearby peasant houses.

Eventually, Joaquín ordered everyone to get their knapsacks

1. See page 169.

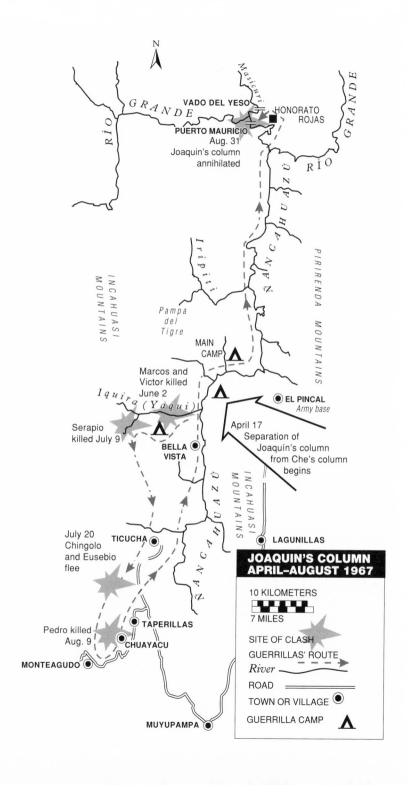

N

Masicurí

R Í O   G R A N D E

VADO DEL YESO

HONORATO
ROJAS

PUERTO MAURICIO
Aug. 31
Joaquin's column
annihilated

R Í O

G R A N D E

R Í O

Iripiti

Ñ A N C A H U A Z Ú

P I R I R E N D A   M O U N T A I N S

I N C A H U A S I   M O U N T A I N S

*Pampa
del
Tigre*

MAIN
CAMP

Marcos and
Victor killed
June 2

I q u i r a   (Y a q u i)

Serapio
killed July 9

● EL PINCAL
Army base

April 17
Separation of
Joaquín's column
from Che's column
begins

BELLA
VISTA ●

Ñ A N C A H U A Z Ú

*I N C A H U A S I
M O U N T A I N S*

July 20
Chingolo
and Eusebio
flee

TICUCHA ●

LAGUNILLAS ●

Pedro killed
Aug. 9

● TAPERILLAS

● CHUAYACU

MONTEAGUDO ●

MUYUPAMPA ●

**JOAQUIN'S COLUMN
APRIL–AUGUST 1967**

10 KILOMETERS

7 MILES

SITE OF CLASH

GUERRILLAS' ROUTE

River

ROAD

TOWN OR VILLAGE ●

GUERRILLA CAMP ▲

ready for leaving. At about 7:00 a.m. they prepared an ambush for the army. Almost everyone left, with just Alejandro, Tania, Serapio, and Chingolo remaining. The ambush was set up near the peasant houses, along the bank of the Ñancahuazú river. Guevara and Paco stayed in the rear guard on lookout.

The ambush failed because Joaquín fired his rifle too soon in the direction of the woods where he had heard a noise. After a series of discussions, criticisms, and commentary, they abandoned that site. They walked all day, always along the riverbank, always moving farther away from the houses. They came to a deep ravine that came out some four hundred meters from the river. They made camp atop the walls of the ravine. Climbing a very high hillock, they had a perfect view of the whole vicinity.

There they set up a permanent watch post. They named the slope Observatory Hill. (These places were chosen by Braulio during his scouting missions.) From this site they could monitor all the movements of the army along the river and the houses of the peasants. For ten days there were helicopter flights over the houses. It was assumed that the army landed there to leave provisions for the troops who were occupying the area. In addition, peasant guides or soldiers dressed like peasants also made incursions along the river, searching for tracks. After these searches ended, four army planes bombed the zone on the other side of the river, that is, the side opposite from the guerrilla encampment. They did this for four days. Afterwards they again began tracking, until several peasants on horseback crossed the river and passed through the area that had been bombed.

Another watch post was set up overlooking the riverbank, at the exit of the ravine. Beginning on that day, they also sent out reconnaissance missions to look for Che and to scout the terrain. In one of these scouting missions, Braulio and Polo stumbled on two peasants and took away their horses. This event was happily greeted at the camp because the horses could be eaten, since all they had by this time was a little bit of corn.

Two days later several peasants were once again seen going down by the river. They went right by where the comrades keeping watch were posted. Learning of this, it was thought that the peasants had discovered them, and orders were issued to immediately abandon the camp to escape to another place. This was done and after walking for a night and a day they came to a glen where there was a small stagnant lagoon. There they set up a new camp, from which they sent out more frequent scouting missions in search of Che and also kept watch on the movements of the army.

One day a volunteer group went to peasants' homes to get food, because they no longer had anything to eat. When the group returned, they reported welcome news that the army had abandoned the peasants' homes.

They bought a large amount of corn, and even carried a full sack halfway back on a mule loaned by a peasant. The next day several comrades were selected to go pick it up. Marcos and Pedro carried out the customary scouting mission. Braulio was head of the group, and his aim was to catch a horse seen in the area. On the way back they brought the corn but could not find the horse. Pepe, who was part of the group, fell way behind while climbing a hill. When they got to the hillcrest, the rest of the comrades decided to rest to wait for him and then continue on. Braulio said he wanted to get to the camp early. He went on ahead and left Ernesto in charge of the group. After a while, when Pepe had still not arrived, Ernesto sent Polo and Paco to a designated place with the aim of finding him. They went, but Pepe did not appear anywhere and they returned to the group. Ernesto ordered them to get to the camp as fast as possible to inform Joaquín what had happened.

Learning of this, Joaquín was greatly concerned and started to ask Eusebio, Paco, and the others if they had heard Pepe talk about his intentions of fleeing. Marcos and

Pedro went looking for him in the direction of the peasants' houses. The next day they returned very agitated and said that Pepe had deserted. He had gone by a peasant house and said that he had fled because the guerrillas were a bunch of murderers.[1]

They stayed a few more days at this place, which they called Lagoon Camp, and then abandoned it to move to Observatory Camp or somewhere near it. There, by a small ravine, they set up a new camp. This happened, more or less, in the middle of May.

The death of Marcos and Víctor

Later they sent a group of combatants to the house of a peasant and were successful in returning with plenty of food. Two days later [June 2] Marcos, Pedro, and Víctor returned to that house. When they got close they fell into an army ambush. Marcos and Víctor were killed, while Pedro managed to escape unharmed. The loss of the comrades was deeply felt, especially Marcos.

After that they did not return to the peasants' houses. As time passed, the corn, which was the only thing they had to eat, began to get scarce. Joaquín was very worried and nervous. Braulio, together with other comrades, went out scouting almost every day.

Everyone was very worried by the absence of Che.

The group stayed in that location until the middle of July.

When very little corn remained, they decided to go to the houses of peasants to get food, even if it meant firing gunshots. The situation was very difficult, and there was a great deal of hunger.

---

1. Pepe deserted on May 23. The following day he was captured by the army and murdered.

A group of several fighters went out, and along the way they found the bodies of Marcos and Víctor. Only their bones remained; they were recognized by their shoes. After burying them, the group continued and found abandoned houses and the army's tracks. In the first houses the soldiers had piled up the corn and set it on fire; they had cut up the calabash into pieces so it would rot.

The group had to sift through the corn and gather up what had not been burned. They got together a good amount and had to make two trips. The problem of hunger had been solved.

While Alejandro and Polo were doing guard duty on Observatory Hill, they clashed with the army coming up the slope. After a brief exchange of fire, they retreated to the camp and reported that the army was advancing. Joaquín ordered them to abandon the camp, but first they had to move the corn. One group did that while the rest prepared the ambush. After moving the corn a safe distance, everyone retreated. They walked a night and a day, until reaching Lagoon Camp. Before arriving there, right as they were coming down off a hill to enter the camp, Paco heard some voices, but they did not pay it much importance.

After a little while, Moisés Guevara, who was on sentry duty, saw the army coming down a hill and approaching the camp. He and Polo fired and succeeded in containing them until the other comrades reinforced them. The battle lasted several minutes while the rest of the group packed up the knapsacks, the corn, and the .30-caliber machine gun. Then they retreated one by one. That night they rested on a small hill, and the army did not advance.

The next day [July 9] they continued walking and came to the Yaqui, or Iquira, river. They walked in the water upriver, to avoid leaving tracks. The march was extremely arduous. All the comrades were exhausted because of the weight they were carrying. Serapio suffered the most since his foot was injured and it swelled up on him considerably.

The death of Serapio

While the group was resting Serapio went on ahead to gain time, followed shortly after by Pedro and Eusebio, who were helping him with his knapsack. When they were just about to reach him, Serapio signaled to them and shouted that they should not advance because the army was there with an ambush. He was shot and killed. In this way he saved the whole group from falling into an ambush.

The guerrillas had to turn back and prepare a defense in case the army advanced. Since it did not advance, they retreated downriver. At that moment planes flew over the area but did not attack.

The group headed into the woods and camped near the river for the night. They cooked an abundant supply of corn, enough for two days. In the morning they abandoned that location and climbed a steep hill. Joaquín ordered them to leave behind a large part of the corn and all the things that were a heavy burden and of no use in moving rapidly and trying to break the encirclement the army had woven around them. For several days they walked rapidly without any more encounters. They had succeeded in breaking out of the encirclement and came to a settlement where they made every attempt not to be seen. The group's aim was to reach the road to Sucre and obtain food supplies, and they did not want anyone to inform on their presence there. They were discovered, however, so they interrogated the residents about the army's position and the name of the place. The residents said the soldiers were in a nearby village called Ticucha, and that the settlement they were in was Taperillas.

In Taperillas and Monteagudo

They continued the march and came to a hillock. From there they sent a small group to the houses to buy provisions, while five comrades moved things and looked for a place to set up camp.

At about ten o'clock that night, the group returned with supplies and confirmed that the army was far away. The peasants had asked them to return if they wished to buy more food, that they would be happy to sell it to them.

Joaquín was willing to have the people go back to buy some more, but since every one was exhausted, they did not go. (A fortunate occurrence, since the army had already arrived at the houses that night.) The next day, as they were dividing up the loads and the food, the enemy, having followed their tracks, found the location of their camp and fired on them. Joaquín and his people reacted immediately and returned fire. Despite it being a surprise attack, there were no casualties, thanks to the dense forest.

As was customary, one group kept the army at bay, while the others transferred the packs far from the place. When they got back together, they discovered that Eusebio and Chingolo had deserted. The two of them had discarded their knapsacks and taken advantage of the critical moment to flee.

The group looked for a safe place and camped for several days. Then they continued on, with long days of walking, toward Monteagudo. On August 5 they camped on a high mountain (Iñao, as they found out later). The group went down to the village of Chuayacú, where they bought a considerable amount of food supplies. Tania stayed at the camp by herself. On their return, after a night and two days, they immediately prepared an ambush, thinking the army was following them. They waited two days, but the army did not appear and the ambush was lifted. Nevertheless, that same day, the sentry caught a peasant looking for tracks and took him prisoner. The man confessed that the army was nearby and that they had forced him to follow the tracks.

Several army companies were trying to surround the guerrilla group.

The next day, twenty minutes after they left, the army

started to bomb the camp. The peasant prisoner marched ahead and escaped during a moment of carelessness by Braulio.

After a few hours, the army caught up with the column and demanded their surrender. The only escape route was an exposed hillside, but Joaquín was lagging behind with almost half the group. Braulio said they could not wait for Joaquín, that it was necessary to find a favorable position, and he started climbing the hill, followed by the others. At that moment the army began to fire in their direction, but they all continued climbing until they reached the top. Pedro, who was repelling the attack and keeping the enemy at bay with the .30-caliber machine gun, was struck and killed by a bullet.

When they got to the other side, they waited until Joaquín caught up with them. Voices were heard over the hill; they had succeeded in passing by before the army could surround them.

That night they resumed the march to find a safe place to rest. After walking over the tallest hills, they turned back around (from those hills they observed the town of Monteagudo, which was very close) and returned to erase their tracks. They continued on again to the area around Taperillas and arrived at a peasant house to buy food.

Immediately afterward, without leaving any traces, they left the place and walked for many days until they reached the hill where they had left corn and various other things. They did not find anything; the army had gotten it. Then they headed toward the Iquira to get to Lagoon Camp. From there they went out to scout the area. There were army units throughout the territory, and they were building a road to Ñancahuazú.

Because of this they abandoned camp and crossed the Iquira river. Joaquín directed the group to head toward the Río Grande. They entered a region full of high mountains and dangerous cliffs and finally reached a densely wooded flatland. Braulio worked and guided the group each day until he was worn out, clearing paths all day long.

The next day they moved very rapidly through the area of the main camp. They walked hard, but without incidents, other than hearing some machine gun bursts and mortar fire. (They presumed that the camp had been occupied and the army was conducting target practice.) The group was in very poor shape. Joaquín could barely walk and looked much older. Tania had bad pains in her ovaries.

Toward the ford of betrayal

They continued downriver toward the Río Grande, walking three days with absolutely nothing to eat. They were all practically barefoot, their shoes fastened together with ropes or rags. They had almost no clothes; Joaquín was half naked. They did not stray from this march along the river except to rest, which they did with great caution, but always in a disorderly fashion. In this way, before arriving at the mouth of the river, they ran into a peasant who was bringing donkeys from Valle Grande. They stopped him and bought one to eat. Then they left for the Río Grande.

After a day of walking along the riverbank, they arrived at the house of Honorato Rojas, who was said to be a friend. Two men were sent to his house. They returned, reporting they could not enter because shots were heard, although they did not see anything. Alejandro spoke up and told Joaquín that they could try one more time and if two men accompanied him, he would go to the peasant's house. Joaquín agreed and the three headed out. A little while later Walter returned and reported they had met with the peasant, and that he offered to collaborate in whatever way he could, because he was against the army. The other two comrades had kept a watch on the house to see if anyone came out.

That night, after reporting to Joaquín everything they had discussed with the peasant, and having made camp for the night, Joaquín and the others returned to Honorato's house.

They returned very late at night and said that the peasant had promised to show them a safe place, where there was water and they could camp while they sent out a search party to look for Che. He had also agreed to go to a nearby town to buy supplies, and they left him 100 pesos for this. That night they ate fish bought by the peasant.

The next day [August 31] at the time indicated by him, 4:00 p.m., they left camp and headed to Honorato's house. He was waiting for them with two pots of corn and invited them to eat. Later he took them to the riverbank. They headed upriver and followed around a big curve. Then, after walking about three hundred meters, the peasant stopped and with hand signals pointed out to them a hill they could see in front of them. He said goodbye, shaking hands with those near him. He shook hands with Joaquín and then stared at Tania, who tried to keep him from seeing her face. Afterward Honorato left rapidly.

Braulio continued walking a little more and started to cross the river. The order was given to cross as quickly as possible in single file. When Braulio got to the shore, heavy firing broke out. The army had ambushed the group of guerrillas from both sides of the river simultaneously.

They all fell in the water, some already dead or badly wounded. Joaquín managed to return to the bank and ran along it trying to escape, but he was riddled with bullets. Paco let the current carry him a short distance and hid behind a rock jutting out of the water. Ernesto swam to his side. Bodies were carried off by the current. At that moment, the army started firing at Ernesto and Paco. The latter was hit by two bullets, one in his forearm, the other in his shoulder, and then another one passed through his armpit.

The soldiers advanced slowly and shouted at them from the riverbank to come out of the water with their hands in the air. Ernesto did so, but Paco was unable to lift his hands in the air, plus he had his knapsack on. Ernesto helped him out of the water.

Once they were on the bank, the soldiers separated them

and began kicking them around. Then one of the sergeants, who was from Trinidad, recognized Ernesto. Ernesto said something to him, and they immediately started shouting at him and kicking him in the face. Then they shot him and split open his arm. At that moment, an officer shouted from the opposite bank, ordering them to bring the prisoners there, to which they replied, "Very well, Captain."

The two were taken to the other side and placed next to the bodies that had been gathered up. They were asked to identify the bodies. Ernesto fell to the ground complaining about the pain. They took him to a corner and the medic bandaged his arm with a rag. It was getting dark. Ernesto kept complaining about the pain. The same ones who had kicked him before now approached along with Capt. Mario Vargas. They took him to the riverbank and murdered him, riddling him with a machine gun burst.

This whole scene was observed by Paco with great difficulty, since he was bleeding from his wounds and was in a lot of pain. He tells how he spent the night next to the bodies of his comrades, who were stacked up along with their belongings. At sunrise the soldiers started moving about, and Honorato Rojas arrived with fried pork for the troops.

They found the body of Polo, which was all swollen. Paco was in bad shape from his wounds and felt worse on seeing his comrades, whose bodies were lying almost shattered to pieces at his side.

Later peasants with mules came and carried off the bodies. The peasants went with their heads down and in silence.

Paco walked barefoot an entire day and night toward the village of Masicuri. They had bandaged his wounds with an old shirt. Once on the highway, at about 3:00 a.m., they transferred him to Valle Grande in one of two trucks they had picked up.[1]

---

1. From military sources it was learned later that a CIA agent of Cuban origin, Gabriel García, participated in the interrogation of Paco.

This brief narrative of the stoic — and at the same time heroic — deeds of the rear guard is an example of determination and decision. It is a story of individuals who were consistent in word and deed.

Other facts learned later show more clearly the treachery of Honorato Rojas and its consequences.

The day Alejandro went to Honorato's house, there was a man there introduced as a trusted friend. This man was a soldier disguised as a peasant in his work of investigating guerrilla activities.

This situation posed two alternatives for the peasant. He could either turn the soldier in to the guerrillas, or he could betray them to the army. He opted for the latter, that is, for the side that seemed stronger to him. But not just that. He personally selected the positions for the soldiers to make sure there were no survivors, because he knew how dearly this betrayal could cost him.[1]

A FATAL RENDEZVOUS MISSED

It should be recalled that our column, headed by Che, arrived at the Vado del Yeso ford [on the Masicuri river] on September 1. The ambush of Joaquín's group occurred on August 31 at the Puerto Mauricio ford [on the Río Grande]. The fact that we had animals with us and had to clear a path for them delayed us and prevented both columns from arriving simultaneously. Had this not been the case, the outcome would have been dif-

---

1. For his services rendered to the army in the massacre at Puerto Mauricio, Honorato Rojas received a medal from the government. In 1969 he was executed by an ELN commando unit.

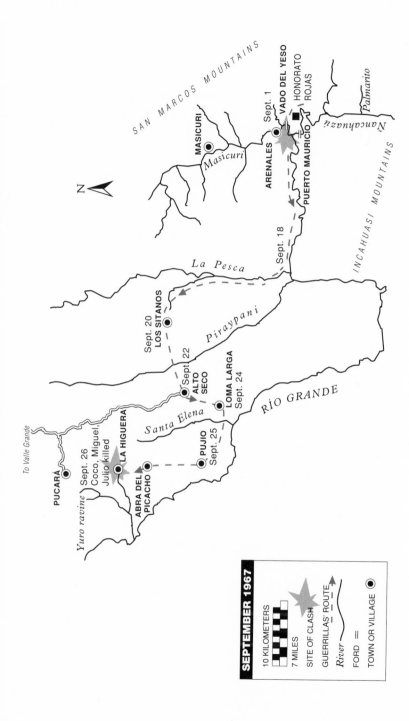

SAN MARCOS MOUNTAINS

MASICURI

Masicuri

Sept. 1
ARENALES

VADO DEL YESO

HONORATO
ROJAS

PUERTO MAURICIO

Ñancahuazú

Palmarito

INCAHUASI MOUNTAINS

N

Sept. 18

La Pesca

Sept. 20
LOS SITANOS

Piraypani

Sept. 22

ALTO
SECO

LOMA LARGA
Sept. 24

RÍO GRANDE

Santa Elena

PUJIO
Sept. 25

To Valle Grande

PUCARÁ

Yuro ravine Sept. 26
Coco, Miguel,
Julio killed

LA HIGUERA

ABRA DEL
PICACHO

SEPTEMBER 1967

10 KILOMETERS

7 MILES

SITE OF CLASH

GUERRILLAS' ROUTE

River

FORD ═

TOWN OR VILLAGE ●

ferent. One must remember Che's opinion about Honorato Rojas on February 10, the first time we came across him: "He is unable to help us, but also unable to foresee the dangers he can cause, and thus potentially dangerous."

Logically enough, no one could be absolutely sure about the ambush, since the army had taken every security measure so that nothing would be known about it. That's why we considered it to be false. When we heard the news on the Voice of America (the local press maintained absolute silence), we tried to check its accuracy, but none of the peasants in the vicinity had heard the battle or even seen any troop movements. We had not heard shots or found any evidence of the event that we assumed, given the magnitude of the news, would have to be known throughout the region. Everything indicated the information was false.

For our part, on September 4, we set up an ambush headed by Miguel on the road from Masicuri to Honorato's house. Volunteers were requested to go find supplies to purchase, and Coco, Chapaco, Arturo, Julio, and Aniceto were selected under the command of Inti. Urbano and Camba went on a scouting mission upriver.

We heard on the radio news of the death of the Peruvian doctor Negro at the Vado del Yeso, near where Joaquín fell.[1] He was identified by Ciro Roberto Bustos. Everything indicated that Bustos was collaborating with the army.

We waited all day for the comrades' return. They arrived in the early morning and brought some food. They had practically bumped right into the army.

An ambush was set up again. When Urbano went to tell Miguel to withdraw, he ran into an army patrol that had sneaked between the ambush and the camp. They fired a few shots in Urbano's direction, so we set up a defense and took positions.

---

1. The Peruvian combatant Restituto José Cabrera (*Negro*) had escaped from the August 31 ambush, but was captured and murdered on September 4.

After a few minutes, Che ordered me, together with Camba and Chapaco, to take charge of the sick men. Just then we heard a noise about three hundred meters from our positions. We thought it was the army trying to surround us and got ready to defend ourselves. Moro forgot all about his illness and took Camba's rifle, who gave it to him gladly. To our relief it was Miguel who, on realizing the situation, decided to circle around through the woods. We informed Che, who was at the head of the defenses, and he organized our retreat.

After crossing several fords (some of them very dangerous) we stopped for the night and killed one of the cows we had taken with us during the retreat. That day it was my turn to work in the kitchen, which I did with Che. As punishment, he had assigned himself to be kitchen helper for having gotten his rifle wet in the river. That was the penalty that everyone who was negligent in some matter was sanctioned with.

The next day we walked just a little due to the difficult trail. We set up camp to be able to go out scouting the following day.

Radio Cruz del Sur reported that Tania's body had been found on the banks of the Río Grande, and it referred to Paco's statements against Debray.

We organized a rotating ambush and sent Chapaco and Aniceto out scouting.

We heard about Barrientos's visit to Honorato Rojas's house. Barrientos also offered to guarantee the lives of the Bolivian guerrillas, on condition that they present themselves with their hands on their head. Nothing was offered to the Cubans, since he knew that none of them would surrender alive.

Antonio and I spent the day [September 9] at the head of eight men on ambush. Everything went uneventfully.

ALONG THE LA PESCA RIVER
TO MASICURI

We set out early to cross the river at a ford that Miguel had found the day before. The river's current was very strong and the mules swam across, except for the male, which flatly refused. Che lost his shoes while trying to get the mule across. A helicopter flew over us three times, and we saw a small plane in the distance. Che commented that it was possible the army had set up an ambush ahead, since it was feasible for a helicopter to be used for that.

Two scouting parties were organized: one downriver and the other upstream. The first one was successful, finding out that it was possible to cross when the water level went down. The other party could barely advance at all. An ambush headed by Antonio was set up in the morning, and one headed by me was organized in the afternoon. At night we slaughtered one of the oxen. Ñato, Darío, Julio, and Pablito ate a whole fillet. Che was annoyed with Ñato for not having asked authorization and with Chino for having permitted it. Chino asked to be replaced from this assignment, and Che named me head of provisions, in addition to continuing as head of services.

In the morning [September 12] the alarm was sounded personally by Che with the shout of "The army." Everyone mobilized and occupied our positions. It soon became clear that it was all a confusion by Antonio, who apparently fell asleep and thought he had seen several soldiers.

Chapaco was punished with three days as kitchen helper for refusing to go scouting along the edge of the river. Two scouting teams were sent out and returned the next day. The one that went along the river learned that it was possible to cross after going around the cliff. We believed we were about three hours from the Piraymini river (La Pesca).

Those scouting the creek reported that the animals could

not cross it due to very difficult fords. They reported that the creek began in a mountain range that could be seen in the distance in front of our position.

After waiting to hear from Miguel, who had gone out early, we set out in the afternoon on an arduous march to where a raft was being built to cross the creek. Ten comrades had already crossed, and the rest of us hoped to do so the next day.

We advanced several kilometers without reaching the La Pesca river. Che banned us from making fires to combat the cold. Some comrades were cooking meat, claiming they had saved it from the previous meal when in reality they had removed it from the collective reserve.

On the radio we heard about Loyola's arrest. They presented photos in which she appeared with the guerrillas.[1]

Che began an evaluation of the troop's state of mind.

Barrientos's proposition to pardon the lives of the Bolivians who surrendered had made some of them think. A series of small conflicts and arguments arose repeatedly. Chapaco refused to allow Aniceto to give him orders. That led to his being punished by Antonio with six days as kitchen helper. Che ratified the punishment. Some were saying that Moro was faking illness and should change his attitude, because it hindered the guerrillas' mobility (this claim was false). There were also problems over food.

Che summoned Inti and Coco. Afterward he asked me for a general map of Bolivia and raised that the reports about Joaquín appeared to be true, and that morale was falling. He reviewed all the incidents that demonstrated this. He explained that we needed to strike a blow in order to raise morale and enable us to obtain food supplies and other things, and then abandon the zone and hide out for a time. During that interval we would make contact with the city and incorporate forty or

1. Photos of Loyola Guzmán at the guerrilla camp during her stay in late January were found by the army in the guerrillas' caves after these were seized on August 4. This helped lead to her arrest on September 14, together with Norberta Guilar and Paca Bernal Leyton. She was jailed until 1970.

fifty men from La Paz who were ready to join the guerrillas. The plan consisted of going up the La Pesca river to Masicuri and from there to Valle Grande, skirting around it in search of a road that, according to the map, would take us to Puerto Breto and from there to Chapare or Alto Beni.

We soon started the march to the La Pesca river. By the time we started the descent, Miguel had gotten lost without leaving anyone to guide us. We stopped some peasants, and Benigno committed the mistake of letting them go look for some traps after promising to return. Che gave Benigno a real dressing-down, to the point that Benigno started to cry. These peasants had reported that Aladino Gutiérrez and others were fishing on the bank of the Río Grande. We had informed them previously that they would be leaving with us in the morning along the La Pesca river toward Los Sitanos, a place where Aladino had a farm and a grocery store.

Che authorized another peasant to go look for his animals. Later we learned that three months before the man had guided the army through the zone. We went looking for him with some urgency and brought him back.

In the afternoon a small plane made two suspicious passes overhead.

We divided ourselves into three groups for the march: the forward detachment, which had an hour's head start; one part of the center group; and the rear guard, with the rest of the comrades of the center group who were sick. Chino was in very poor shape and fell behind. We had to leave him waiting for the rear guard or for Che, who was the only one capable of making him advance, since no one was authorized to criticize him.

When we reached the river, we found the forward detachment resting and the peasants fishing. We continued and came to a chancaca store, where we found Miguel. We bought a pig, rice, and a large amount of chancaca, which allowed us to make a good maté, which we had been drinking unsweetened for several days.

In the afternoon we set out and came to a farm along the

way, where we had lunch and then continued on toward Los Sitanos.

One of the peasants, anxious to arrive rapidly at his house, fooled Eustaquio. As a result, Che and the rest of the people of the center group got lost. I went out looking for them, and they turned up across the way. When he got up to the hill-crest, Che realized that he had been fooled, since he did not find the farm or the fields where we had been cooking.

After several stumbles and falls, we arrived late at night at Aladino's house where we bought cigarettes, soft drinks, and other things. We took over the house of the mayor, Alejandro Vargas, and cut the phone line, even though it was not work-ing. At daybreak we headed toward Alto Seco. We pulled back a little and camped at the edge of the Piraypani.

In the morning [September 21] we came to the first houses on the way down. We arrived at the mayor's house, where we bought some animals and two quintals of corn to take for grinding to a hydraulic mill on the edge of the river near the road up to Alto Seco. Its owner was named Manuela Durán Peña.

Che ordered that he be woken at 10:00. But he was so tired and weak that we let him sleep until 11:00. (Tremendous out-burst by Che.) This brought me a scolding.

Along the way to the house where we were to pick up the flour, we got lost. We therefore did not leave until 2:00 a.m.

FROM ALTO SECO TO PUCARÁ

In the early morning hours [September 22] we arrived at the village of Asunción (Alto Seco). There we purchased a huge quantity of merchandise (food, clothing, candy, etc.). It was so much that we thought we could not carry it all; in bread alone we each had twenty-three rolls.

We set up two ambushes; one on the road coming from Valle Grande and the other on the road from Los Sitanos. News of our arrival in the village had been communicated to Valle Grande the day before by a peasant from Los Sitanos who arrived before us. The mayor, Vidal Osinagas Aguilar, had disappeared, apparently to inform on our presence there. For this reason we confiscated all the merchandise that had come from his grocery store. The plan of capturing a vehicle to take us to Valle Grande, supply ourselves with medicine, and continue on to Puerto Breto had failed, since the army had set up checkpoints along the roads.

In the evening a small meeting was held in which Inti spoke to the population. The attitude of the peasants was courteous enough, although somewhat reserved. In the early morning, we set off for a place known as Santa Elena.

We arrived at 10:00. It was a day of rest and guard duty until dawn. Then we headed toward Loma Larga. We arrived exhausted, and camped at the junction of the road to Pujio.

We left at 4:00 p.m. Che's idea was to reach the top of the heights and follow it to Pujio without being seen from the opposite slope, where we could see a fire that might be from the army. Very early in the morning we were on the heights, where we ran into a peasant. Upon arriving at Pujio several more peasants saw us and fled, as always. We stopped some from fleeing, and others, watching from afar, gained trust in us and returned. They invited us to have maté, coffee, and *chicha*.[1] We learned that a carabinero had been there a short time before to arrest a peasant.

There was a beautiful view from that spot. The Río Grande could be seen, and in the distance one could make out the place where three departments converged: Cochabamba, Santa Cruz, and Chuquisaca.

---

1. A homemade alcoholic beverage made from fermented corn.

There was discussion on the coming departure of Camba (who had raised his desire to abandon the struggle) and who we would try to utilize as a messenger. He would thus provide us a service while at the same time — by not cutting him off entirely from revolutionary circles — we would avoid throwing him into the arms of the enemy as a collaborator.

We continued the march to a hamlet where we made tea and bought a piece of pork. We found out that the mayor of La Higuera, Aníbal Quiroga, had been in these parts the day before. We continued and camped for the night at an exposed and open-air site. The peasants called out to us when we crossed by their houses, but to avoid bringing harm to any of them Che rejected staying in their homes.

At noon we arrived at Abra del Picacho. The peasants of the area were having a celebration and greeted us with glasses of chicha and gaiety. We received confirmation that the people from the little village of Pujio had arrived ahead of us, saying they had passed in front of our sentry post. Coffee and sandwiches were ordered.

We continued the march along the road to La Higuera. We arrived at about 12:30. The residents had abandoned their houses. There were only some women. One got frightened on hearing an explosion and began shouting that it was a gunshot. Julio tried to calm her down, saying it was a firecracker tossed in Picacho for the town celebration.

We captured a peasant who had come down the path from Pucará. Che questioned him and he affirmed that "all is quiet" — that is, there were no soldiers. Che said he did not trust the man, who he thought was lying. Che felt tempted to take the path along the river, which would make us alter all the plans and venture through much more inhospitable regions. He decided to run the risk and continue along the path to Pucará.

THE BATTLE OF SEPTEMBER 26

Miguel, Coco, and Julio are killed

At 1:00 p.m. Miguel set out at the head of the forward detachment. Che had given them instructions to advance with great caution. They were to maintain a distance of no less than ten meters between each member of the column, and the platoons were to leave at thirty-minute intervals. This would guarantee that when the center group began its march, the forward detachment would already have occupied the ridge.

At 3:30, when the entire guerrilla unit was on the march, heavy gunfire was heard. Soldiers could be seen running along the ridge, trying to reach the road that ascended to our left. Che gave orders to retreat back to the village and organize the defense, which meant that we had to cross a road and withdraw; but the army had a perfect aim at the place. We came under intense fire, which forced us to throw ourselves to the ground, except for Chino, whose instincts of self-preservation no longer functioned. We all managed to cross except for Inti and León, who threw themselves into a ravine that opened there and remained separated from the group. Benigno, Pablito, and Darío met up with us (Camba had disappeared) and informed us of what happened in the ambush:

Benigno had fallen behind because a pebble had gotten in his shoe and was bothering him when he walked. This saved his life, since he was at the point position of the forward detachment. When he fell behind, Miguel, Coco, and Julio passed in front and were already crowning the crest of the Batán ravine. At that instant the army, which was waiting in ambush, opened fire. Miguel was killed. Coco and Julio were wounded but could still move. Julio tried to reach a stone fence that was to his right, some fifteen to twenty meters away. The soldiers, noticing him, concentrated their fire and riddled him with bullets. Benigno tried to get Coco away and slung him over his shoulder, but a bullet finished him off. Another grazed Benigno's shoulder. The rest of the forward detachment — Pablito, Darío, and Aniceto — retreated behind a stone fence.

Che realized that we could not continue up the path, because everything indicated the enemy had arrived at the ridge before we had. He decided to abandon that road and remain with Pacho and Urbano in containing the army's advance. Meanwhile, I and the rest of the men prepared the defense on a hill located some six hundred meters away and that could be reached only by a narrow path, whose sides were steep cliffs.

We did this, until Che gave the order to lift the defense and continue the march. As we did so, we saw in the distance, by the ravine to our left, a man heading toward the river. We looked through our binoculars and saw that it was León. He looked at us and we signaled him to come back, but he kept going. At 5:00 p.m. we stopped to tend to Benigno, while Antonio set up an ambush a hundred meters away.

Inti arrived with his feet wrapped in a piece of blanket, because he had lost his shoes when he flung himself into the ravine. He tried to walk without shoes, but it was practically an odyssey, since the area contained round prickly pears, full of thorns ranging from three to five inches long, looking almost like giant hedgehogs.

Urbano went scouting to see if there was any sign of the army. He went far down and saw nothing.

Che decided to take a ravine that lay to our right and go back through it to La Higuera. We tried to throw the army off the track by sending some comrades with the animals to walk to the edge of the Río Grande and then, after having let the animals loose, return to the point of separation without leaving any traces. The walk was very rough, since the ravine was rocky. We camped high up in a canyon.

The outcome of the ambush was disastrous for us, since we lost three men of enormous value.

Miguel was our iron arm with the machete, and he was an exemplary combatant. He joined the revolutionary struggle in the Sierra Maestra, where he reached the rank of captain. At the time of his death he was undoubtedly, after Che, the man with the most experience among the guerrillas. He was the type of man whose temperament could be defined with the phrase "in bad times, a happy face."

Coco stood out as a Bolivian of the highest political and military quality. He had worked with us since the beginning.

Julio, for his part, showed promise of being a good combatant.

All three were communist militants from a very early age. They were eloquent examples of tenacity and firmness of ideas, because in offering their lives, they did so with complete confidence in the triumph of the revolutionary cause.

In addition to these losses, Camba and León had disappeared.[1] We thought they had turned themselves in. León's action surprised many of us, because he seemed to be convinced of the mission and had earned Che's trust.

After walking for part of the early morning, we reached the summit of a ridge. From there we could see a small house that we had been watching for a long time. Later on we saw a soldier and a peasant playing around as they left. Through them we discovered a path that in all likelihood went down to the river. At noon we heard a few shots, bursts of machine gun fire, and shouts of "There he is!" "Look at him there!" "Give yourself up!" We thought it must have been Camba.

It appeared as if a little above the houses the army had set up an observation post or an ambush, because we saw the movement of soldiers in the ravine above. They were detected by the reflection of the sun on their canteens or some other object.

1. Camba was taken prisoner the following day as he was trying to rejoin the guerrillas. León surrendered to the army the day after his desertion and turned informer.

In the afternoon, with great caution, we moved to a hollow filled with taller bushes, at the mouth of a ravine. We listened to news of the death of Coco, Julio, and Miguel and how they had moved the bodies to Valle Grande. The radio reported that the clash had been with the Galindo company.[1]

Nerve-racking moments
September 28

This was a day of extraordinary tension, because we could have been discovered at any moment. A total of 123 soldiers, divided into two groups — one of 46 and another of 77 — passed by. Just when the second group was right in front of our hiding place, a shot was heard. They dropped back and took positions, while an officer ordered them to go down into the ravine. They shouted, "There they are, look at them!" Che, looking absolutely calm, ordered us not to move and to wait until they opened fire.

I do not know exactly what happened. Apparently they communicated by radio what had occurred and then continued their march, but not without first glaring down at where we were.

Had they discovered us, it would have been a complicated situation, since we were in a kind of mousetrap with no chance of defending ourselves.

Che explained the need to look for another place and to remain hidden for a few days to make the enemy think we had retreated from the area. It was also necessary to look for another way down to get water. He designated Inti and Willy for this task. It started to rain.

The army, accompanied by peasants, patrolled the road continuously.

The search for a suitable place to hide was successful. Antonio, Arturo, Pacho, and I went down to get water.

1. The Tiger Company, under the command of Lt. Eduardo Galindo, was part of the Bolivian army's Eighth Division.

At night, we climbed up to the place chosen for our new campsite. Watching Chino was pitiful. He tripped and fell again and again. Then he couldn't find his glasses and would begin to shout: "Fernando, Fernando, I've lost my glasses," because without them he could see nothing at all. Che was the one who went back and helped Chino whenever he called out.

Once Che put Chino under my care. I told him to tie the frames of his glasses with a cord or a small piece of rope to keep them from falling. He didn't do it, for which I upbraided him. Che reprimanded me for doing so, saying that no one had the right to address harsh words to Chino. To keep that from happening, from then on Che himself was the one who looked after him. In truth, it was painful to say anything to Chino, since he was the one who made the most sacrifices of the group, carrying out with stoicism an almost superhuman effort. Due to his age and physical state, Chino represented the polar opposite of the conditions a guerrilla fighter should be in.

For the first time in four days we ate solid food. We suffered terrible diarrhea, and the water we drank was pure magnesium. Che authorized us to eat the reserve supply of sardines we had (three-fourths of a can per person). He ordered it to be rationed in the following manner: half a can that day and a quarter of a can the following day. As a result of confusion on my part, half a can was eaten in the morning and the remaining quarter in the afternoon. (Tremendous outburst by Che.)

The situation had improved, because our new encampment was on a plain, with some vegetation that made it possible to cook without the smoke being seen from the house. Chapaco, who said he was "a master of the fritter," was assigned to the task. We also roasted a piece of charqui.

Two lookouts were stationed: one on top of the hill and another on the high part of the small plateau. In the afternoon a group of soldiers went into a canyon that lay to the right of the house and we heard a few shots.

Ñato, Darío, and Eustaquio were assigned to go down and get water.

Che summoned Inti and me to tell us what he had heard on Radio Balmaceda of Chile. The army high command was reporting that guerrillas under Che Guevara were surrounded by 2,000 soldiers in a jungle canyon. Che expressed the view that since the local broadcasts had said nothing, it looked as though there had been a betrayal. Moreover, the army's precise concentration of forces and resources in the area indicated they were sure of our presence in the area. He asked us not to say anything about this, to avoid demoralization.

The next day [October 2] in the afternoon, Che gave the order to go down by the creek, cook something, and then continue on out of the ravine. He withdrew the ambush that was set up on the hill, made up of Pacho, Willy, and me. We were a little late. Che had already set out, leaving the rear guard to wait for us.

They strayed from the path without leaving anyone to point out which direction to take, so we remained separated in two groups. Ours went down through the creek and spent the day hidden in our previous campsite.

In the early morning hours [October 3], Inti and Ñato — who had come down in search of water — woke us up. They had orders from Che to collect the cans we had and fill them. It turned out that their group had gone astray because of a mistake by Ñato, and they had camped on high ground. Later we went up to see if we could find a spot on the hill where we could defend ourselves against the army.

In the afternoon we went down to the creek and prepared coffee, flour, and rice with charqui. In the early morning we left to cross the road that led to some houses and descended into a very deep ravine. In this way, we managed to get out of what we assumed to be the front line of fire.

We listened to the statements by León and Camba concerning Fernando's identity, the number of us, and how many were sick. To our surprise, Camba conducted himself more firmly than León. The latter said he had turned himself in because he trusted in the honorable word of President Barrientos to respect the lives of every guerrilla no matter what they had done.

We moved downward, stopping in the ravine to make breakfast out of a plate of food we had in reserve. We continued until we came to another ravine that joined up on the right with the one we were in. We took that one, heading upward, and we put three men on lookout for three-hour shifts. Pacho, Inti, Eustaquio, and I left with the mission to scout out two ravines that branched off two kilometers away. Neither one had water or a way to descend into them. In the afternoon we continued the march until 8:00 p.m., when it was impossible to advance due to darkness and lack of visibility.

We walked from three until six in the morning [October 5], when we hid in a small thicket. Two lookouts were placed, one watching over the cattle path by which we had come, and another by a hollow that lay to our right. Pacho and Benigno went out to scout for water and found a house. As they retreated, they heard dogs barking and saw six soldiers coming.

We listened to the news that Camba would be testifying in the trial of Debray.

This was quite a night for Che, because Chino fell more than twenty times and Che was the one helping him.

In the morning [October 6] Urbano and Ñato went out as scouts, bringing news that six kilometers away was a creek with water. We went there in groups of three. In plain daylight we cooked in a stone house, taking measures to avoid smoke. Three ambushes were set up: one downstream under Antonio, another upstream under Aniceto, and the last one in the ravine with Pacho in charge. We spent the night there. We heard over the radio that there were 1,800 soldiers looking for us in the area.

We moved up to where our ravine connected with another one that lay off to the right. At around 12:00 noon [October 7] we took into custody an old woman named Epifania, who herded sheep.[1] At first, she pretended to be deaf, then that she did not speak Spanish. We made her stay with us and in the afternoon she gave us concrete information about the army. She also told us how far the wide road went, which we presumed was the one that went to Pucará, where there might be troops. We made some fritters out of flour and yeast and let the old woman go. She was escorted to her house by Inti, Aniceto, and Pablito. She did not want them to come and cried, pleading with them. The portrait they witnessed was a desolate one. The old woman had two daughters; one was paralyzed and the other was a dwarf. They gave her 50 pesos.

We advanced at night through the ravine. The first obstacle was a very dangerous cliff. Everyone said it was impossible to cross. Giving yet another example of his iron will, Che crossed it, clawing the walls as if he were a cat. He made it all the way up and organized the rest of the troops to cross with a rope. Then he leaped to the other side, jumping over a gap about a meter and a half long that formed a well of icy water.

Che's demonstration greatly inspired us in our determination to overcome all obstacles. In spite of being ill, he managed to do what many healthy comrades considered impossible.

We made tea and at 1:30 a.m., we saw a light. Chapaco, Willy, and Antonio reported that it appeared to be a person because it moved. Che asked me if I saw it move. I told him no, that everything indicated it was the residue of a brush fire. We stopped at 2:30 a.m. and rested until 4:00. The road was a bramble patch.

---

1. It was later thought that the peasant woman Epifania had been the one who informed the army of the guerrillas' presence. It was actually another peasant, Pedro Peña, "who saw a group of seventeen men" that had set up a camp nearby. He told this to Aníbal Quiroga, mayor of La Higuera, who informed the army.

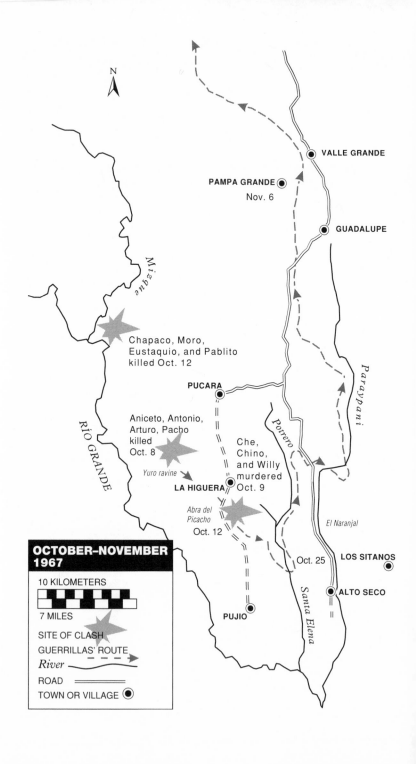

N

Chapaco, Moro,
Eustaquio, and Pablito
killed Oct. 12

*Miz*que

VALLE GRANDE

PAMPA GRANDE
Nov. 6

GUADALUPE

RÍO GRANDE

PUCARA

Aniceto, Antonio,
Arturo, Pacho
killed
Oct. 8

Potrero

Paraypani

Che,
Chino,
and Willy
murdered
Oct. 9

Yuro ravine

LA HIGUERA

*Abra del
Picacho*
Oct. 12

El Naranjal

Oct. 25

LOS SITANOS

Santa Elena

ALTO SECO

PUJIO

**OCTOBER–NOVEMBER
1967**

10 KILOMETERS

7 MILES

SITE OF CLASH

GUERRILLAS' ROUTE

River

ROAD

TOWN OR VILLAGE ⦿

THE YURO RAVINE

We resumed the march and at 5:30 in the morning of October 8 we reached the junction of the Yuro and San Antonio ravines.[1] Che ordered three scouting parties; one to the left flank, one to the right flank, and a third in the middle. The rest of us hid.

A short time later, Benigno and Pacho came back and reported they had seen soldiers moving atop the ridge. Che ordered the scouts called back and lifted an ambush that he had set up under Antonio's command. We retreated lower into the ravine. Che decided to abandon the central ravine and hide ourselves in another one, which was to our left, with the aim of spending the day unnoticed. He sent Pacho and Benigno on reconnaissance. They reported that the La Tusca ravine ended in cliffs and had practically no way out. Che organized the defense as follows: The rear guard consisted of Antonio, Chapaco, Arturo, and Willy at the entrance of the ravine. Benigno, Inti, and Darío were on the left flank, with the mission of protecting the entrance (if it were necessary for us to retreat, this is where we would do it). On the right flank, he positioned Pacho, practically as a lookout. On the highest position were Urbano and I.

The instructions were the following: If the army tried to enter the ravine, we would retreat through the left flank. If it tried to penetrate along both flanks, we would retreat down into the ravine through the positions defended by Antonio. If it attacked through the entrance, we would go through the left flank where Inti, Benigno, and Darío were positioned. If the attack began at the top, we would retreat down into the ravine, until we could leave the Yuro ravine. The ridge along the left was set as the meeting point.

1. The San Antonio ravine runs about 300 meters long and is located between the La Tusca and Jagüey ravines. The Yuro ravine is also called "Churo" by some local inhabitants.

This decision was based on the application of the law of possibilities, since we thought we knew the position and location of the enemy, and there was a possibility that the army would not discover us. In the event we were discovered, we would have the possibility of retreating until we could find a more advantageous position. But if they did not discover us, we would have the possibility of sneaking through and breaking the encirclement during the first hours of nightfall, which would be in our favor since we would have more time to get as far away as possible from the enemy while it was still dark.

At approximately 1:30 p.m., heavy firing began just as Che sent Ñato and Aniceto to relieve us. They were discovered moving in the ravine, and the shooting became generalized along all the flanks, except for the left one. Faced with this unforeseen situation, in which the army overlooked the ravine and made it very difficult to move, we decided to ask Che for instructions and sent Aniceto. The latter reached the place where the command post was situated, but did not find Che there; he had already retreated. Aniceto returned and informed Ñato of what had happened, but when he tried to get to our position, he was shot in the eye.

Ñato was making signals, trying to explain the situation, but Urbano and I did not understand them. We did not want to retreat unless Che gave the order. The shooting became more distant, and was becoming heavier in the upper part of the Yuro ravine. (Later we understood what had happened — Che was retreating from the ravine; he was spotted and was being pursued.) At 4:00 p.m. Ñato made signals to us that indicated: "The commander says to retreat." I left first and they showered me with bullets. I thought Urbano would be unable to leave and he thought I had been wounded. The jacket I was wearing received bullet holes in front and in back, but I was able to make it over to Ñato's position, where Aniceto's lifeless body lay.

The army concentrated its fire on Urbano's shoulder, which they could see, without hitting their objective. They threw a grenade. In exploding, it raised a cloud of dust that gave Urbano the chance to get out.

In search of Che

We met up and continued on toward the command post. When we arrived, we confirmed that they had retreated without haste; they had taken a radio from Inti's pack, and from mine they had removed a wallet containing 20,000 dollars, as well as the documents and diaries that I carried. Everything indicated that Che had retreated down into the ravine, because we heard a series of shots coming from that direction, and later, sporadic firing. That was the moment we lost contact with Che for good.

Urbano, Ñato, and I were trying to climb up to the left ridge when Benigno saw us, made signals, and shouted to us at the top of his lungs not to advance or the army would kill us, because it overlooked our position from the front slope. We climbed down and took positions.

From there, we listened to the voices of the soldiers. One of them shouted: "There are three of them in the ravine." "Let's get them out with bazookas and flame throwers."

At 7:00 p.m. Inti, Darío, and Benigno, taking advantage of the moment when the enemy was firing shots, climbed down all at once. In this way they prevented the soldiers from learning the spot from which they had been fired upon, causing them a number of casualties.

We asked each other about Che. No one had seen him leave. Faced with this dilemma, we lightened up our knapsacks and started to climb up the hill to reach the regroupment point Che had designated. At 9:00 p.m. we arrived and confirmed that a group of our comrades had been there, because we found traces of food (apparently to lighten their knapsacks). Then we remembered that Che had told us of his intention of breaking the encirclement during the night and heading to the Piraypani river in order to reach Valle Grande, looking for the road to Puerto Breto.

We advanced upward, trying to reach the junction with the road going from Pucará to La Higuera. We wound up in a ravine filled with thick vegetation and water, and climbed up to a completely open ridge. Crossing over a hedge atop the summit, we were able to confirm that we were on the road to Pucará. We crossed it with great caution, without leaving footprints, and stopped to rest. Here, I asked a question that was on everyone's mind: Which would be the best road to take? I asked each comrade to give his opinion. Even though the group was very small and I had been elected leader, decisions needed to be made collectively as much as possible.

Following Benigno's proposal, we marched to the right to make the crossing as far from the army as possible. The path was hellish, completely open. There were only small, thorny bushes. The earth was sandy. We were advancing three steps only to take ten steps back.

When day came, we hid ourselves better and stationed lookouts. We were in front of the little schoolhouse in La Higuera. At 7:00 a.m. on October 9, a helicopter began to hover above, protected by an airplane. At that time, we thought it might be due to the visit of some high military leaders, including Ovando and Barrientos.

We listened to news on the radio about the army's capture of a guerrilla fighter who might be Che. We thought it was not possible. At noon, they denied the story and said it was his lieutenant. The description they gave made us think it could be Pacho, because of his physical resemblance to Che.

We heard heavy firing on the other side of the slope.

At night, we decided to go down and cross the valley that was occupied by the army, since we had detected the presence of troops in three places.

During the night, using great caution, we climbed down and saw how the soldiers were singing and dancing and holding a happy celebration. At 9:00 p.m., they were called to formation, which surprised us somewhat. The dogs began to bark. We descended until we reached a creek that had some vegetation and drank a little water with sugar (we had not eaten anything since October 6, when we ate the fritters). We rested and resumed the march at midnight, eventually stumbling into an impassable ravine. We tried to cross it in various places, and in all of them it turned out to be impossible. Then we understood why the army was so confident, because they had made a cordon along the head of the ravine, which was the only place one could get through.

Tying the ropes of the hammocks to the exposed portion of a root, Urbano lowered himself down a cliff. We were able to get down into the ravine, even though the descent was not easy. We walked until approximately 5:30 a.m. and decided to hide in a small ravine to the left of the camp. Scouting was conducted by Urbano and Darío.

To the right, some two hundred meters away, was a road on which some peasants were descending, accompanied by soldiers.

In the afternoon of October 10, we heard the news of Che's death. There was no room for doubt; they gave his physical description and the way he was dressed. They mentioned the sweater that belonged to Tuma, which he carried as a keepsake; the two watches: his own and Tuma's (he was keeping this to give to the son Tuma had never seen); the sandals Ñato had made for him; two pairs of socks (Che always wore two pairs because he had very fine skin and these protected him).

There was a deep silence, we felt indescribable and profound pain. For the first time in my life, tears flowed without needing to have another person cry beside me. I understood more than ever that Che had been a father for me.

We held a meeting in which I communicated the news to the rest of the comrades. I asked Darío and Ñato to decide what course of action they intended to follow, and I asked Inti, as political leader, to give a presentation. I proposed to carry forward the struggle until death and to continue on under the slogan put forward by Che of "Victory or death."

The following oath was taken: "Che, your ideas have not died. We who fought at your side pledge to continue the struggle until death or the final victory. Your banners, which are ours, will never be lowered. Victory or death."

A second oath was taken, according to which none of us would abandon the group, much less the struggle. We would continue on together and no one would be taken prisoner.

LT. GARY PRADO'S VERSION

Among the versions known of Che's death that have been made known, we consider one to be fairly accurate, based on personal knowledge of Che and the conditions of the terrain. This version came to us by way of the Italian filmmaker Rosi, who received it from then-lieutenant of the Bolivian army Gary Prado, who participated in the actions at the Yuro ravine.

Everything seems to indicate that Che, knowing that the army was combing the area and that combat would begin, carried out the first phase of his instructions, which was to retreat along the bottom of the ravine. Sensing that the army was right on top of him, and knowing that with him were a group of sick men, he selected those in the best condition to fight. Putting them in front of the sick ones, he created a line of defense to contain the army. In this way, the sick men were able to move a good distance away from the point where the enemy would descend and cut off their retreat. Logically, during the course of the battle, the army maneuvered and succeeded in completing the encirclement.

Continuing to march, they clashed head-on with the army

inside the ravine. During the opening shots, Che — the one acting as leader — was wounded in one leg. The rest of his comrades took positions and established a tight defense. One of them, Willy Cuba,[1] helped Che go down along the right flank. The rest followed, defending their positions until they were gravely wounded or killed. Those who were not dead were finished off by the army later on.

According to this version, Che escaped from the army, and they later came across him by accident while installing a mortar. At the moment they ran into him, he was tending his wound. They fell upon him by surprise and prevented him from defending himself, even though his ability to defend himself was nil since his gun had been rendered useless and he had lost the magazine of his pistol. He was taken on foot to the little schoolhouse of La Higuera.[2]

AT THE MIZQUE RIVER

Moro, Eustaquio, Pablo, and Chapaco are killed

On October 13 we heard the news that the army had wiped out one of the groups of survivors. The group of sick comrades consisted of Moro, Eustaquio, Pablo, and Chapaco. After two days of continuous walking, thirsty and without food, they

---

1. Simón Cuba (*Willy*).
2. Guevara, together with Willy and Chino, was taken to the La Higuera school-house on October 8. Word of Guevara's capture was quickly passed on to Barrientos and the high command in La Paz. After consultation with Washington, the three captured guerrillas were murdered the following day. One of those on the scene during the hours Guevara was held and then murdered was CIA agent Félix Rodríguez.

made a desperate attempt to get water where the Mizque river flows into the Río Grande. The spot they chose was being watched by the army, and as they approached, the soldiers opened fire on them. They fought back, advancing on the enemy position. As a result, they were riddled with bullets.

AT ABRA DEL PICACHO

Our group, with little desire to keep walking, crossed three very difficult ravines after nightfall. In one of them we made a little coffee and cooked some flour. We continued on and made camp in a ravine located inside the valley, and therefore still within the army encirclement.

We cooked some more flour and, to lighten our load, hid Moro's surgical instruments and some of my photographic equipment under some rocks.

Leaving the ravine we scaled a very jagged cliff. Ñato slipped, but the timely help of Urbano prevented him from falling. At 11:00 p.m. we crossed the last hill in a horseshoe-shaped chain.

We didn't know where we were, only that we could see the Río Grande to our right. We walked an hour and found an uninhabited house. We went inside but found only a piece of chancaca to eat.

We went nearby to sleep. Seeing a calf, we decided to wait for someone to come get milk from its mother. At about 6:00 a.m. a young boy of about fifteen arrived and we took him prisoner. In our interrogation he stammered a lot, saying that "the army had not been in the area for a week." He told us we were in Abra del Picacho, in other words, we had gone in a complete circle around the horseshoe formed by the hills of

La Higuera, and had come out in the same place we had entered. The boy asked to join the guerrillas, which at that moment seemed inexplicable to us.

A peasant came by. When he realized who we were, he fled. We gave chase but failed to catch him.

We left in a hurry, taking the youth with us, and came to another house where we offered to pay a peasant to guide us. He agreed.

The peasant who fled from us had gone to Abra del Picacho to inform an army company camped there of our presence. This caused us to move quickly in order to beat them to the path leading to Pujio over the ridge. When we got there we had a choice of two routes: the one we had been taking, that is, toward Pujio to later head down to Santa Elena; or by way of the El Potrero river. We chose the second.

As we rested, I noticed that the peasant looked scared (the "hunted look," as Che would say). I asked him what was wrong, and he began to shout, "Soldiers, soldiers!" It was true; the army was moving along the ridge trying to block our retreat. We dashed down the ravine at full speed, while the peasant and the boy chose that moment to flee. We decided to leave the ravine. Once outside of it, Urbano, acting as point man, ran head on into the army as he climbed a hill. Fortunately, when he ran into them they were sitting and resting, with their rifles a yard or two away. "There they are!" they yelled. We opened fire and seemed to scare them, as they were unable to hit us. A real hail of bullets was showered on us for the whole length of the ridge and the other side. Running hard, we went back to the ravine and began climbing. We ran into big obstacles and were forced to abandon our knapsacks to be able to continue. Benigno, our rear guard, had passed to the point position. We scaled an almost vertical cliff and erased our tracks. There we heard the voices of the soldiers fighting over our belongings found in the knapsacks. Later they began tracking us.

We managed to climb up to the ridge and tried to hide in a

wooded area. I ended up barefoot since my boots would not take any more and fell apart.

Leaving there, we reached a thicket. Urbano scouted the area in front of us and Ñato to one side. Urbano discovered some peasants with dogs tracking the hillcrests. We deliberated on our situation, and decided to wait for nightfall to break the army's encirclement around the thicket. There were about three hundred soldiers.

At about 5:00 p.m. the enemy opened fire on the thicket with mortars, grenades, and rifle fire.

We moved over to a small hill with a flat summit. This was the highest spot, a type of rise.

At 6:30 they began to comb the small woods. Several frightened soldiers yelled: "Let's get out of here; there's no one here. The guerrillas can't be so dumb as to hide in this little thicket."

Our orders were to hold our fire if we weren't seen.

A man accompanying the army spotted Benigno, who shot him. The man fell, apparently dead. The soldiers retreated in a hurry. Later the encirclement was tightened around our little hill. Ñato sighted a soldier and shot him in the forehead.

Soon after, another soldier was spotted. Urbano fired and the soldier fell wounded. The man cried desperately for help, and when one of his comrades came he too was shot. The dead body of the second man rolled down toward us. We took his shoes and gave them to Urbano who, as the one assigned to march in the lead, had to flatten down thorny bushes. Since I was barefoot, I got Urbano's shoes. As night fell the army pulled back a little, expanding the encirclement.

Unfortunately for us, a beautiful moon lit up the area as if it were daytime. We decided to wait for cloud cover in order to leave. In the meantime, the six of us slept huddled together to conserve body heat, as it was intensely cold. We awoke at 1:00 a.m.; it was still clear. At last, at 3:30, the moon disappeared. We ate the last of the food (a little chancaca). Inti proposed to me that we bury the money and watches so the enemy would not get them. I did not agree to this, explaining to him that these were the only resources we had to get the peasants to help us reach Puerto Breto, Beni, or Cochabamba to make contact with Rodolfo. Then we could meet up with the fifty men in La Paz who were prepared to join us, and return to the mountains. Those were our plans, although we did not know how difficult it would be to carry them out.

Amid the cold and darkness of the night, we crept up trying to cross the army's line along the ridge. We spotted a soldier on guard who was smoking. We sneaked up, planning to kill him. He saw us, but instead of firing, stammered, "You bastards, who goes there?" His yell alerted the troops and produced confusion. The army was aligned on both flanks with a corridor in the middle, apparently with the idea that we would enter and face intense fire from both sides. The sentry opened fire and fierce but wild shooting began. We threw ourselves to the ground rolling, changing direction, mixing with the soldiers. At one point Inti shot two soldiers with his rifle right in their stomachs. I, on the other side, amid the confusion, sat on a rock trying to orient myself, for I didn't know who was who. For his part, Benigno, also disoriented, approached someone on the ground and asked him, "Are you wounded?" thinking it was one of us. Seeing the man had short hair and no beard, he realized it was a soldier. Amid a torrent of bullets in which the soldiers were firing at each other, we managed to regroup and escape the encirclement.

Later we reached a shack and erased our tracks to throw off the search that would surely begin in the morning. We entered a wooded area with a deep ravine that descended to the place through which we had come. Keeping on, we arrived at a smaller woods, where we rested. We could hear peasants and soldiers tracking the area. Climbing up trees, we saw them in the distance, bringing dogs.

Continuing the march, we waded into a creek to throw the dogs off the scent. We came to a house with a woman in it. We told her we were soldiers and bought a pig, flour, and a cooking pan. We knew she wasn't fooled, for it would be odd indeed for soldiers to have long hair and beards, and no cooking utensils.

AT THE SANTA ELENA RIVER

Before dawn we reached the banks of the Santa Elena river, somewhat below El Naranjal where we had crossed earlier. We hid in a real woods. The plant growth had changed considerably; now it was quite lush.

At night we went down to the river to cook; we roasted the pig and made a fricassee.

Continuing on, we crossed an area similar to a *marabú*[1] patch. Reaching the ridge above, we found a house; we tried to go around it but couldn't. We went toward the right until we realized we had lost the path. We went back and at 4:00 p.m. we heard dogs barking. Deciding to hide, we conducted a thorough search to determine the best place to go back down. After finding it, now late in the day, we came to another house where we bought a pig and fried it with water. There we learned that a company based in Alto Seco had participated in the clash at the El Potrero river. We offered the peasant 1,000 pesos to get us to Piraypani. He agreed, but led us only as far as the hillcrest, and only because we forced him. We bought a pair of scissors from him.

We kept going and by early morning arrived at the river. We went into a creekbed and made camp. Spending an entire day there, we took the opportunity to cut our hair and shave.

1. A dense, thorny plant that grows wild in Cuba and other tropical climates.

The following day we reached a house where a woman lived with her two children; a very pretty girl and a boy named Fidel. That tickled us and Benigno kept saying, "I'll be damned; look at Fidel; look at Fidel." We left before dawn and began to climb the hill on October 25. From there we planned to get to the La Pesca river after passing through the ravine where we had camped with Che during our trip there. The chancaca producers periodically left to work their fields, and we had considered spending a month hidden in their homes.

At sunset we left, intending to reach Los Sitanos while it was still dark. When we got to the summit we heard whistles, causing us to go back and hide. Two soldiers were speaking as they neared us, "It must have been cattle." They turned back right before reaching our ambush position. After waiting a little, we moved from there. It was necessary to put a cover over Darío's mouth; he had an attack of nerves and wanted to cough. We advanced a little and entered the woods.

Very early the following day the army came searching for us, using peasants as trackers. We kept quiet in a little ditch near a pool of water. At eight o'clock a patrol arrived with a peasant. They were less than five meters from us on the edge of the ditch, in other words, right on top of us. The peasant said, "They haven't been here," and they left. We moved in the afternoon. Our diet was balanced in the following manner: chancaca, fried pork, and coffee.

We spent an entire day there resting, and at night we went down to the water to make hot tea.

Analysis of the situation

We held a discussion to analyze the situation. Looking back at where we had been several days before, we noted that the enemy stationed there was trying to force us into areas we were unfamiliar with. This posed great disadvantages for us, but also one advantage. In areas we had not operated in, the army had not organized the peasantry or appointed mayors. The peasants therefore did not feel pressured to inform on us. In addition, in these areas the army had not offered a reward of 5,000 pesos for the capture of each one of us, dead or alive.[1] (This sum represented more than five years of work for a peasant.) This meant that in areas we had not operated in, the peasants were apathetic and indifferent, but they would be interested in earning money and therefore would sell us food. In fact, it was not a good idea to keep marching toward Los Sitanos, for troops would surely be stationed all along the hillcrest where we had been on October 25. They would also be watching carefully our previous campsites.

For all these reasons, it would be better to advance toward Valle Grande by the route we were on, following the Piray-pani to Guadalupe. By this maneuver we would surprise the army and reach the highway. If possible we would buy new clothes in Guadalupe.

TOWARD VALLE GRANDE

During the early morning hours we walked downstream, later crossing the path we had climbed the night before, as planned. At three o'clock we descended a cliff and made camp.

We spent the evening catching and slaughtering a cow, under Urbano's direction.

The next morning we moved to a creekbed about three kilometers away. We chose a dry ravine to avoid being discovered by some peasant looking for water.

---

1. See reproduction of poster in third photo section.

Due to fatigue, the following day we again moved to another nearby stream, where we slept.

In the early morning we hiked some seven hundred meters upstream to distance ourselves from where we had killed the cow. Along the way we came upon a peasant and his dog grazing some cattle. We hid, but the dog, having caught our scent, came right up to us and took a piece of roast meat from Darío, who was daydreaming. It then barked several times. The peasant called the dog; it left but returned a little later, this time taking a bone in its mouth.

This incident surely aroused the interest of the dog's owner, who must have figured out that someone was there.

At night we moved as far away as the darkness permitted and threw ourselves down to sleep.

At the first light of day, we headed toward a place that was very difficult to climb. Due to Urbano's skill, we managed to scale it. There we found various paths that we presumed led to homes or nearby farms. Although it was still daytime, we decided to cross the main path and headed on our way. We entered a thick forest and walked until nightfall. After passing through many thorny areas, we found a trail that led to a nearly dry creek. Since we could barely see, we made a fire to warm up and drank water with chancaca.

Very early we followed the creek looking for better cover. In the afternoon we climbed to the top of the bank, which was well covered but near a little trail. We crossed it at a spot where the fields had been burned off before the rain. The night was very dark and we made camp in a little gully.

In the early morning we walked some two kilometers to a hill, with a house in front. We observed it a while, trying to determine the prospects of obtaining food.

We went up to the house claiming to be soldiers. The owner and his children were alone and had nothing to eat. At first we considered taking them prisoner and bringing them with us, but we later felt sorry for the children and didn't.

We advanced some seven kilometers and hid during the

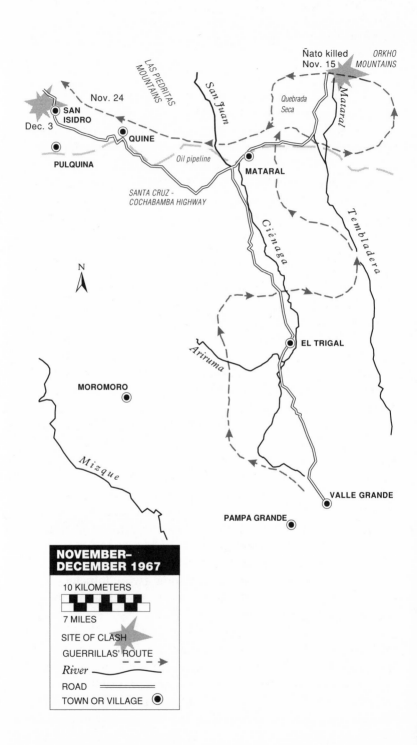

Ñato killed
Nov. 15

ORKHO MOUNTAINS

LAS PIEDRITAS MOUNTAINS

San Juan

Quebrada Seca

Mataral

Nov. 24

SAN ISIDRO

Dec. 3

QUINE

PULQUINA

Oil pipeline

MATARAL

SANTA CRUZ - COCHABAMBA HIGHWAY

Ciénaga

Tembladera

N

Ariruma

MOROMORO

EL TRIGAL

Mizque

VALLE GRANDE

PAMPA GRANDE

NOVEMBER–DECEMBER 1967

10 KILOMETERS

7 MILES

SITE OF CLASH

GUERRILLAS' ROUTE

River

ROAD

TOWN OR VILLAGE

morning. At night we walked to another house where we were treated very well. The peasant we visited the day before, we were told, had denounced us and later followed our tracks to the earlier river crossing, where he lost them. (This was due to our walking in the river.) He also told us of the presence of soldiers garrisoned in a corn mill. We cooked and left.

In the morning we entered a ravine and hid facing some fields. At noon a boy came to graze sheep. Later, owing to darkness we chose to wait for daylight to continue.

Avoiding houses, we resumed the march. A torrential rain started to fall, so strong that Urbano got lost without knowing it. We found a rock cave where we sheltered ourselves from the rain for more than thirty hours. We departed at night, climbing a steep hill from which we observed a hut up on the ridge. When we got there we found no one and came across only a little corn. Still at night, we reached a creek, but could see nothing. Groping our way, we came across a big jutting rock that afforded us protection from the persistent rain.

We left early. Since we had not eaten in two days, we looked for signs of cattle along the way. That day we found and slaughtered a pig.

The next day we climbed to some high clearings. From the top of a hollow we saw some houses. We then came to a ravine, where we determined which house to approach.

At night we went down to the settlement. After walking around a bit, we tried to enter the house we had chosen, but an old woman who lived there yelled out. At that moment her son, Honorato, arrived and sold us some things. He seemed very interested in money, and we offered him 1,000 pesos to take us to Valle Grande. He agreed.

We left at 11:00 p.m. on November 5. We walked all night until eight in the morning. My foot was getting more and more sore and swollen.

We were three kilometers from a road leading to a settlement called Raya. We cooked a delicious locro and continued on with the idea of reaching Pampa Grande, on the outskirts of Valle Grande. Our guide informed us that the road entering the city was under surveillance, and we proposed that he take us around Valle Grande to Mataral, avoiding the settlement. We did not make it. We were all exhausted and decided to make camp at 1:00 a.m. on a small hill near a house.

In the afternoon we climbed a ridge that, according to the peasant, would save us several kilometers. He did not know the route well, however, and we got lost. We approached a nearby house, and its occupant gave us directions. Finally, in the early morning, we saw the lights of the city of Valle Grande, which cheered everyone a great deal.

We paid the peasant. We walked all day and reached a hill, where we heard the music of the provincial band of Valle Grande. The view was beautiful. The city was completely lit up, contrasting with the dark reflection of the hills in the background.

Ñato expressed his desire to visit the cemetery and leave flowers for our fallen comrades. We explained that while this would be a lovely gesture, it was also a crazy idea that could bring terrible consequences. Convinced, he abandoned the idea.

En route to Mataral

We continued toward the highway and crossed it. We had managed to skirt around Valle Grande. Walking some more, we stopped in a ravine to map out our direction and future plans. We would follow the highway very carefully, avoiding the settlements, and thus moving faster. In Mataral we would send a messenger to the city. All this was calculated in accordance with a map we were carrying.

Resuming the march, all the guidelines were followed except those involving security measures when passing by houses. We were following a path when some dogs began to bark. Later we saw a red light approaching. We left the path and saw a peasant walking along smoking.

We walked all morning and went down into a ravine. We had gone quite a way in and were far from the highway. We looked for a place to camp, since we had heard sounds. Our scouting revealed two houses.

In the afternoon a peasant came to our encampment. Urbano, on watch, detained him, and we offered him 2,000 pesos to take us to the highway.

He agreed, but first asked to go to his house to tell his wife he would be gone and to bring us clothes, charqui, and cheese that his brother-in-law sold. We told him that one of us would have to accompany him to ensure his return. The peasant, it seemed, evaluated each one of us and asked that Darío accompany him. We sent Urbano instead. After arriving at his home, the peasant did not want to leave and had to be dragged.

We reached a place called Rancho Grande, which is on the way to El Naranjal. Benigno, Ñato, and Darío went to the store claiming to be new residents who had bought a farm in El Naranjal. The purchase was explained as a *tapeque* (food prepared for a trip).

We spent the night and the following morning off the road, resting. In front of us was a heavily traveled path that led to two houses; it seemed there was a wedding. At noon it rained hard, and we set out again at night. It was exhausting. We camped in a field of marabú.

The following day we again went along the highway. This detour added about twenty kilometers to the trip but avoided a little town on the highway that had an army checkpoint. At five in the morning we reached the Santa Cruz-to-Cochabamba highway.

We went into the riverbed trying to hide and found a hut, where we took some jocos.

In the afternoon we freed the peasant and paid him 3,000 pesos for his services. We advised him not to return along the highway, for it would risk his falling into the hands of the army.

Escape plan

At night we went down to the river and cooked in a safe place.

There we discussed our plan of escape, how to make contacts, etc. We agreed that Inti and Benigno would head for a city. Prior to that, Urbano and Ñato would go to the town of Mataral to buy clothes and investigate government security measures. Depending on the results, we would decide whether to go to Santa Cruz or to Cochabamba. Under all circumstances we were to avoid party channels; for greater security, we were to establish ties with the ELN.

The next day Urbano and Ñato left for Mataral. The rest of us stayed hidden. Arriving in town they went to a grocery store to make the purchases, and the woman who served them (as if trying to collaborate) said: "The guerrillas are around. A peasant was arrested and said he had guided them near here." They immediately returned to apprise us of the situation. Moreover, three trucks of soldiers had arrived to reinforce the garrison.

We retreated hurriedly. In the afternoon, as we walked, we heard a metallic sound (apparently a soldier drinking from his canteen) and stopped to look. About six hundred meters away we saw the army headed in our direction. We rushed down into a ravine and began climbing a little hill. Halfway up we hid and took defensive positions. Night was falling over the top of the ravine and we could see the shadows of the advancing soldiers.

At night, we continued the march, stopping only to cook by a pond.

When we set out once more, we saw fresh tracks of soldiers. We took precautions and advanced with great care, for we expected an ambush. But apparently they just passed right by. Since the pond could not be seen from the road and they were unfamiliar with the area, they continued on their way. We walked the entire night, and dawn found us crossing the highway. We walked about a kilometer upriver where vegetation was scarce, virtually nonexistent. Due to our exhaustion, however, we threw ourselves down to rest.

COMBAT IN MATARAL

The death of Ñato

Between 9:00 and 10:00 a.m., Ñato, who was on guard, woke us and signaled us to listen (touching his ear). It was the army approaching. Darío coughed from nerves; the soldiers heard him and said: "Who's there? Answer, you bastards!" They opened fire and we did too. We immediately retreated, abandoning our provisions in order to jump over a hedge of thorns. We began the climb, but when we reached the top we realized that Ñato had stayed behind to retrieve a bag of food and had been hit in the spine by a bullet. We went back and set up a line of defense around him to try to take him with us. It was impossible; he was unable to move. His spinal cord had been severed and he was in terrible pain. There was no hope. The wound was fatal, and he could not be moved.

It was a very difficult moment. On the one hand, Ñato was demanding we end his life, asking that we not allow him to fall prisoner. On the other hand, this was the life of our comrade, with whom we had shared dangers and difficulties, with whom we were united by great love and respect, a comrade long faithful to the cause. Since he was Bolivian, I first consulted with Inti and Darío. The painful decision was to comply with our agreed-upon commitment, as Ñato requested. As Che would say, he had reached the highest level of the human species, that of revolutionary.

We continued and went through a narrow pass, where the enemy shot at us from a distance. We managed to get through and climbed down to go around them. We headed off along the highway, toward Cochabamba. En route, we found ourselves face to face with the soldiers. They shot at us, but both sides had the same response: to run away from each other. By the time they had recovered, we had already climbed and circled the hill above them (our speed was impressive). We went around the ridge and crossed on the same side as the soldiers. Later we took the road that follows an oil pipeline, and by morning we managed to be about twenty kilometers beyond where we had clashed. The plan was to seize a vehicle and get to Cochabamba at whatever the cost. This was impossible, since the army had set up checkpoints along the highway and was stopping every vehicle that went by.

We walked a good stretch. Suddenly we threw ourselves into a ditch because a group of soldiers was advancing from the opposite direction. But before passing the spot where we were hidden, they turned onto a path that led to a pool of water. We crossed the highway and climbed a very steep hill. From there we heard the voices of the soldiers at the checkpoint.

In the afternoon we were able to eat something, and at midnight we resumed the march. Benigno and Urbano had an argument about which way we were headed and where Cochabamba was. We decided to consult the map when the sun came up. We spent the night in a ravine containing a hut next to a man-made pond. The soil was a thick clay that prevented water from filtering through, allowing the water to accumulate and permitting the cattle to drink from two sides. The area was very dry, without grass. The cows fed on the leaves of some small plants or bushes similar to marabú.

IN PULQUINA AND SAN ISIDRO

At night we resumed our march. Daylight found us in an open area facing a little village. We circled around it to avoid being seen by the peasants who worked there.

We hid from a young boy who was walking along the river with his dog. Watching him, we saw that he was working on the irrigation system, made up of canals or ditches designed to bring water from the river. The area was essentially agricultural; we saw big fields of tomatoes, cabbage, peppers, etc. We crossed the river and on reaching the ridge above we saw a town. Consulting the map, we identified it as San Isidro. The one we saw earlier was Pulquina, which is a little smaller. The river has the same name.

From there we heard a loudspeaker announcing the movie they were going to be showing: *We, the Poor* with Pedro Infante (I had seen it fifteen years earlier).

We went down into a ravine, unpopulated and dry. We later found an orchard with a small pool of water. The earth was cracked, contrasting with the other side, where the river flowed.

As we were drinking water, Benigno caught sight of two men; they approached the edge of the ravine, and on spotting us yelled: "Guerrillas!" Seeing the soldiers, we rapidly retreated. We walked from eleven until three without a halt. After stopping, we continued at night until we came to a hut, where there was corn and potatoes. We toasted the corn and cooked the potatoes. While we waited for the food, Inti asked me what our plan was and expressed the opinion that it would be best to turn back since to go forward was suicidal. The land was open and would get worse the farther we went. Moreover, the zone was under the control of the agricultural unions, and therefore Barrientos, since the leaders of these unions were sellouts. (There was one exception — a peasant leader with over a thousand men under arms who would surely help us if contacted.) In short, Inti felt we should return to where we had spent the previous night and once there, decide which plan was best: either head to the Mizque river, where we had come from, or find the road to Puerto Breto, and take it to Beni. If we were not near the road, we would go to the Piraypani river and the house of Honorato and wait there several days or even months.

Speaking with the other comrades, we explained the plan and asked their opinion. We decided to return on a forced march. At 8:00 a.m. we arrived at the hut. There we caught a cow and roasted it. Later we moved to a little house further in, where we rested an entire day.

The following day, while Inti was on watch, two peasants arrived on horseback. Dismounting, they carefully observed the remains of the cow we had slaughtered. After being informed of this, Benigno and I left to circle around the pond and prevent them from reaching the path they had taken. When we got there, the unexpected visitors were far in the distance. We left with the idea of asking in the next house where we were and the distance to the Río Grande.

At 2:30 in the morning of November 24, we arrived at an inhabited hut where a little dog greeted us with his insistent barking. Soon a man came who claimed to be seventy-six years old but looked no more than fifty. I don't remember his name but he was a civil engineer. He offered us all he had. We worked hard to convince him to sell us things while he, for his part, refused to budge, in order to get more money. Finally he agreed to collaborate and supply us with food, clothing, and later a radio. Afterward we left to hide.

At dawn of the next day we returned to the old man's house. He was asleep. He had brought us food for a week and trousers. Our situation was improving; we were no longer so ragged-looking.

He told us there was a major leading the troops in Pulquina. (They were Rangers.) He also told us that he had been arrested by the lieutenant of the post because a soldier had seen us and reported it. The lieutenant, who was drunk, told him, "Look, it doesn't matter, today is Sunday. We don't work Sundays. We'll go after them tomorrow." The engineer explained how dangerous it was to collaborate with us. He gave the impression of wanting to turn tail and run.

He later told us he would help out of humanitarianism and agreed to bring us shirts and underwear within three days, because to get all that, he would have to go to town. We stayed hidden three days to get the promised clothing. In the middle of the afternoon, taking all precautions, we went to the agreed-upon meeting place. The man brought us shirts and some food. He had bought the rest but had left it at home, he told us. He assured us he would bring it within three days. We worked out with him a little plan to get it.

We stayed hidden three more days hoping for the return of our new supplier. On the third day we set up a lookout to signal the old man's arrival. In a little while we heard a shot (the agreed-upon signal in the event we saw him first). We ran at full speed to catch him but it was impossible. A man tending cattle saw us going by. We approached the man pretending to be soldiers, though with little hope of deceiving him.

On December 3, in the early morning, Darío and I went looking for water. At six o'clock, while we were preparing water with chancaca, Inti heard footsteps and the sound of breaking branches. We got ourselves all together. It was a company of Rangers combing the ravine. At full speed, we gathered some of our things. Benigno was the first to open fire; he aimed at a soldier and shot him. The other soldiers, hearing the shots, threw themselves to the ground hiding their heads, which we took advantage of to escape. Later, we heard the tremendous firefight they were having by themselves. They failed to find the place where we had gone. We advanced several hours without stopping. In the afternoon, while drinking water, Urbano sounded the alarm. We thought it was the army but it was a peasant, and we didn't know if he saw us. We walked the whole day and night.

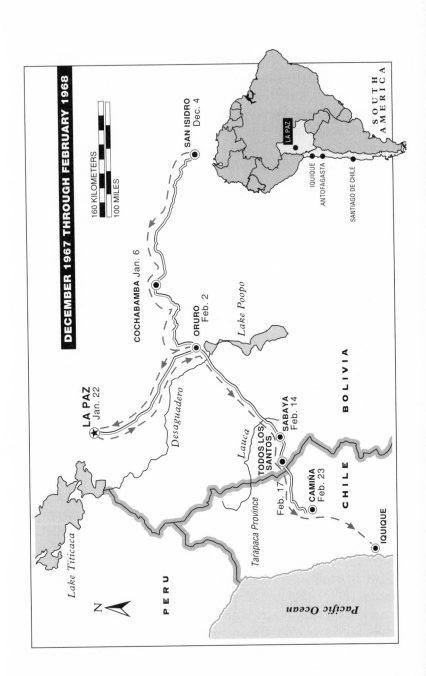

DECEMBER 1967 THROUGH FEBRUARY 1968

160 KILOMETERS
100 MILES

SAN ISIDRO
Dec. 4

COCHABAMBA Jan. 6

ORURO
Feb. 2

Lake Poopo

LA PAZ
Jan. 22

Desaguadero

SABAYA
Feb. 14

Lauca

TODOS LOS
SANTOS

Feb. 17

CAMIÑA
Feb. 23

BOLIVIA

CHILE

IQUIQUE

Lake Titicaca

PERU

Tarapaca Province

Pacific Ocean

N

SOUTH
AMERICA

LA PAZ

IQUIQUE
ANTOFAGASTA

SANTIAGO DE CHILE

The next morning we found a locked hut. We broke down the door and found flour, rice, and pans; we took it all, since we had nothing. We kept going and at noon, after climbing a hill, we found another hut. We did the same thing here too, taking lard and alcohol. We moved to a nearby pool of water, where we cooked and ate a delicious locro. Later we looked for a safe spot to wait for nightfall and continue the march.

Don Víctor

As we rested, a peasant came upon Urbano carrying out a physiological necessity. We spoke with him; his attitude was friendly and he invited us to chew coca and drink alcohol. We offered him the alcohol we were carrying. We asked him if he knew who we were, and he answered: "The good ones." "And who are the good ones?" "You are!" It went around and around like this, until he finally said that the "bad ones" had searched his house and broken a bed. This calmed us, for we had not done it, the army had; they were the bad ones he was referring to. He invited us to his house and offered us alcohol, cheese, and coffee. We bought a pig from him but he refused to take money. For the first time in recent memory, we had come upon a man with an honest and selfless attitude.

We said goodbye and returned to the woods, but it soon began to rain and we went back to his house. A little later his wife arrived, and she was very nice to us. We chatted with them a while and tried to convince them to go buy some things for us. The next day was rainy. They were unable to make the purchases.

The following day they brought us many things they had purchased. But the woman was worried because she had seen tracks on the road and had run into a man from town who was an army collaborator.

Taking precautions, we left and hid ourselves on a ridge. At 6:20, Darío gave the word: "Soldiers!" They were barely ten meters away, but did not see us due to our camouflaged position. They only heard the sound, and didn't shoot.

We left there immediately and about an hour later we heard fierce gunfire. Apparently they were attacking the ravine they thought we were in.

Through all of this we were followed by one of the dogs of Don Víctor, the name of our friend.

The next day we arrived at a ravine where Inti and Urbano bathed; the water was excessively cold. We continued the march, and after many obstacles we got to a field of vegetables and quinces, although these were very sour. We made camp a little below there. As we prepared our lunch, Urbano detained a peasant tending cattle.

We tried to interrogate him but it turned out the man spoke no Spanish, only Quechua. Fortunately, Darío spoke that language and asked him some questions.

This proved to us again how right Che was in insisting we study that language, which is predominant in many areas of South America.

We set out in the afternoon toward the settlement to speak with the mayor of the area and ask his help. He was not home, but we were told he could be found in another house he owned on the riverbank. We went there but still could not find him. We resumed the march and a torrential rain began to fall, which forced us to seek refuge in a little house. The peasant was polite but refused to sell us anything in spite of having identified ourselves as soldiers.

New actions

We overslept and left late, which spoiled our plans to reach Siberia that night. We spent the day in a forest. At 3:30 Darío announced he had seen several soldiers pass by; we got ourselves ready and prepared for the retreat. We began the ascent. Just when we were near the summit, we bumped into a group of soldiers who appeared to be assigned to close the encirclement behind us. When they detected us, there was heavy firing. We managed to break the encirclement and lose sight of them. Heading downhill, we arrived at a farm on the riverbank. There were peasants working there, and we had to wait for them to finish and leave. (In this area, due to the intensity of the sun, the peasants begin work before dawn to take advantage of the moonlight and quit at noon.)

At about five o'clock, we were forced to leave our cover, as the enemy was headed directly toward our hiding place. The shooting was sporadic since they were not able to see us well. Our flight was rapid until we reached a small wooded ridge, where we stopped and took positions. We then returned for the dog[1] and clashed again with the army. Later we continued on to a place where the houses were far apart. There it began to rain and we huddled up together against the cold.

When we awoke, we discussed what plan to follow. We could not continue constantly under siege by the army, constantly scampering from one place to another. We unanimously decided to return to Don Víctor's house.

We set out toward San Isidro, spending a part of the day en route. On the afternoon of December 12 we reached the area of Don Víctor, whom we met camping in the woods with his dogs. The dogs greeted us with joy. Don Víctor arrived later, happy to see us, and related his wife's concern about us. He said that the day of our departure, while looking for a cow, he was detained by some soldiers who asked him about the guerrillas. He responded that he knew nothing, but they insisted. They told him they knew we had been in his house because a peasant had heard us talking there. He denied it and a lieutenant slapped and kicked him. The officer tried to beat the truth out of him while a major and the rest of the troops watched.

Later, the major hit him several times with a baton and or-

---

1. One of Don Víctor's dogs was accompanying the guerrillas.

dered him held prisoner to guide them to the guerrillas. While they were following tracks, he asked permission to carry out a necessity and fled. He wandered all night, arriving home in San Isidro in the morning. There he was again arrested and held until the day before our return. In other words, he had been free only one day.

THE DEPARTURE

Inti proposed to me that he set out on his own to make contact, saying that for the five of us to do so together would be suicide. I told him that in my view what was suicide was precisely to disperse the group, since the Cubans had no chance of getting out. We also did not know anyone in the city with whom to make contact and continue the struggle in the event that the comrades were willing to do so; or if not, to be able to get out of the country. We agreed to discuss the question with everyone that night.

We hid near the house and began the meeting with a report by me analyzing the situation. I proposed that Inti and Urbano set out, and that the rest of us wait fifteen days for the contact. If there were no news after this period of time, we would begin the plan of leaving separately. Darío would leave first since, as a Bolivian, he could mix with the people more easily. Then Benigno would go, followed by me. Being Black, I would have the least chance of passing unnoticed.

Then came the question on everyone's mind: "Why not confide in Don Víctor?" It really was necessary to confide in someone, although always with reserve.

After a thorough discussion centered around the departure, we arrived at the following agreement:

Inti and Urbano would leave on the afternoon of December 15, taking care not to leave tracks. We would await contact with them every third day from December 20 to 29. On the last day, if nothing happened, we would proceed to leave one by one. Inti left addresses if this were to occur: that of his father-in-law; that of the editor of a newspaper in Cochabamba; and that of a girl who had grown up with him in Santa Cruz. The money I was carrying would be taken by Darío and Benigno (50,000 pesos and 3,000 dollars). Their physical appearance gave them a better chance of not being caught.

If contact were made, the comrade sent would explain the escape plan and work out the date and manner in which the rest of us would be picked up.

Benigno would go to the place chosen to make the contact, I decided. Being white and owing to his overall appearance, he would stand out less. When the vehicle stopped and the driver got out to fix a simulated problem in the right front tire, he would approach the driver and say, "Is the tire low, friend?" to which the driver would respond, "How are the three?"

The following day I arranged with Don Víctor to go buy us supplies.

He left on the afternoon of December 15, and then we said goodbye to our comrades. This type of life truly develops a heightened sense of human feeling. Darío cried, and before leaving Urbano too had tears welling up in his eyes. Don Víctor had not yet returned, and we decided to sleep in the house, although we were on the alert.

Don Víctor arrived in the early morning, very nervous and without our supplies. "Don Pedrito, Don Panchito," he said, addressing Benigno and me, "I saw footprints on the road. Please leave the house quickly."

We asked what the footprints were like. He responded that there was one set made by shoes and another made by sandals. We explained that these footprints were made by the shoes he had given to Alberto (Urbano), who had gone out on a mission with Pepe (Inti).

This calmed him considerably, and he told us he had hidden the goods, in case he was being watched. To change the subject, we arranged to organize a family party for December 24 (Christmas Eve), since Don Víctor and his family had never celebrated it.

On December 17 the old man's relatives arrived: a son, his son-in-law, and Don Víctor's wife, who brought two little grandchildren. To avoid suspicion, we asked his wife to go to the town of Camarapa to buy the goods. She explained that people there were saying that two guerrillas had passed through. The reason was that they had gone into a store with a 50 peso bill. (Those bills became known in the area as *guerrilleros*, since we always had to pay for things with 50 and 100 peso bills as we didn't have any others.) She added that the owner of the store had informed the authorities who, thinking it impossible, refused to believe her.

Peasants frequently came through the area following tracks, looking for us and asking about us in the house. Some claimed we were in Siberia and that after the last clash there were four of us left, since one had been wounded, died, and was buried.

That same day I spoke with Don Víctor, asking him to send his son-in-law to Cochabamba to buy us a shortwave radio so we could listen to Radio Havana Cuba. The one we had was a small, battery-operated set that only received local stations. We also asked him to buy items needed for Christmas Eve (wine, sweets, etc.) and, if possible, underwear and a jacket.

We spent December 20 on a ridge where the whole area was visible. If the army approached, we would have about a two hours' head start on them.

Benigno went with the old man to the rendezvous point. No one appeared who acted in the agreed-upon fashion. The rest of us returned to the woods and stayed the whole day until

Benigno came back. Everything went peacefully. On December 23 we tried to establish contact, but no one came.[1]

We had to postpone the party of December 24 because on that day the old man's son was arrested on suspicion of robbery. We were greatly worried, for it could bring complications.

Don Víctor refused to go see his son, saying it was shameful to have a son who was a thief. We had to make a great effort to convince him, finally explaining that the boy could make things worse for himself if he hinted at our presence in the house.

On December 25 the whole family came. Don Víctor's daughter, a married woman, was very pretty. She was taller than most of the inhabitants of the area. Don Víctor, for his part, was very happy. We drank Italian and Chilean wine. The food too was excellent. The daughter promised us books and magazines, since the boredom was terrible. She told us that two people had been arrested in Cochabamba for having hidden guerrillas. That darkened the holiday for us, and we got very worried. That night we listened to the news on Radio Havana.

On December 26 Benigno left again for the contact point.[2] The contacts came, and they informed him that they would come for us between December 30 and January 30, and that the contacts would be attempted every five days, beginning January 5. In other words, we had nearly ten days until the first contact.

We returned to our spot in the woods. There, as long as we

1. In his book *Guerrillero Inti,* Bolivian writer Jesús Lara — Inti Peredo's father-in-law and at the time a member of the Communist Party — recounts that a rescue committee of five people was formed, among them members of the ELN and the PCB. The contact expedition was organized, but was unsuccessful on December 20 because Benigno did not show; he did not think the emissaries were trustworthy. On the second try (December 23) the highway was heavily patrolled.
2. For the third and last attempt at contact, Roberto Asner, first secretary of the Bolivian CP in the region, chose the individuals and the procedure.

were not betrayed, problems were unlikely. It was a flat area between two ravines that each came to a point. It would be very difficult to approach from the sides, and if the enemy came, we would have more than enough time to escape safely.

On December 28 the old man's son was freed, through paying a fine of 1,000 pesos, which we provided.

On December 31, we listened to Radio Havana's year-end review of the news.

We celebrated the new year with roast pork and wine and something unusual happened: we fell asleep before twelve and missed the arrival of the new year. We wanted to bathe but a peasant of Quechua origin arrived and we were unable to. Don Víctor's wife had invited him for cheese and coffee.

On January 2 we listened to the rally commemorating the triumph of the Cuban revolution, and a little later a group of peasants arrived, saying they had seen soldiers in the area. They asked Don Víctor about us and our earlier stay.

Two days later, other peasants came and offered Don Víctor half of the reward money for our capture if he simply told them where to find us. They brought flyers with our photographs and underneath them the reward: 10,000 pesos for each of us.

That same day, Benigno became a member of the family, for he baptized one of the old man's grandchildren (baptism is done there with the symbolic act of the child's first haircut).

When the old man's daughter was saying goodbye, we practically had to cover her mouth as she began to shout: "My child has a Cuban godfather! My child has a Cuban godfather!"

Later five individuals in civilian dress showed up carrying rifles; upon seeing them we left quickly for the woods. When they left, Don Víctor's wife came looking for us and told us she had invited them to eat and insisted we return to the house. We decided to spend the night in the woods.

We were quite worried, because the next day the three of us were to leave together as already planned. The situation was a difficult one, for if they did not come to get us, it would be almost impossible to return. In addition, we were worried about this peasant who had risked his life for us so many times without asking for a cent, his only interest being to help us.

Operation Rescue

At dusk on January 5 we said goodbye to them and gave them 6,000 pesos, with the promise that if we managed to get out we would leave more. This promise was fulfilled.

Don Víctor had organized a line of security along the whole route from his house to the rendezvous point. The line was made up of his children and relatives, with the goal of warning us of anything out of the ordinary that might endanger our plans. At 9:00 p.m. we arrived at the bridge where a truck was to pick us up. We had arranged that the vehicle would stop at that point, and we would ask the driver: "Hey friend, do you have a flat?" He, in turn, would answer: "No, I'm just checking the tires."

Within a short time, as we were drinking coffee, a truck arrived, stopped, and the driver began throwing tools to the ground. We approached him and asked, "Hey friend, do you have a flat?" The young man looked very scared and said, "Yes, yes, get on in. It's us."

The truck, a large one, was set up as follows: the rear of the truck was piled halfway up with long wooden boards. The middle section was loaded with the same wood but cut in two parts, one part facing the front and the other facing the back. There was a space in between, a type of cage, which was where we traveled. Finally, the hole was covered and the load was topped off with full-length pieces of the wood. This made it appear that the truck was loaded normally.

We began our trek jammed together because the three of us could barely fit in the space.

Our driver later related to us how the trip went: we passed

the first checkpoint smoothly, but at the second one the truck was stopped and the officer asked the driver for papers. A soldier climbed up on top of the load and began to throw the boards to the ground. When he had removed two whole layers, our driver invited first the captain and then the other soldiers to smoke a cigarette. They accepted and stopped to smoke. Next, the one who was still on the truck asked for a bar and began to poke it between the boards. We had a small piece of wood in our hiding place which we used to block the blows. This was a very tense moment; there had been three layers of wood above us, but only one was now left before we would be discovered. Apparently, the activity of smoking and the cold altered their plans, which would have been fatal for both them and us. We would have been discovered, but they would not have lived to tell about it, for we were armed.

In total our truck passed through ten army checkpoints without any more problems.

The young men who did the job were members of the PCB and conducted themselves with great calm. One of them worked as a helper on the truck. To arrange its use, he got the owner drunk and later convinced him not to drive in an inebriated state. The owner then gave him permission to drive the vehicle to Cochabamba the next morning.

On January 6 we arrived in Cochabamba and hid in a house on the outskirts. There several comrades from the party were waiting for us. They were jubilant about the success of the mission they had been given. We asked to see Inti and were told he was in La Paz. We gave the ELN representative money for documents and other expenses.

The departure of Inti and Urbano

Later we learned how Inti and Urbano had managed to make their way out. They first walked three hours to the outskirts of San Isidro. There they bought a meal and coffee in a hotel, paying with a 50 peso bill. Next they went to the check-point leading onto the highway and, pretending to be peas-ants from the countryside, chatted with the soldiers.

They were told there were 350 soldiers that had relieved the Trinidad Regiment. Later they went to see a movie; 80 percent of those in the theater were soldiers. At the end of the movie they returned to the checkpoint to wait for the bus. A little later it began to rain and the soldiers left the arm of the road barrier up. At two o'clock a truck passed by; they hailed it, and, as luck would have it, the cab was empty and they got on. At that moment Urbano's hat fell off. A peasant picked it up to return it, and Urbano gave it to him as a gift. Inti criti-cized him for that, since no peasant would so easily give away a new hat, and the gesture could have aroused suspicions.

They continued on to Mataral, where the truck stopped. That was the most dangerous place, because Urbano had been there with Ñato. The soldiers looked at him and nothing hap-pened; they did not recognize him. In Santa Cruz the arm of the road barrier wasn't down, and they arrived without problems.

There they bought clothes, suits, and shoes and changed in a public bath. Then they made a telephone call to Lloyd Aéreo Boliviano and reserved two seats for Cochabamba. They went to the airport, bought two tickets in the names of Alberto Tor-res and José Gutiérrez, and during the entire flight they chat-ted with an officer of the Special Forces, who told them anec-dotes of his role in the antiguerrilla actions.

His story explained in part how it was that we escaped the army. He said that we had changed ourselves into dogs and become invisible in order to escape the encirclements. He de-scribed me as a Black man of tremendous size who fought with two machine guns, one in each hand. It was obvious they had woven a whole legend around us to justify their own ineffectiveness. The aim was to show that a stroke of luck, not consciously planned action, was responsible for everything that happened.

Finally, on reaching Cochabamba, our comrades found refuge in the home of a sister-in-law of Inti and other family members and friends.

FROM COCHABAMBA TO LA PAZ

During the night we were placed in different homes, having been warned that the residents did not know our identities. Nearly all were intellectuals and trusted people, although not party members. It was assumed that our stay in these houses would be short, since a house belonging to a family was being readied for us.

Our plan was to send a man to Cuba, get our documents, and try to make contact with Rodolfo to see if the forty men were still prepared to go off to fight. If so, we would not leave and would continue the struggle.

On the night of January 21 two comrades belonging to the ELN came to pick us up in a car.[1] They decided to do this, they explained, because the news of our escape was common knowledge, even in La Paz, and had been known for several days. To avoid our discovery, it was best to move us quickly. We picked up Urbano and then Darío. Benigno was moved two days later.

We traveled to La Paz. Urbano drove the car for three hours to allow the driver to rest. At eight in the morning we reached Alto de La Paz. As we got out of the car, a pair of carabineros passed in front of us on the sidewalk. We went right by them with our bags.

1. The car belonged to Juvenal Castro (1926–), a leader of the Bolivian Communist party's peasant work. He is currently a senator in Bolivia.

We were treated very well in the home we stayed at. Living there was a married couple: a German television actress who spoke Spanish quite well and a Bolivian geologist who ended up betraying the ELN, making false and slanderous charges against the organization, the Cuban revolution, and us.

At night a conflict arose, since the apartment had only one bedroom, where the couple slept. They insisted on sleeping on the floor, giving us the bed. We of course flatly refused.

Rodolfo arrived the next day. He looked very different; his hair was combed to the side and he was not wearing glasses. We asked about Inti. He said he had not seen him, that he was safe, but exactly where he was staying Rodolfo didn't know, other than it was in the home of a congressman, and thus under immunity. Rodolfo instructed us to wait for him to make contact with Inti. That annoyed us somewhat.

He spoke about the organization of the ELN and the possibilities that existed. He told us that he himself was making contact with the group of students. This was not the best procedure, but there was no alternative. He thought they had some twenty to thirty rifles and about thirty men, although he was not sure of the total. He added that the group of forty had been won over by Zamora. It was said they were hidden on a farm in Chapare ready to rise up in arms. Rodolfo therefore thought it necessary to make contacts in Chile to guarantee our escape, with the objective of reorganizing our forces without pressure and without the risk of being caught.

Later we raised the need for the ELN to organize its general staff, in which each comrade would have responsibility for specific activities. We talked about practicing mutual vigilance as a way to combat infiltration. We also spoke of applying Ramón's guidelines for the urban struggle.[1]

At the end of the discussion we listened to several sambas sung by our hosts. They later played records of poetry by

1. Guevara's "Instructions for Cadres Assigned to Urban Areas." In *Bolivian Diary*, pp. 299–304.

Nicolás Guillén and popular music that reminded us of the programs of Radio Havana Cuba that we had listened to up in the mountains.

On January 24 Jorge René Pol Álvarez-Plata arrived; he was the comrade responsible for making contact with Chile. He announced his departure by plane to Santiago at the end of the week, to return the following Thursday.

We expressed to him our desire to speak with Benigno and Sánchez.[1] He explained that it would be better for them to come and talk to us, since Benigno's physical appearance made it easier for him to move around, and that he could locate Sánchez.

On January 25 Sánchez came. It was very difficult to recognize him. He was very happy to see us and consulted with me about giving a certain amount of money to Rodolfo. We explained to him that we had no instructions on the matter. But according to a message he carried, it would be better not to turn over all of it, but only 20,000 pesos for the moment and to await instructions. He had to leave for Arica to meet some comrades. He was worried that Loyola had talked a lot, that documents and photos had been taken from her. I explained to Sánchez that everything he described had been taken by the army from the caves, that Loyola had not talked.

As Sánchez began to tell us about the development of events in the city, he was summoned to other work. He proposed to come at another time, but as a security measure we told him we were leaving the house that very day, and it would not be possible for him to see us again.

The next day Jorge Pol proposed to us that we leave on February 1 and that Miguel Ballón would go to Chile to inform people of our departure.

An attempt was made to organize a structure in the city responsible for our escape, but this was impossible. We decided

---

1. Sánchez — Julio Dagnino Pacheco — was the Peruvian revolutionary working in the guerrillas' clandestine network in La Paz.

to utilize the party because Kolle had promised to get us out, as he would anyone who might want to leave. He wanted virtually everyone from the ELN to leave. We felt he would do this enthusiastically and safely, for it was an opportunity to vindicate himself in something.

It was the responsibility of the Bolivian party to get us to the border; once inside Chile we were on our own. It was left open whether it would be the party or the Chilean ELN that would take charge of our security and documents.

We moved to another house on Ecuador Street, in La Paz, which we paid for with the money we had left.

We argued with Rodolfo about a note from Pol informing us that the departure would be organized in two groups: in the first would be Inti, Urbano, and Rodolfo; in the second, Benigno, Darío, and me.

I did not agree to this. I explained to him that if something unexpected happened, it would be impossible for the Cubans to hide, since they could not pass unnoticed in the city. Benigno and Urbano might be able to hide if they kept their mouths shut; I couldn't even if they painted me. The logical thing was for the six of us to leave together, or, if necessary, the three Bolivians would go separately and we would all meet up again in Chile. We believed the Bolivians should leave first, and the Cubans later. I had to guarantee that no one remained behind. Separations had not brought good results.

FROM LA PAZ TO CHILE

On February 2 in the afternoon, they picked us up and gave us a farewell tour of La Paz.

Early the next morning we arrived at the house of Efraín

Quicañas[1] in Oruro, closely followed by a group that included Inti. There we were told that everything was ready for us to leave the next day. Shortly after we arrived, it started raining and did not stop. The temperature that night dropped to four degrees [centigrade].

Petiso arrived the next day, assigned by the party to our departure. He said we should wait for the other group and continue ahead the following day, since the Desaguadero river had overflowed its banks. We told him it would be crazy for a group of eight people to leave on foot in a completely desolate zone.

A meeting with Inti

That night Inti visited me. We discussed the situation and agreed not to leave until the rain had abated. This would also enable us to spend more time organizing the ELN apparatus.

He told me of his plan to write a response to an article by Kolle entitled "Secret Interview," in which Kolle lied shamelessly.

We discussed future plans and took up the need to leave and reorganize the ELN. If possible we would receive training in Cuba and then return to implement Che's initial plan:

The people's war had to be organized everywhere, that is, the guerrilla struggle in the mountains needed to be carried out simultaneously with urban warfare (actions, sabotage, kidnapping, and broad use of psychological warfare, such as rumor and propaganda). All these actions should be combined, so that the war would not be limited to one region of the country, but would be extended and make itself felt in every corner of Bolivia.

It was necessary to ensure that once guerrilla actions began, they should not become isolated from the rest of the country.

1. A member of the Bolivian CP, who traveled under the alias of Efraín Aguilar Quiñones.

We needed to examine the characteristics of the most suitable regions for guerrilla warfare. For this we needed to take into account the inhospitable and inaccessible areas that would make large-scale military operations difficult (a favorable factor for guerrillas but a negative aspect insofar as it would make it possible to isolate the zone). We also had to consider control over the roads, villages, and so forth.

It was necessary to concentrate our forces in one place and for everyone to go off to the mountains at the same time, not gradually. This would ensure that the enemy's intelligence network in the zones would be unable to detect us until we were ready for combat.

We should establish a reserve supply of materials in caves. Physical contact with the city would be made two months after actions began.

The largest possible quantity of explosives needed to be gathered, with the aim of using them for booby traps, controlled antipersonnel mines, and other applications.

We did not envision the use of antitank grenades, because vehicles could not travel easily in the region selected. Moreover, this would ensure two fundamental principles: aggressiveness and economy of life.

We agreed to carefully study the country's characteristics and draw up a plan to minimize contingencies.

We sent Petiso to La Paz to discuss the new situation with the leadership of the PCB and return in three days. Meanwhile, Inti went to Santa Cruz for meetings and to organize the ELN's urban apparatus.

En route to Chile

Three days later Petiso returned with Enrique Hinojosa (Víctor), an ELN delegate. They had contacted the Chilean party and had come to an agreement for them to wait for us at the border between February 15 and 17. If contact were not made then, they would wait for us on February 21 in the Chilean town of Camiña, 150 kilometers from the border. A party member would drive around in a truck, waiting to pick us up at the Lauca river, if it was possible to get across.

In the afternoon of February 10 we were taken by truck and dropped off near the Desaguadero river. We planned to cross by raft. Villca[1] was in charge of logistics, and Quicañas would take care of political contacts.

For three hours we walked over terrain flooded from the river's overflow. Due to the altitude, Benigno and I felt very sick and my leg was hurting. Our hearts were bursting from our chests. The water rose over our knees, which caused quite a shock since it was so cold. Twice I fell, and the second time I plunged in up to my head. I lost my hat and a French pistol.

At twelve o'clock we reached the river and entered a small house we found there. It was built of clay and was round (Eskimo style) with almost no door. Protected from the cold, we made a fire to warm up. At 1:30 we crossed the river. The boatman asked for 750 pesos. We gave him 700 when we got to the other side, explaining that we were just getting the business started. (He thought we were smugglers.) We continued walking until 4:00. We were exhausted and unable to continue, so we stopped.

In the morning we walked as fast as we could for a stretch. Then I got a charley horse and couldn't walk. Urbano rubbed me down with liniment and all of us took drops of coramina. (The Cubans had to take it continuously to combat mountain sickness.) Villca went down to a small village at midday to buy food. He returned and we continued ahead to cross the river. Reaching the spot where we were to be picked up, we rested on the riverbank. Suddenly Urbano realized that the river was rising and we went across rapidly. The river's rise was brutal, making it impossible for a truck right behind us to cross.

---

1. Estanislao Villca, a university student from Sabaya and a member of the ELN.

At 7:00 p.m. we got on a truck to speed up our progress a bit.

After a few hours on the road, we reached the Lauca river. There the road turned, and we made the mistake of offering the driver ten times the price the trip was worth. He agreed to continue on the next day.

On the morning of February 14 we hid near Sabaya to avoid being seen by the inhabitants. But riding in the truck with us was a townsman who seemed to suspect something, and spoke of it in the village.

Villca went down into town and saw the driver, Teodoro Araníbar, who was supposed to pick us up. The man said he was running late but he was getting ready to go find us. He agreed to pick us up in the afternoon outside town. By now there was quite a stir, since the whole town knew of our presence in the area. Peasants began to go out on bicycles to look for us; their aim was simply to find us.

A torrential rain began to fall and at night we moved closer to town. Villca went back to look for the driver. He returned to report that he had spoken with the telegraph operator, who was a member of the party and who told him that the driver was on his farm outside town and would return tomorrow. At that time we would be able to leave without problems. The man offered to let us hide in his house overnight.

We went to his house. The owner made us coffee and fritters. Later, Villca returned from a trip to town. He told us that the town authorities had called to demand that we report to them and show them the goods we were carrying. Given that smuggling is quite common around there, they took us for smugglers. We decided to report to them and straighten out the situation, presenting ourselves as merchants.

Benigno, Urbano, and Quicañas reported to the authorities on February 15, and I remained in hiding, to avoid having my skin color draw attention to us.

When they arrived they were told that people in town wanted to know who they were. Our people explained they were Chileans, but said that they did not have papers on them, and would present these upon their return. There was a man there who identified himself as a merchant like us (a real smuggler[1]), and he really pushed them to demand our papers. Then he went up to Quicañas and said, pointing to Benigno and Urbano: "They don't have Chilean accents."

Finally the authorities decided to interrogate them separately. While they were interrogating Benigno, a sergeant approached to search him. Benigno jumped back, drew his pistol, and a number of soldiers tried to tackle him, forcing him to fire a shot through the ceiling. That action put a halt to their threatening behavior, and they decided to settle things peacefully. At that point Urbano burst in; on hearing Benigno's shot he had seized a soldier's rifle. It was quite a surprise to Urbano when he checked the rifle and discovered it wasn't loaded.

Then we began haggling over the price of our freedom. Finally they settled for a 400 dollar guarantee.

We ate lunch in a restaurant. While there we heard news from Oruro that army troops were being brought in, and we began looking for a truck to get us out of there. It was useless, however. Some people said they had no gasoline, others that their trucks were broken down, etc., etc. Everything indicated that they were delaying us, and that at the very least the smuggler had identified us.

A resident soon approached us to say that a report had been sent to Oruro detailing the incidents here. We immediately left the town. Along the way Villca's uncle caught up with us on bicycle to advise us to take the road through the hills. We went that way, and an hour later we heard planes flying overhead and thought we saw a light airplane land on a wide plain. We hid all afternoon until sunset, since we had seen a number of vehicles moving about. We lightened our load a bit and at night we set out, changing our route. We crossed a

1. His name was Juan González.

Castro delivers speech at meeting paying tribute to
Guevara and other slain combatants in Havana's Plaza of
the Revolution, before a crowd of hundreds of thousands,
October 18, 1967.

RECOMPENSA

$b. 10.000.—
(DIEZ MILLONES DE BOLIVIANOS)
POR CADA UNO VIVO

$b. 10.000.—
(DIEZ MILLONES DE BOLIVIANOS)
POR CADA UNO VIVO

ESTOS SON LOS BANDOLEROS MERCENARIOS AL SERVICIO DEL CASTROCOMUNISMO
ESTOS SON LOS CAUSANTES DE LUTO Y DOLOR EN LOS HOGARES BOLIVIANOS
INFORMACION QUE RESULTE CIERTA, DARA DERECHO A LA RECOMPENSA

Ciudadano Boliviano, Ayúdanos a Capturarlos Vivos en lo Posible

| Pombo | Benigno | Urbano | Inti | Darío |

Nacionalidad: cubana. — Edad Aprox. 26 años. — Estatura Aprox. 1.71 m. — Color de la piel: Moreno oscuro. — Rasgos faciales finos. — Cabellos crespos — Cicatriz de bala en la pantorrilla.

Nacionalidad: cubana — Edad Aprox. 25 años. — Estatura Aprox. 1.80 m. — Color de la piel: blanca. Tiene herida de bala en la espalda. Espalda ancha, camina a zancadas.

Nacionalidad: cubana. — Edad: 28 años. — Estatura Aprox. 1.65 m. Color de la piel: Moreno oscuro. — Rasgos faciales: De raza negra. — Nariz ancha. Boca grande.

Nacionalidad: boliviana — Edad Aprox. 35 años. — Estatura Aprox. 1.70 m. — Cara delgada. Ojos grandes sombreados. Cejas gruesas tupidas. Frente ancha, cabello ondulado.

Nacionalidad: boliviana. — Edad Aprox. 28 años. — Estatura Aprox. 1.62 m. — Color de la piel: blanca (trigueño). — Labios gruesos. Cabellos negros lacios. Barba tupida.

NOTA.– Pueden usar barba o llevar otros nombres falsos

EDITORA POLÍTICA

Facing page, top, Col. Joaquín Anaya (left) and Maj. Arnaldo Saucedo exhibit Guevara's captured diary at Bolivian army Eighth Division headquarters in Valle Grande, October 10, 1967. **Bottom,** pages from Pombo's field diary for October 9, 1967.

In a gruelling five-month odyssey, five of the six surviving combatants succeded in eluding the army's encirclement (one, Ñato, was mortally wounded in combat at Mataral). **This page, top,** guerrilla collaborators Régis Debray (left) and Ciro Roberto Bustos on trial in Camiri, Bolivia, 1967. On November 16, 1967, they were sentenced to 30 years' imprisonment; they were amnestied in 1970. **Above,** poster issued by Bolivian government offering a 10,000 peso reward (US$842) for each guerrilla captured alive. Poster reads: "Bolivian citizen, help us capture them alive if possible. These are mercenary bandits at the service of Castro-Communism. These are the ones who cause mourning and pain in Bolivian homes. Information that turns out to be true will be subject to a reward. Note: they may have beards or use false names."

The three Cuban veterans crossed over into Chile February 16–17, 1968.

Top, left to right, Pombo, Benigno, Urbano, guides Estanislao Villca and Efraín Quicañas, upon their arrival in Chile. **Bottom,** at the Carabineros Hospital in Santiago de Chile, where they were given medical examinations. Left to right, Benigno, Pombo, Quicañas.

Top, aboard plane en route to Santiago de Chile, February 23; left to right, unidentified, Quicañas, Pombo, Urbano. **Middle,** Salvador Allende, president of the Chilean senate, greets the guerrillas in Santiago de Chile. From left to right, their guide Efraín Quicañas, Urbano, Benigno, and Pombo. **Bottom,** meeting with Fidel Castro at the José Martí airport in Havana, March 6; clockwise, Fidel Castro, Urbano, Pombo, Benigno. Also in meeting were Quicañas and Villca.

"Wherever death may surprise us, let it be welcome if our battle cry has reached even one receptive ear, if another hand reaches out to take up our arms," Guevara wrote in his Message to the Tricontinental.

Top, scene from the Sorbonne university in Paris, during mass student upsurge and general strike by workers, May 1968. **Bottom,** marchers in Chicano Moratorium demonstration of 30,000 in Los Angeles, August 29, 1970, protesting Vietnam War.

In the years following the crushing of the revolutionary front in Bolivia massive social upheavals swept the Southern Cone of South America.

Top, workers demonstrate in Tucumán, Argentina, June 1969, in weeks following the *Cordobazo* uprising. **Bottom,** farmers demonstrate in La Paz, 1971.

Top, Brig. Gen. Harry Villegas (at right) continuing Cuba's internationalist traditions in Angola, 1980s. **Bottom,** Villegas as commander of troops defending Cuba's border with U.S. military base at Guantánamo, 1970s.

plain and then the terrain turned to mud and water until we reached a ridge on another mountain range.

A heavy rainstorm began in the early morning. We stopped to put on rain gear and continued forward until twelve. At that time we rested and resumed the march until 3:00 p.m., when we found a cave in which to weather the shower. While inside, we heard what seemed to be an airplane with at least a twin engine. It was clear we had to cross the border that very night because the plane was very possibly a troop transport.[1]

At 5:00 p.m. we began an exhausting march that lasted until midnight, when we halted at the outskirts of Todos los Santos, a small village about fifty or sixty kilometers from the border.

The radio was reporting our presence in the town of Sabaya, and they were also saying that we had already crossed.

In the early morning hours of February 17 we were at the border, still uncertain which country we were in.

A WEEK IN CHILE

To find out, Villca headed to a settlement we could see about two kilometers away, while we remained hidden. He returned with good news: the village was in Chilean territory.

There all we came upon were some children and an old man, who sold us canned peaches and made us soup with dried llama meat. In the afternoon we continued moving deeper into Chilean territory and came to a house about

---

1. According to reports, on February 15 military planes transported troops to exterminate "the daring ones." It was announced that the guerrillas were near the zone of Pichiga, between Sabaya and the Chilean border, and that "they will be captured at any moment."

fifteen kilometers from the border. We were greeted there by a friendly peasant. We noted the change in living conditions between the Bolivian and Chilean peasants, even though there is still great poverty among the latter.

We decided to bury the weapons under some rocks and camp out in the woods.

The next day a peasant boy told us that a truckload of carabineros had arrived and were looking for us. We went to see his father, who showed us a place to hide. We climbed up a ravine and then a ridge, where we observed vehicles moving about. We continued on and hid between two snow-capped peaks. The cold was so intense that our hands and feet turned numb, even though they were wrapped in blankets.

We resumed the hike at night, and Benigno became so sick he could hardly move. We camped in a ravine.

In the afternoon we covered a long stretch and ran into a man on the road who was from Sabaya and knew Villca. He sold us bread, toasted wheat, quinces, and other items. We continued on looking for a river, since thirst was beginning to ravage us.

In the morning we reached a ravine ten kilometers from Camiña. There we waited for Villca, who had gone to the town to contact his cousin, who lived there. The cousin told him there were a large number of soldiers, carabineros, and agents of the political police searching for us.

The radio carried a statement by the Communist Party appealing for the support of the masses and government to grant us asylum. Furthermore it rebroadcast statements by Salvador Allende, president of the senate, expressing support for our asylum and about his efforts to locate us. Toward this end, he had sent out envoys to places where we might appear.

Later we listened to Barrientos's statements, in which he blamed himself for our escape since he had ordered us to be captured alive. Ovando's declaration was much more sensible. His opinion was that we escaped because of the heavy rains in the zone, which prevented them from sending paratroopers against us. Future decisions were put off to the following day, when the Bolivian congress would meet to consider the question of our escape.

At night Benigno and Villca went into town. The latter's cousin refused to sell him goods and threatened to inform the authorities if Villca returned to the man's home, since he did not want to take any more risks.

That day they announced that Bolivia's Council of Ministers had decided not to request our extradition, since they concluded that Chile would never grant it. They also began an investigation to determine who was responsible for our escape and punish them.

On hearing this news we felt relief, and gave up the idea of going to Iquique since it's a desert and we did not have enough food. Moreover, we had to make contact that day.

Benigno and Villca went to the agreed-upon contact point. Finding no one, they returned and on the way back ran into the army. They escaped by losing them in a cornfield.

The Communist and Socialist parties had sent high-ranking members to the border. On February 22 the Communist deputy Antonio Carvajal and the Socialist leader Leonel Valcarve met with us a short distance from Camiña.

The next day, February 23, we concluded that it would better to turn ourselves in. At 12:00 we began the march and two hours later reached the outskirts of the village near Camiña in the desert of Tarapaca province.[1] There we ran into a reporter for *El Mercurio*[2] and told him we were the guerrillas and that we wanted to accept the hospitality of the Chilean people. We told him we were unarmed and our main objective was to turn ourselves in to the authorities and request asylum, trusting in the democratic traditions and hospitality of the Chilean people.

---

1. This was the first contact point with the Chilean commission assigned to their rescue.
2. Luis Berenguela.

A boy on a bicycle rushed to the police station to inform them of our presence. Soon a captain named Caupolicán arrived. He was very friendly, and took us to the carabinero station in town.

Along the way all the residents greeted us warmly. I remember that some of them called out, "Don't be afraid, we Chileans are civilized people. We're on your side." "We love you, stay here with us."

At the station they were ordered to take us to Iquique. Before that we were introduced to a leader of the Chilean Communist Party, Senator Volodia Teitelboim, who told us the people would support us.

In another small village we passed through, all the residents lined the road to greet us and shout out their support, since the party had announced we were coming through.

Along the way we encountered and spoke with Roth, the man who claimed to be an English reporter and was in the mountains, and who left with Debray and Bustos. He said he was presently working as a photographer for *Life* magazine. A strange encounter.

Arriving in Iquique, we listened over the shortwave to the orders from the Ministry of the Interior. They ordered that we not be taken into the city, because the people were in the streets there demonstrating their support; to avoid disturbances, it was best to take us to the Los Cóndores base. There, some local officials visited us.

The municipality of Iquique declared us Illustrious Sons, the highest local honor bestowed on a visitor.

That night they allowed local dignitaries to visit and greet us. There was a large number of people at the entrance to the base requesting to see us.

At 6:oo p.m., after dinner, they told us to gather our things because we were leaving for Antofagasta.

We arrived at midnight, and they handed us over to the political police. They were the ones who treated us most rudely. Until then everything had been courteous. They took off our clothes to do a search. Luckily they didn't search Benigno very carefully, since he had the money hidden next to his testicles.

We flew to Santiago de Chile. We were handcuffed and shackled to the seats, which really bothered us because it had never happened to us before.

Once in Santiago we were taken to the Carabineros Hospital and given a complete medical checkup. Then we were brought to the Bureau of Investigation, where the central police headquarters was also located.

In the Bureau of Investigation we met with Salvador Allende, who explained that we shouldn't worry, that we had the support of the Senate. He said he would accompany us out of the country and he had already requested permission for it. We talked about Fidel and the Cuban revolution.

For two hours we were kept in cells with the doors open. Then began the job of booking us and preparing the documents.

We spoke with the chief of police about things in general, and he told us that the minister had ordered that we leave the country that very day, if possible.

In the meeting with the minister of the interior, he explained that a request for asylum would not be convenient. The North Americans were demanding we be sent back to Bolivia. They planned to get us out on a special flight via Peru-Ecuador-Cuba, and they were getting in touch with our government.

The head of the Bureau of Investigation asked about our personal circumstances and if we knew the identity of someone named Iván.[1] Later he asked if we knew a Mike Ballón, who was being held prisoner in Chile and was said to be a close friend of mine. They brought us face to face. We did not recognize each other and for that reason they dropped the charges. He was Miguel Bayón, the comrade Pol had spoken

1. A Cuban who had been working as a contact person with the guerrillas.

to us about when we were in La Paz. I did not want to implicate him in our escape.[1]

At night they showed us the decree expelling us from the country. They explained in detail that we would have to leave the South American continent via Isla de Pascua [Easter Island], a Chilean possession in the Pacific. The objective was to distract the attention of the United States from our presence there and thus avoid the demand that they hand us over to the Bolivian government.

At the same time, they were making approaches to the Peruvian and Ecuadoran governments to obtain authorization for a Lan Chile (the Chilean airline) plane to land in those countries in order to fly directly to Cuba. These requests were turned down, however, with the threat that if we landed at those airports we would be returned to Bolivian territory.

On February 25, 1968, we departed for Isla de Pascua. Our stay there extended to nearly a week.

On the island was a satellite-tracking station operated by North Americans. When they learned of our presence, they wanted to meet us. We spoke and they explained what they did and expressed interest in learning about Cuba, the Cuban revolution and its achievements. These were things we knew, but were not up to date on.

FROM TAHITI TO CUBA

In the course of the week Allende arrived and we joined his delegation. Then we continued the trip.

1. The person being held was actually Miguel Ballón's brother Coco, who was not a member of the urban network.

We arrived on the island of Tahiti, a French possession. There we were greeted by a group of women who performed the native dances of the country and sang their songs. Then they placed a beautiful shell necklace around each of our necks.

We stayed at a hotel and were visited by the Cuban ambassador to France, Baudilio Castellanos, who from that point on was the person responsible for us.

We stayed in Tahiti for three days. There we met a very pretty Cuban woman from Pinar del Río who was married to the director of the French center for nuclear testing at Mururoa Atoll. Meeting her made it possible to reacquaint ourselves with Cuban cooking, since they invited us to their home and entertained us with the traditional Cuban dish of congrí, roast pork, and yucca. We felt like we were in Pinar del Río or any other Cuban province.

In Tahiti we also had the opportunity to spend more time with Allende. We talked with him, and he explained his ideas, his conception of taking power by peaceful means. In addition to these things of a political nature, we got to appreciate the human side of this leader and his concern for the people. We saw a happy Allende. We spent an evening with him dancing the hula-hula, telling jokes, and having fun. All this helped establish closer ties and enabled us get to know better this great man from Chile.

We bid farewell to Allende, deeply grateful for the solidarity and militant assistance he offered as a true revolutionary.

We continued the trip forced upon us, which went nearly around the world, since we had to leave the Americas and pass through Polynesia, Asia, to Europe, and from there back to the Americas.

We departed Tahiti for Nouméa, a small island in the Pacific where we ran into another Cuban. We were in the airport talking about how things were going in Cuba, listening to Baudilio Castellanos (Bilito). There was a gentleman working in the post-office who heard us speaking. He immediately ran out and hugged us, overjoyed, yelling, "You're Cubans! What a joy!" He was a Cuban, a compatriot of ours.

We also went to Sydney, to Sri Lanka, and we made a stopover in Addis Ababa. From there we went on to Paris.

We arrived at Orly airport. They had taken a whole series of security measures, having been through the experience of Ben Barka's kidnapping.[1] The French authorities wanted to prevent any irregularities with us.

We had planned to tour Paris with the ambassador, see the Arc de Triomphe, visit the Seine, in short, see the city. But as we used to say, "To Orly I fly, and then goodbye," since we never got to do any of that. Upon our arrival, the authorities cordoned us off and drove us straight to the other airport, where for more than an hour and a half they held up the Aeroflot flight that was to take us to Moscow.

After our arrival in the Soviet capital, we spent two days at the home of one of the Cuban embassy officials.

Finally we set off from Moscow to Havana. What a deeply moving experience it was to spot the Punta de Maisí, in Cuban territory. Seeing the lush foliage, the beauty of our land, made an extraordinary impression on us.

But the greatest surprise of all was when we arrived at the airport and were met there by our commander in chief [Fidel Castro], who greeted us with an embrace full of understanding and confidence in us. This did not make us feel self-satisfied; rather we felt sure that one day we would return to fulfill the commitment we had made on October 10, 1967, in front of the little schoolhouse in La Higuera.

There, for over five hours, we explained to our commander in chief the circumstances of Che's death and the battles that followed. He then said something we will never forget:

1. Mehdi Ben Barka, a political exile from Morocco living in France, was kidnapped and evidently murdered in Paris in October 1965. At the time of his death Ben Barka was president of the International Preparatory Committee for the Tricontinental Conference to be held in Havana in January 1966.

"You are alive because you were aggressive, because you fought. Had you been scared, had you shown fear, you would have perished. It is precisely your ability to resist, your capacity to fight, that shows your revolutionary strength and convictions."

List of combatants *and* Glossary

List of combatants

FROM CUBA
Alejandro
Antonio
Arturo
Benigno
Braulio[†]
Joaquín (Vilo)
Marcos (Pinares)
Miguel
Moro (El Médico, Muganga)[†]
Pacho
Pombo[†]
Ramón (Fernando, Mongo, Che)[†]
Ricardo (Mbili, Papi, Chinchu, Taco)[†]
Rolando (San Luis)
Rubio
Tania
Tuma (Tumaine)[†]
Urbano

FROM PERU
Chino
Eustaquio
Negro (El Médico)

FROM BOLIVIA
FROM BOLIVIAN CP/CP YOUTH
Aniceto
Benjamín
Camba*
Carlos
Chapaco
Coco
Ernesto
Eusebio*
Inti
Julio
León*
Loro (Bigotes)
Ñato
Pedro
Polo
Serapio
Walter

FROM MOISÉS GUEVARA GROUP
Chingolo*
Daniel*
Darío
Moisés (Guevara)
Orlando*
Pablito (Pablo)
Paco*
Pepe*
Raúl
Salustio
Víctor
Willy

---

* Deserters or expelled.

† Fought in Congo, 1965

Division of column (as of April 1, 1967)

FORWARD DETACHMENT	CENTER GROUP	REAR GUARD
Miguel (*head*)	Ramón (*head*)	Joaquín (*head*)
Aniceto	Alejandro	Braulio
Benigno	Antonio	Ernesto
Camba	Arturo	Marcos
Coco	Chapaco	Pedro
Darío	Chino	Polo
Julio	Eustaquio	Rubio
Loro	Inti	Víctor
Pablito	León	Walter
Pacho	Moisés	Chingolo (*expelled*)
Raúl	Moro	Eusebio (*expelled*)
	Ñato	Paco (*expelled*)
	Negro	Pepe (*expelled*)
	Pombo	
	Ricardo	
	Rolando	
	Serapio	
	Tania	
	Tuma	
	Urbano	
	Willy	

Prior to April 1, 1967
died: Benjamín, Carlos
captured: Salustio
deserted: Daniel, Orlando

JOAQUÍN'S COLUMN (after April 17, 1967)

Joaquín	Moisés	Tania	Chingolo (*expelled*)
Braulio	Pedro	Víctor	Eusebio (*expelled*)
Ernesto	Polo	Walter	Paco (*expelled*)
Marcos	Serapio		Pepe (*expelled*)

Glossary

(Bolivia combatants are in bold type, listed under the pseudonyms used in Pombo's diary and account.)

Acuña, Vilo. See *Joaquín*

Adriazola, David. See *Darío*

Alejandro

> *Gustavo Machín* (1937–1967) – Active in movement against Batista at University of Havana, and a leader of Revolutionary Directorate. In February 1958 he organized landing of Directorate guerrilla column, which established base in Cuba's Escambray mountains. Fought in battle of Santa Clara December 1958 under Guevara's command. Ended war with rank of commander. Held a number of government posts after 1959, including vice minister of industry, before returning to active military duty. Joined column in Bolivia December 11, 1966. Assigned as head of operations, with responsibility for planning and coordination of military logistics. Originally part of center group, he became a member of Joaquín's column. Killed at Puerto Mauricio ford August 31, 1967.

Algarañaz, Ciro – Owner of property next to Ñancahuazú farm. Arrested by Bolivian troops charged with being guerrilla collaborator. Acquitted November 1967 in trial of Debray, Bustos, and others connected to guerrillas.

Allende, Salvador (1908–1973) – Leader of Socialist Party of Chile. Elected president of Chile September 1970. Killed during right-wing military coup September 1973.

Almeida, Juan (1927–) – *Granma* expeditionary and Rebel Army
commander during Cuba's revolutionary war. Held numerous
posts after 1959 including commander of air force, vice minister
of armed forces, and vice president of Council of State and of
Council of Ministers. Longtime member of Central Committee
and Political Bureau of Communist Party of Cuba.

Aniceto

Aniceto Reinaga (1940–1967) – Student from La Paz, and member
of national leadership of Bolivian Communist Youth. Studied in
Cuba after triumph of revolution. Joined column in Bolivia by
early January 1967, assigned to center group. Expelled from
Executive Committee of Bolivian Communist Youth February
1967. Killed at Yuro ravine October 8, 1967.

Antonio

Orlando Pantoja (1933–1967) – Native of Maffo, Jiguaní in eastern
Cuba. Veteran of anti-Batista struggle and early member of July
26 Movement, jailed for underground activities. Joined Rebel
Army October 1957, becoming a captain in Guevara's column.
Headed Las Villas Regiment no. 3 of Central Army January-
June 1959, then served in Ministry of Interior, later heading up
border guards. Joined guerrilla column December 19, 1966.
Member of center group. Killed at Yuro ravine October 8, 1967.

APRA (American Revolutionary Popular Alliance) – Revolutionary
nationalist movement founded in Peru 1924, with followers
throughout Latin America. In its early years called for Latin
American unity and opposed U.S. imperialist domination but
moved to the right in 1950s. Pro–Cuban revolution wing of
Peruvian APRA party split away in 1959 to form APRA
Rebelde, which later became Movement of the Revolutionary
Left (MIR).

Arguedas, Antonio – Bolivian interior minister in Barrientos
government during period of guerrilla campaign; provided
microfilms of Guevara's Bolivian diary and typescript of
Pombo's diary to Cuba early 1968. Subsequently fled to Chile.

Ariel – Code name for one of guerrilla movement's contacts
with Cuba.

Arismendi, Rodney (1913–1989) – General secretary of Communist Party of Uruguay 1955–88.

Arturo

René Martínez Tamayo (1941–1967) – Born in Mayarí, Holguín, in eastern Cuba. Jailed for underground activities against Batista dictatorship; joined Rebel Army November 1958. After 1959 served in Cuban air force, Rebel Army Department of Investigations, and Ministry of Interior, achieving rank of lieutenant. Joined column in Bolivia December 11, 1966. Assigned as radio operator attached to center group. Brother of Bolivia combatant Ricardo. Killed at Yuro ravine October 8, 1967.

Baigorría, Paulino – Peasant from Abapó who accompanied guerrillas for several days in June 1967 and asked to join. Volunteered as messenger; captured by army in Camarapa. Tortured but refused to talk.

Barrera, Pastor. See *Daniel*

Barrientos, René (1919–1969) – Bolivian air force general; vice president under Paz Estenssoro, he led November 1964 military coup. President of Bolivia 1966–69; died in helicopter crash.

Béjar, Héctor (1935–) – A leader of Peruvian CP, expelled 1958 for opposition to party's electoralism. Founding leader of National Liberation Army (ELN) in Peru 1962. Led guerrilla front in department of Ayacucho, September-December 1965. Arrested 1966 in Lima and imprisoned until 1970. While in prison wrote *Peru 1965: Notes on a Guerrilla Experience.*

Benigno

Dariel Alarcón (1939–) – Peasant from Cuba's Sierra Maestra. Joined Rebel Army July 1957, serving under Camilo Cienfuegos. After revolution's triumph, continued working in armed forces, reaching rank of lieutenant in Cuban army. Joined guerrilla column in Bolivia December 11, 1966. Assigned to forward detachment. One of five surviving veterans of guerrilla front, he reached Cuba March 6, 1968. Retired from Ministry of Interior 1979 with rank of lieutenant colonel. Defected from Cuba 1996.

Benjamín

Benjamín Coronado (1941–1967) – School teacher from La Paz and member of Bolivian Communist Youth. Studied in Cuba, returning to join guerrilla column January 21, 1967. Assigned to forward detachment. Drowned in Río Grande February 26, 1967.

Bigotes. See *Loro*

Blanco, Hugo (1935–) – Leader of Peruvian Trotskyist Revolutionary Left Front (FIR). In early 1960s led peasant unions in La Convención valley that seized land and organized militias to defend themselves. Captured in 1963 and sentenced to death. Amnestied in 1970 following international solidarity campaign.

Bolívar, Simón (1783–1830) – Latin American patriot, born in Caracas. Led armed rebellion that helped win independence from Spain for much of Latin America.

Braulio

Israel Reyes (1933–1967) – Born in Cuba's Sierra Maestra, where he worked as sharecropper and day laborer. Joined Rebel Army in 1957, serving in Raúl Castro's column. After revolution's triumph served in Raúl Castro's escort and in National Revolutionary Police. Returned to armed forces as lieutenant and was liaison officer of Eastern Army's general staff. In 1965 volunteered for internationalist assignment to Congo with Che, under name of Azi. Joined guerrillas in Bolivia November 27, 1966. Assigned to rear guard. Became second in command of Joaquín's column. Killed at Puerto Mauricio ford August 31, 1967.

Bravo, Douglas (1933–) – Member of Political Bureau of Venezuelan Communist Party. Leader of guerrilla front in Venezuela organized in 1961; a founding leader of Armed Forces for National Liberation (FALN) in 1963. Expelled from Venezuelan Communist Party in 1967 for refusing to suspend struggle to overthrow Venezuelan regime.

Brizola, Leonel (1922–) – Leader of bourgeois nationalist Brazilian Labor Party and former governor of Rio Grande do Sul. Went into exile in Uruguay following 1964 U.S.-backed military coup.

Bunke, Haydée Tamara. See *Tania*

Bustos, Ciro Roberto (Carlos) – Painter and journalist from Argentina
who helped raise funds for 1963–64 guerrilla movement in
northern Argentina led by Jorge Masetti. Asked by Guevara to
come to Bolivia to discuss support activities in Argentina, he
arrived in early March 1967. Captured by Bolivian army April 20
in Muyupampa. After capture adopted stance of having been
"taken in" by guerrillas, testifying about his discussions with
Guevara and providing sketches of guerrilla fighters for
Bolivian authorities. Tried and sentenced to 30 years
imprisonment; amnestied in 1970. After release involved in
support activities for various guerrilla groups in Southern
Cone.

Calixto. See *Béjar, Héctor*

Camba

Orlando Jiménez (b. 1934) – Born in Riberalta; a member of
Bolivian Communist Party. Assigned as worker on guerrilla-
owned farm near Caranavi in mid-1966. Incorporated as
combatant at Ñancahuazú December 11, 1966, assigned to
forward detachment. Deserted September 26, 1967, and
captured by army next day while attempting to rejoin guerrilla
unit. Sentenced to 10-year prison term; amnestied in 1970.

Carlos

Lorgio Vaca (1934–1967) – Native of Santa Cruz and member of
Bolivian Communist Party. A national leader of social security
workers union and of Bolivian Communist Youth. Studied
economics in Cuba following revolution. Returned to Bolivia to
participate in guerrilla struggle, arriving at Ñancahuazú camp
December 11, 1966. Assigned to rear guard. Drowned in Río
Grande March 16, 1967.

Carlos. See *Bustos, Ciro Roberto*

Castellanos, Baudilio (Bilito) – Childhood friend of Fidel Castro. One
of defense attorneys in 1953 trial of Moncada attackers.
Underground combatant during Cuban revolutionary war.
Cuba's ambassador to France in 1960s.

Castillo, José. See *Paco*

Castro, Fidel (1926–) – Central leader of armed insurrection against

U.S.-backed Cuban dictator Fulgencio Batista and of socialist revolution carried out by Cuba's workers and peasants. Led 1953 attack on Moncada garrison; founder and leader of July 26 Movement; organized *Granma* landing December 1956 and commanded Rebel Army during revolutionary war. Cuban prime minister 1959–76; president of Council of State and of Council of Ministers since 1976; commander in chief of armed forces; first secretary of Communist Party of Cuba.

Castro, Juvenal (1926–) – Leader of Bolivian Communist Party's peasant work; currently a senator in Bolivia.

Catalán, Elmo (Elías) – Member of Bolivian ELN; journalist from Chile who led support network in Chile for movement led by Guevara. Abducted and murdered by Bolivian police together with wife Jenny Koeller in June 1970.

Chapaco (Luis)

Jaime Arana (1938–1967) – Native of Tarija in southern Bolivia. A leader of Revolutionary Nationalist Movement (MNR) at University of San Andrés. Went to Cuba in 1963 to study hydraulic engineering, and became member of Bolivian Communist Youth. Joined column in March 1967 and was assigned to center group. Killed at Mizque river October 12, 1967.

Chinchu. See *Ricardo*

Chingolo

Hugo Choque – Arrived at Ñancahuazú March 1967 as part of Moisés Guevara's group. Expelled from guerrilla ranks March 25, under escort of Joaquín's column. Deserted in July 1967. Collaborated with Bolivian army after capture, leading them to guerrilla supply caves. Acquitted November 1967 in trial of Debray, Bustos, and others connected to guerrillas.

Chino

Juan Pablo Chang (1930–1967) – Peruvian revolutionary of Chinese ancestry, he joined youth movement of APRA party in 1945 and was active in movement against the military dictatorship. Arrested in 1948, he was jailed for two years, the first of many periods of imprisonment and exile. Joined Communist Party of Peru in early 1950s, becoming a member of

Central Committee. Expelled from CP in early 1960s.
Participated in Puerto Maldonado guerrilla movement
organized by National Liberation Army (ELN) of Peru in 1963;
after its defeat he escaped through Bolivia and spent two years
living clandestinely in La Paz. In January 1966 he attended
Tricontinental Conference in Havana, after which he began
organizing a new ELN front in Peru. Arrived in Ñancahuazú in
February 1967 and became part of revolutionary front, assigned
to center group. Captured at Yuro ravine October 8, 1967, and
murdered next day.

COB (Bolivian Workers Federation) – National federation of Bolivian
trade unions, founded during 1952 revolutionary upsurge.
Leading role played by tin miners. Led by Juan Lechín since its
founding.

Coco

Roberto Peredo (1938–1967) – Native of Beni and brother of Inti
Peredo. Joined Bolivian Communist Party in 1951 at age 13 and
was active in student movement. Helped found Bolivian
Communist Youth after moving to La Paz. There he organized
printshop in his home for CP's newspaper. Imprisoned several
times for political activities. In 1963–64 assisted guerrilla
movements in Peru and in northern Argentina. One of original
cadres assigned by Bolivian CP to prepare front, he was the
legal proprietor of Ñancahuazú farm. Assigned to forward
detachment. Killed at La Higuera September 26, 1967.

Communist Party of Bolivia (PCB) – Constituted 1950. General
secretary during period of guerrilla front and preparations for it
was Mario Monje. Replaced by Jorge Kolle December 1967.
Published weekly newspaper *Unidad*.

Communist Party of Bolivia (Marxist-Leninist) (PCB-ML) – Party
formed by forces that looked to Beijing leadership; founded
April 1965 following expulsion previous year of minority led by
Oscar Zamora from Communist Party of Bolivia. Refused to
support 1966–67 revolutionary front led by Che Guevara.
Minority led by miners' leader Moisés Guevara split and joined
combatants.

Coronado, Benjamín. See *Benjamín*

Daniel

> *Pastor Barrera* – Native of Oruro, Bolivia. Bricklayer. Arrived at guerrilla camp February 1967 as part of group led by Moisés Guevara. Deserted March 11 and captured by army three days later, becoming informer.

Danton. See *Debray, Régis*

Darío

> *David Adriazola* (1939–1969) – Mine worker from Oruro. Former member of Bolivian Communist Party, recruited to guerrilla struggle as part of Moisés Guevara's group. Arrived at guerrilla camp March 1967 and assigned to forward detachment. One of two Bolivian surviving veterans of the struggle together with Inti Peredo, lived clandestinely in La Paz reorganizing ELN and preparing new front. Hideout located through an informer; killed December 31, 1969.

Debray, Régis (Danton, Frenchman) (1940–) – Journalist from France; author of *Revolution in the Revolution?* Conducted survey of Alto Beni zone of Bolivia at Guevara's request in late 1966. Asked by Guevara to come to Ñancahuazú camp to discuss support activities, he arrived in early March 1967. Captured by Bolivian army April 20 in Muyupampa. Tried and sentenced to 30-year prison term; amnestied 1970.

de la Puente, Luis (1929–1965) – A leader of Peruvian APRA party. Broke with party following Cuban revolution and formed APRA Rebelde, which became Movement of the Revolutionary Left (MIR) in 1962. Led MIR guerrilla front in department of Cuzco September-October 1965. Killed in battle October 22, 1965.

Don Víctor (Víctor Céspedes) – Peasant who assisted five surviving guerrilla fighters in their escape from Bolivian army, December 1967 to January 1968.

El Médico. See *Moro*

El Médico (Negro). See *Negro*

ELN (National Liberation Army, Bolivia) – Name adopted in March 1967 by revolutionary movement led by Guevara in Bolivia.

Also used by guerrilla movements in other Latin American countries, including Peru and Colombia.

ELN (National Liberation Army, Colombia) – Colombian guerrilla movement whose leaders included Fabio Vázquez and Camilo Torres. Began operations January 1965.

ELN (National Liberation Army, Peru) – Guerrilla movement founded in Peru 1962 by former members of Peruvian CP and others. Organized short-lived Puerto Maldonado guerrilla front in May 1963 led by Javier Heraud. Established guerrilla front in Ayacucho September-December 1965 led by Héctor Béjar. Juan Pablo Chang (*Chino*) and other ELN members participated in 1966–67 Bolivian front.

Emiliano. See *Francisco*

Englishman. See *Roth, George Andrew*

Ernesto

Freddy Maymura (1941–1967) – Native of Trinidad, department of Beni, in Bolivia, of Japanese ancestry. Went to Cuba in 1962 to study medicine. Member of Bolivian Communist Youth. Returned to Bolivia to join guerrilla column November 27, 1966. Assigned to rear guard under Joaquín. Captured and murdered at Puerto Mauricio ford August 31, 1967.

Estanislao. See *Monje, Mario*

Eusebio

Eusebio Tapia – Born in La Paz. A member of Bolivian Communist Party assigned as worker at guerrilla-owned farm near Caranavi, mid-1966. Joined guerrilla column January 21, 1967. Expelled from guerrilla ranks March 25, he accompanied Joaquín's column. Deserted in July 1967, captured by army; amnestied in 1970.

Eustaquio

Lucio Edilberto Galván (1937–1967) – Born in Huancayo, Peru. Worked as bakery worker, pharmacy hand, and radio technician. Member of National Liberation Army (ELN) of Peru and participant in 1963 guerrilla movement in Peru. Arrived at Ñancahuazú with Juan Pablo Chang February 1967. Assigned to center group in March. Killed at Mizque river October 12, 1967.

Facundo. See *Tellería, Luis*

FALN (Armed Forces of National Liberation) – Guerrilla organization formed February 1963 by members of Venezuelan Communist Party, dissident military officers, and others. Leaders included Douglas Bravo and Fabricio Ojeda. Its political front was FLN (National Liberation Front). Formally broke with Communist Party in 1967 after Bravo and others were expelled from CP for refusal to abandon guerrilla effort to overthrow Venezuelan regime.

FAR (Rebel Armed Forces) – An alliance of Guatemalan guerrilla forces formed December 1962 with close ties to Guatemalan Communist Party. Led by Luis Augusto Turcios Lima and César Montes. Broke with CP in 1967.

FARC (Colombian Revolutionary Armed Forces) – Guerrilla movement established early 1966 with close ties to Colombian Communist Party. Led by Manuel Marulanda.

Fernando. See *Guevara, Ernesto Che*

Flaco. See *Francisco*

Francisco – Cuban internationalist volunteer who helped prepare Bolivian guerrilla front; backed out before actions began.

Frenchman. See *Debray, Régis*

Gadea, Ricardo – Leader of Movement of the Revolutionary Left (MIR) in Peru. Participated in guerrilla effort led by Luis de la Puente; arrested in Peru April 1966 and imprisoned until 1970. Brother of Che Guevara's first wife.

Guevara, Ernesto Che *(Ramón, Mongo, Fernando)* (1928–1967) – Born in Argentina. Both before and after graduating from medical school in 1953, he traveled extensively through the Americas. While living in Guatemala in 1954, became involved in political struggle, participating in resistance to CIA-organized rightist coup against government of Jacobo Arbenz. Escaped to Mexico. In July 1955 met Fidel Castro and volunteered to be troop doctor for expeditionary force being organized by Cuban July 26 Movement to overthrow dictator Fulgencio Batista.

One of 82 expeditionaries to set sail from Tuxpan, Mexico,

aboard the yacht *Granma* in November 1956. Landed on Cuba's southeastern coast in Oriente province on December 2 to begin revolutionary war from Sierra Maestra mountains in eastern part of island. Named commander of second Rebel Army column (Column no. 4) in July 1957. From late August 1958 led Column no. 8 toward Las Villas province in central Cuba. Commanded battle of Santa Clara, capturing Cuba's third largest city at the end of December, helping seal fate of U.S.-backed dictatorship.

Following Batista's fall on January 1, 1959, Guevara carried a number of central responsibilities in the new revolutionary government, including president of National Bank and minister of industry, while continuing duties as an officer in armed forces. Frequently represented Cuba internationally, including at United Nations and in other world forums. As a leader of July 26 Movement, he helped bring about political regroupment that led to founding of Communist Party of Cuba in October 1965.

Resigned his government and party posts, including his military commission and responsibilities, in early 1965 and began preparing to return to South America to help advance anti-imperialist struggles sharpening in several countries. Along with a number of volunteers who would later join him in Bolivia, Guevara went first to the Congo to aid anti-imperialist movement founded by Patrice Lumumba. Arrived in Bolivia November 3, 1966, and led internationalist revolutionary movement there for eleven months. Wounded and captured on October 8, 1967; murdered following day on orders of Bolivian government following consultation with Washington.

Guevara, Moisés

(1939–1967) – Bolivian miner from Huanuni, in department of Oruro. A leader of miners union in Huanuni; was arrested for union activities in 1963. Joined Bolivian Communist Party in 1956. Sided with Oscar Zamora in 1964 split, then expelled together with supporters from Communist Party (Marxist-Leninist) for support to guerrilla line. After meeting with Che Guevara in January 1967, led twelve members of his group to join revolutionary nucleus, arriving in February-March.

Originally assigned to center group, he became part of Joaquín's
column. Killed at Puerto Mauricio ford August 31, 1967.

Guillén, Nicolás (1902–1989) – Noted Cuban poet; member of National
Committee of Popular Socialist Party before revolution. Became
president of Union of Writers and Artists in 1961. Member of
Communist Party Central Committee at time of death.

Guzmán, Loyola (1942–) – Leader of urban support network and
head of finances for ELN. Joined Bolivian Communist Youth in
1956 and became member of national leadership. Expelled from
Executive Committee in February 1967 for work in support of
guerrillas. Arrested September 14, 1967; released 1970 in
exchange for hostages held by ELN combatants. Currently
president of international Association of Relatives of Arrested,
Disappeared, and Martyred Persons for National Liberation.

Heraud, Javier – Peruvian poet; member of ELN; killed May 1963
leading guerrilla effort in Puerto Maldonado, Peru.

Honorato. See *Rojas, Honorato*

Inti

Guido Alvaro Peredo (1937–1969) – Born in Cochabamba and
grew up in Beni. Joined Bolivian Communist Party in 1951 at
age 14; became alternate member of Central Committee in 1959
and regular member in 1964. Imprisoned several times for
political activities. Helped give logistical support to guerrilla
front in northern Argentina 1963–64. Became secretary of CP
regional committee in La Paz in 1965. Joined Guevara's
revolutionary front November 27, 1966. Together with Rolando,
assigned as political commissar — a member of general staff
with responsibility for political leadership of unit; assigned to
center group. One of two Bolivian surviving veterans of
struggle. Worked to reorganize ELN and relaunch guerrilla
front. Wrote *Mi campaña con el Che* (My campaign with Che).
Tipped off by an informer, army raided house where he was
staying in La Paz. After determined resistance he was wounded,
captured, and executed September 9, 1969.

Iván – Member of guerrilla support network in La Paz working as
contact person with Cuba.

Jiménez, Antonio. See *Pedro*

Joaquín (Vilo)

Juan Vitalio Acuña (1925–1967) – Peasant from Cuba's Sierra
Maestra, he joined Rebel Army in April 1957. Promoted to
lieutenant, he served in Guevara's Column no. 4, where he
headed rear guard and became a leading recruiter of peasants
to rebels. Promoted by Castro in November 1958 to column
commander in Rebel Army's Third Front. Held a number of
posts in armed forces after 1959. Elected to Central Committee
of Communist Party of Cuba in October 1965. Joined
revolutionary front in Bolivia November 27, 1966. Second in
command of unit, he commanded rear guard, which operated
as a separate column after April 17, 1967. Killed at Puerto
Mauricio ford August 31, 1967.

Julio

Mario Gutiérrez (1939–1967) – Native of city of Trinidad in
department of Beni. A national leader of Bolivian student
movement from 1957 to 1960. Later became a leader of social
security workers union in Trinidad. Member of Bolivian
Communist Youth. Studied medicine in Cuba, returning to join
column March 10, 1967. Assigned to forward detachment. Killed
at La Higuera September 26, 1967.

Kolle, Jorge – Second secretary of Communist Party of Bolivia, who
replaced Monje as general secretary in December 1967, holding
that post until 1985. Currently director of party's newspaper
Unidad.

Lara, Jesús – Bolivian poet and writer; leader of Communist Party in
Cochabamba. Father-in-law of Inti Peredo. Resigned from CP
1969 over disagreement with line toward guerrilla fighters.
Author of *Guerrillero Inti.*

Lechín, Juan (1920–) – Central leader of Bolivian Workers Federation
(COB) since its founding during 1952 revolutionary upsurge. Vice
president of Bolivia in Paz Estenssoro regime 1960–64. Broke
with Paz in 1964 and organized Revolutionary Party of the
National Left (PRIN). Jailed and exiled by Barrientos dictatorship
in May 1965. President of People's Assembly in 1971.

León

Antonio Domínguez – Native of Trinidad in department of Beni, and member of Bolivian Communist Party. Assigned as a worker at Ñancahuazú farm, he was later incorporated as combatant in center group. Deserted September 26, 1967, and captured by army next day, turning informer. Imprisoned until general amnesty in 1970.

Lobatón, Guillermo – Student activist in Peru exiled 1955. Visited Cuba after revolution. Returned to Peru and joined Movement of the Revolutionary Left (MIR), editing its newspaper *Voz Rebelde* [Rebel Voice]. Leader of Túpac Amaru guerrilla front organized by MIR in department of Junín, June-December 1965; disappeared and presumed killed, early 1966.

Loro (Bigotes)

Jorge Vázquez Viaña (1939–1967) – Born in La Paz; son of well-known Bolivian historian and writer. Active in student movement, he joined Communist Party of Bolivia and became alternate member of its Central Committee. Helped provide logistical support to guerrilla movement in northern Argentina 1963–64. At request of Bolivian CP, he received military training in Cuba. One of original cadres assigned in 1966 to help prepare front in Bolivia. Arrived at Ñancahuazú November 7, 1966, carrying out logistical and other tasks. Incorporated into forward detachment January 25. On April 22, 1967, he was separated from column during clash with army; subsequently wounded and taken prisoner. Held incommunicado, he was tortured and murdered, his body thrown from helicopter into jungle.

Loyola (Loya). See *Guzmán, Loyola*

Lumumba, Patrice (1925–1961) – Leader of independence struggle in Congo and prime minister after independence from Belgium in June 1960. In September 1960, after requesting United Nations troops to block attacks by Belgian-backed mercenaries, his government was overthrown in U.S.-backed coup. UN troops supposedly guarding Lumumba took no action as he was captured, jailed, and then murdered by rightist troops in January 1961.

Mario. See *Monje, Mario*

Marcos (Pinares)

Antonio Sánchez (1927–1967) – A native of Pinar del Río province in western Cuba, where he worked as bricklayer. Went to Sierra Maestra in early 1957 and after three-month search encountered Rebel Army, becoming captain and head of rear guard in Camilo Cienfuegos's column. Promoted to commander January 4, 1959. Subsequently held various posts in armed forces, including head of operations in Pinar del Río, corps chief in Camagüey, and military commander at Isle of Pines. Elected to Central Committee of Cuban Communist Party October 1965. He joined column in Bolivia November 20, 1966. Originally head of forward detachment, he was replaced and assigned to rear guard under Joaquín. Killed at Bella Vista June 2, 1967.

Martí, José (1853–1895) – Cuban national hero. Noted poet, writer, speaker, and journalist. Founded Cuban Revolutionary Party in 1892 to fight Spanish rule and oppose U.S. imperialist designs on Cuba. Launched Cuba's 1895 independence war against Spain and was killed in battle. His revolutionary anti-imperialist program is one of cornerstones of Cuban revolution.

Martín, Américo – A leader of bourgeois nationalist Acción Democrática party in Venezuela. Split from party in 1960 under impact of Cuban revolution and helped form Movement of the Revolutionary Left (MIR). General secretary of MIR and head of Ezequiel Zamora guerrilla front in El Bachiller mountain region of Venezuela. Arrested June 1967 on his way to attend OLAS conference in Havana and imprisoned for over a year.

Martínez Tamayo, José María. See *Ricardo*

Marulanda, Manuel (1928–) – Leader of guerrilla movement in Colombia's Marquetalia region from early 1950s until 1964; member of Central Committee of Communist Party; a founder of Colombian Revolutionary Armed Forces (FARC) in 1966 and its leader up to present.

Masetti, Jorge Ricardo (Comandante Segundo) (1929–1964) – Journalist from Argentina who traveled to Cuba's Sierra Maestra in January 1958 and joined Rebel movement. Founding

director of Prensa Latina, press service launched by new
revolutionary government. Killed while organizing guerrilla
nucleus in Salta mountains of northern Argentina.

Maya (Rita Valdivia) – Member of Bolivian ELN. Killed July 15, 1969,
in attack by police on her hideout in Cochabamba.

Maymura, Freddy. See *Ernesto*

Mbili. See *Ricardo*

Méndez, Luis. See *Ñato*

Miguel

Manuel Hernández (1931–1967) – A native of Jiguaní in eastern
Cuba, where he worked as sugarcane cutter and magnesium
miner. A member of July 26 Movement Action and Sabotage
cell, he joined Rebel Army in May 1957. Joined Guevara's
Column no. 8 in August 1958 as lieutenant; promoted to captain
and head of column's forward detachment. Wounded in battle
of Fomento. Held various posts after 1959 in army and interior
ministry, and in 1966 attained rank of first captain in armed
forces. Joined column in Bolivia November 27, 1966, and became
head of forward detachment in March 1967. Killed at La
Higuera September 26, 1967.

MIR (Movement of the Revolutionary Left, Peru) – Founded 1962 by
forces led by Luis de la Puente, who split from bourgeois
nationalist APRA party in 1959. Opened two guerrilla fronts in
1965 led by de la Puente, Guillermo Lobatón, and Máximo
Velando.

MIR (Movement of the Revolutionary Left, Venezuela) – Formed
July 1960 by forces that split from bourgeois Democratic Action
party. Later established two guerrilla fronts. In 1967 general
secretary was Américo Martín.

Miranda, Francisco (1750–1816) – A leader of Venezuela's
independence war from Spain; captured and died in prison.

MNR (Revolutionary Nationalist Movement) – Bourgeois nationalist
party founded in Bolivia in 1941; led by Víctor Paz Estenssoro.

Moisés. See *Guevara, Moisés*

Mongo. See *Guevara, Ernesto Che*

Monje, Mario (Estanislao) (1929–) – Native of Irupana, department of La Paz. Primary school teacher. General secretary of Communist Party of Bolivia until December 1967. Subsequently a leading member of its Central Committee. Currently living in Moscow.

Montes, César (b. 1942) – Replaced Turcios Lima as commander of Revolutionary Armed Forces (FAR) in Guatemala in 1966.

Moro (El Médico, Muganga)

Octavio de la Concepción (1935–1967) – Became active in anti-Batista struggle while studying medicine at University of Havana. Joined July 26 Movement in 1957 and became member of Rebel Army in September 1958, serving in Second Eastern Front as doctor and combatant. After 1959 worked in a number of medical posts, including head of surgery at Baracoa hospital, and as doctor in countryside. From August to December 1965 took part in internationalist mission in Congo with Guevara; upon returning to Cuba was promoted to first lieutenant. Joined Bolivia front December 11, 1966, as head of medical services. Killed at Mizque river October 12, 1967.

MR13 (November 13 Revolutionary Movement) – Guatemalan guerrilla organization formed February 1962. Led by former army officers who had participated in antigovernment revolt on November 13, 1960. Central leader was Marco Antonio Yon Sosa.

Muganga. See *Moro*

Murillo, Pedro Domingo (1757–1810) – Bolivian patriot who led uprising against Spanish rule launched July 16, 1809. Captured by Spanish troops and executed.

Nguyen Van Troi – Vietnamese freedom fighter executed in Saigon, 1965, on charges of plotting assassination of U.S secretary of defense Robert McNamara.

Ñato

Julio Luis Méndez (1937–1967) – Native of Beni and member of Bolivian Communist Party. In 1963 he escorted survivors of Puerto Maldonado guerrilla movement in Peru through mountains of Bolivia. One of original cadres assigned to assist guerrilla preparations in Bolivia in 1966. On request of Bolivian

CP, he received military training in Cuba, January 1966. Incorporated as combatant November 11, 1966, heading up supplies and armaments and assigned to center group. A survivor of Yuro ravine battle, he was mortally wounded at Mataral November 15, 1967.

Negro

Restituto José Cabrera (1931–1967) – Peruvian who studied and practiced medicine in Argentina. Inspired by revolution in Cuba, he moved there in early 1960s. Worked in cardiology department at provincial hospital of Santiago de Cuba until November 1965. A member of Peruvian ELN, he joined combatants in Bolivia in March 1967. A member of center group, he was later moved to rear guard led by Joaquín. Escaped from August 31 ambush at Puerto Mauricio ford, but was captured and murdered September 4, 1967.

Negro. See *Monje, Mario*

O'Higgins, Bernardo (1776–1842) – Leader of Chile's independence struggle from Spain.

Ojeda, Fabricio (1929–1966) – Member of Venezuelan armed forces who became president of junta that overthrew dictator Marcos Pérez Jiménez in 1958. Became a leader of guerrilla movement organized in 1962–63 by Armed Forces of National Liberation (FALN). Captured October 1966 and murdered in prison.

Olivares, René (1938–) – Native of La Paz. University student and member of Bolivian Communist Party; originally assigned to join guerrilla front but did not agree and declined to participate.

Orlando

Vicente Rocabado (1940–) – Native of Oruro, Bolivia. Mechanic. Arrived at Ñancahuazú camp in February 1967 as part of Moisés Guevara's group. Deserted March 11 and was captured by army three days later, turning informer. Acquitted November 1967 in trial of Debray, Bustos, and others connected to guerrillas.

Ovando, Alfredo (1918–) – A leader of November 1964 military coup in Bolivia; commander in chief of armed forces. President of Bolivia 1965–66, 1969–70.

Pablito (Pablo)

Francisco Huanca (1945–1967) – Native of Challapa in department of Oruro. A former member of Bolivian Communist Youth, he was recruited to guerrilla struggle as part of Moisés Guevara's group. Arrived at camp in February 1967; assigned to forward detachment. After Yuro ravine battle, he led a group of four combatants who were killed at Mizque river October 12, 1967.

Pacheco. See Sánchez.

Pacho

Alberto Fernández (1935–1967) – Veteran member of July 26 Movement's urban underground in Santiago de Cuba and then Santa Clara. Joined Rebel Army in November 1958, serving with Guevara's column in Las Villas. From 1961 to 1963 factory administrator in Pinar del Río, then headed state mining enterprise. Held rank of captain in armed forces. Arrived at Ñancahuazú November 7, 1967. Assigned to forward detachment. Wounded and captured at Yuro ravine on October 8, 1967; died from wounds.

Paco

José Castillo (1937–) – Arrived at Ñancahuazú early March 1967 as part of Moisés Guevara's group. Expelled from guerrilla ranks March 25; under escort of Joaquín's column. Captured following ambush at Puerto Mauricio ford August 31, 1967; released 1970. Only survivor among those with Joaquín.

Paniagua, Benjamín – Bolivian peasant from Piray.

Papi. See Ricardo

Paquito. See Paco

Paulino. See Baigorría, Paulino

Paz Estenssoro, Víctor (1907–) – A founder of bourgeois Revolutionary Nationalist Movement (MNR) in 1941. Became president of Bolivia following 1952 revolutionary upsurge, and held that office on three occasions (1952–56, 1960–64, 1985–89). Increasingly corrupt and fractured regime overthrown November 4, 1964, in military coup by Barrientos and Ovando. Fled to Peru.

Pedro

> *Antonio Jiménez* (1941–1967) – University student and native of Tarata in department of Cochabamba. A member of national leadership of Bolivian Communist Youth. After studying in Cuba, he returned to join combatants December 31, 1966. Expelled from Executive Committee of Communist Youth in February 1967. A member of rear guard under Joaquín. Killed near Monteagudo August 9, 1967.

Pepe

> *Julio Velazco* – Arrived at Ñancahuazú early March 1967 as part of Moisés Guevara's group. Expelled from guerrilla ranks March 25; escorted by Joaquín's column. Deserted May 23; captured by army next day and murdered.

Peredo, Coco. See Coco

Peredo, Inti. See Inti

Pinares. See Marcos

Pol Álvarez-Plata, Jorge René – Native of Camiri; member of ELN.

Polo (Apolinar)

> *Apolinar Aquino* (1935–1967) – Factory worker from Viacha in department of La Paz; local union leader and member of Bolivian Communist Party. Originally a worker at Ñancahuazú farm, he requested to become a combatant and was incorporated into unit December 19, 1966. Assigned to rear guard under Joaquín. Killed at Puerto Mauricio ford August 31, 1967.

Pombo (*Harry Villegas*). See biography page 9.

POR (Revolutionary Workers Party) – Bolivian Trotskyist organization founded 1934, with base among tin miners. Wing of party headed by Hugo González supported revolutionary front led by Che Guevara. Banned by Barrientos dictatorship April 11, 1967.

Prado, Gary – Bolivian army captain who participated in antiguerrilla operations and capture of Guevara; later became a general. Has written several books giving his version of events.

Quicañas, Efraín – Bolivian peasant; native of Oruro. Member of Bolivian Communist Party; helped Pombo, Urbano, and Benigno to escape Bolivian dragnet from Oruro to Chile, and accompanied them to Cuba.

Ramírez, Humberto – A leader of Communist Party of Bolivia and of Federation of Mine Workers of Bolivia. CP general secretary 1989–94.

Ramón See *Guevara, Ernesto Che*.

Raúl

Raúl Quispaya (1939–1967) – Tailor from Oruro, Bolivia, of Aymara Indian ancestry. A former member of Bolivian Communist Youth. Recruited to struggle as part of Moisés Guevara's group. Arrived at camp in February 1967; subsequently assigned to forward detachment. Killed at Rosita river July 30, 1967.

Renán Montero Corrales – Member of urban support network.

Revolutionary Nationalist Movement. See *MNR*

Reyes, Simón (1933–) – Leader of Communist Party of Bolivia and mine workers union; CP general secretary 1985–89.

Rhea, Humberto – Bolivian physician. Member of urban support network in charge of supplying medical equipment.

Ricardo (Papi, Chinchu, Mbili, Taco)

José María Martínez Tamayo (1936–1967) – Born in Mayarí, Holguín in Cuba's Oriente province, where he worked as tractor driver. A member of July 26 Movement, he joined Rebel Army in April 1958, serving in Second Front of Oriente. Embarked on first internationalist mission in October 1962, assisting revolutionary movement in Guatemala. Went to Bolivia in March 1963 to help organize logistical support for guerrilla movement in northern Argentina headed by Jorge Masetti. Served in Congo in 1965 with Guevara. Achieved rank of captain in Cuban armed forces. Arrived in La Paz March 1966 to help prepare revolutionary front. Incorporated as combatant on December 31, 1966, assigned to center group. Brother of combatant Arturo. Killed at Rosita river July 30, 1967.

Rocabado, Vicente. See *Orlando*

Rodolfo. See *Saldaña, Rodolfo*

Rojas, Honorato – Bolivian peasant visited by guerrillas in February 1967. Led Joaquín's column into ambush at Puerto Mauricio ford on August 31, for which he received award from government. Executed by ELN commando unit in 1969.

Rolando (San Luis)

Eliseo Reyes (1940–1967) – Native of San Luis in Cuba's Oriente province. Active in clandestine struggle against Batista; joined Rebel Army 1957, serving in Guevara's column and reaching rank of captain. Following triumph of revolution headed military police at La Cabaña garrison, held military responsibilities in Las Villas, and became head of G-2, the counterintelligence division of Cuba's police. Sent to Pinar del Río in 1962 to help lead operations against counterrevolutionary bands. Elected to Central Committee of Cuban Communist Party in October 1965. Captain in armed forces prior to volunteering for internationalist mission with Guevara. Joined revolutionary front in Bolivia November 20, 1966. Member of general staff assigned together with Inti as political commissar of unit, with responsibility for political leadership of troops; assigned to center group. Killed at El Mesón April 25, 1967.

Roth, George Andrew – Anglo-Chilean journalist believed by combatants to have been CIA agent. Followed tracks of guerrillas and met up with them April 19, 1967. Arrested in Muyupampa with Debray and Bustos April 20; released July 8. Appeared in Chile February 1968 when Pombo, Urbano, and Benigno arrived. Later disappeared from public view without a trace.

Rubio

Jesús Suárez Gayol (1936–1967) – Born in Havana. Member of July 26 Movement in Camagüey, Cuba. Forced into exile, he participated in expedition that landed in Pinar del Río in April 1958. After carrying out actions in that province, he went to Las Villas and joined Guevara's Rebel Army column, becoming captain. After 1959 he held a number of posts in Rebel Army and government, including vice minister of sugar industry. Joined revolutionary nucleus in Bolivia December 19, 1966, where he was assigned to rear guard. Killed at Iripiti river April 10, 1967.

Saldaña, Rodolfo (1932–) – Born in Sucre. University student leader. Joined Bolivian Communist Party in early 1950s. Worked as miner and was a union leader. Helped provide logistical support to guerrilla movement in northern Argentina in 1963–64. He then went to Cuba to receive military training, at request of Bolivian CP. One of cadres assigned in 1966 to help prepare guerrilla front in Bolivia. Carried major responsibilities in urban support network. Later arrested; released 1970 in exchange for hostages held by ELN combatants.

Salustio

Salustio Choque – Born in La Paz, he arrived at guerrilla camp in February 1967 as part of Moisés Guevara's group. Captured March 17, 1967, while acting as guerrilla messenger; provided information on guerrilla camp to Bolivian authorities. Tried and found not guilty of sedition in Camiri trial of Debray, Bustos, and others, November 17, 1967.

San Luis. See *Rolando*

Sánchez (Julio Dagnino Pacheco) – Peruvian; member of Peruvian ELN and a leading member of urban support network in La Paz.

San Martín, José de (1778–1850) – Argentine political leader; helped lead struggle that won independence of Chile and Peru from Spain.

Serapio

Serapio Aquino (1951–1967) – Native of Viacha in department of La Paz. Assigned by Bolivian Communist Party as worker at Ñancahuazú farm. Subsequently incorporated as combatant and assigned to rear guard under Joaquín. Killed at Iquira river July 9, 1967.

Shelton, Robert "Pappy" – Major in U.S. Army Special Forces (Green Berets). Arrived in Bolivia March 27, 1967, to command antiguerrilla training camp for Bolivian army Rangers, established near Santa Cruz. Established similar training camps in Laos and Dominican Republic.

Taco. See *Ricardo*

Tania

Haydée Tamara Bunke (1937–1967) – Born in Argentina of German father and Soviet-German mother who had fled Nazi Germany.

In 1952 her family moved to German Democratic Republic, where she later joined German Communist youth and party. Moved to Cuba 1961, working in Ministry of Education and as translator. In March 1963 volunteered for internationalist duty and was trained in clandestine work. Volunteered for Bolivia mission; arrived November 18, 1964. Working under name of Laura Gutiérrez Bauer de Martínez as folklore researcher for Bolivian Ministry of Education, she began preparations for revolutionary front, working with urban network. Under her false identity, she met and socialized with members of Bolivian ruling class and high government officials, including Barrientos and Ovando. Helped arrange for transfer of combatants and others to Ñancahuazú in late 1966 and early 1967. In March 1967, while escorting visitors to Ñancahuazú camp, her cover was blown, leading to incorporation as combatant. A member of Joaquín's column, killed at Puerto Mauricio ford August 31, 1967.

Teitelboim, Volodia (1916–) – Member of Central Committee of Chilean Communist Party since 1940s; elected to Senate in 1965. Fled Chile following 1973 coup.

Tellería, Luis (1925–) – Native of Coripata, Bolivia. Member of Bolivian Communist Party; worked clandestinely on preparations for guerrilla movement. Later joined ELN.

Torres, Camilo (1929–1966) – Colombian priest and dean of Advanced School of Public Administration. Resigned from priesthood June 1965 and joined National Liberation Army (ELN) guerrilla front in eastern Colombia; killed in battle February 15, 1966.

Tuma (Tumaine)

Carlos Coello (1940–1967) – Agricultural worker from eastern Cuba. Joined July 26 Movement in Manzanillo 1956 and became member of Rebel Army in November 1957, serving in Guevara's column. Assigned to Guevara's personal escort from 1959 on, serving with him in Congo in 1965. A lieutenant in armed forces. Went to Bolivia in July 1966 to help with preparations for revolutionary front. Arrived at Ñancahuazú November 7, 1966. Killed at Florida June 26, 1967.

Tumaine. See Tuma

Turcios Lima, Luis Augusto (1941–1966) – Lieutenant in Guatemalan
   army who participated in 1960 barracks uprising against U.S.-
   installed regime. Beginning 1962 he led Revolutionary Armed
   Forces (FAR) guerrilla movement. Killed in traffic accident in
   Guatemala City.

Urbano
   Leonardo Tamayo (1941–) – Peasant from Cuba's Sierra Maestra,
   born in Bayamo. Joined Rebel Army in mid-1957, serving in
   Guevara's Column no. 4. Later second-in-command of "Suicide
   Squad" of Column no. 8 under Guevara. In 1959 became
   member of Guevara's personal escort, which he later headed.
   Subsequently worked as Guevara's adjutant and accompanied
   him on international trips. A first lieutenant in armed forces.
   Joined column in Bolivia November 27, 1966. Assigned to center
   group. One of five surviving veterans of struggle, he reached
   Cuba in March 1968. Later volunteered for internationalist
   missions in Angola and Nicaragua. Currently a colonel (retired)
   in Cuba's Ministry of the Interior.

Vaca, Lorgio. See *Carlos*

Vargas, Epifanio – Bolivian peasant forced to act as army guide;
   killed in ambush at Ñancahuazú March 23, 1967.

Vargas, Gregorio – Young Bolivian peasant from Muchiri;
   accompanied combatants as guide May 31 to June 2, 1967; later
   arrested by army for collaborating with guerrillas.

Vázquez, Fabio – Active in Workers, Students, and Peasants
   Movement (MOEC) of Colombia, formed in wake of Cuban
   revolution. Founder of ELN (National Liberation Army) in
   Colombia in 1965; leader of ELN guerrilla movement until 1976.

Vázquez Viaña, Jorge. See *Loro*

Víctor
   Casildo Condori (1941–1967) – Baker and truck driver from Coro
   Coro in department of La Paz; of Aymara Indian ancestry. A
   former member of Bolivian Communist Party, he joined
   revolutionary front as member of Moisés Guevara's group,
   arriving at Ñancahuazú in February 1967. Subsequently assigned
   to rear guard led by Joaquín. Killed near Bella Vista June 2, 1967.

Villa, Remberto – Proprietor of Ñancahuazú property who sold it to
Coco Peredo. Subsequently arrested by army as guerrilla
collaborator; later released.

Villca, Estanislao (1939–) – Originally from Chile; member of
Bolivian Communist Party and later ELN. Helped Pombo,
Urbano, and Benigno to escape Bolivian dragnet from Oruro to
Chile, and accompanied them to Cuba.

Walter

Walter Arancibia (1941–1967) – Native of Macha in department of
Potosí. A national leader of Bolivian Communist Youth. Studied
in Cuba after revolution. Returned to join revolutionary front
January 21, 1967. Assigned to rear guard led by Joaquín. Killed
at Puerto Mauricio ford August 31, 1967.

Weber, Redmond – Lieutenant colonel in U.S. Army; commander of
Eighth Special Forces group. Arrived in Bolivia March 27, 1967,
to help establish antiguerrilla training camp.

Willy

Simón Cuba (1932–1967) – Born in Cochabamba. Miner and
longtime leader of miners union in Huanuni, in department of
Oruro. Close collaborator of Moisés Guevara. A member of
Communist Party of Bolivia, he subsequently became a leader
of Moisés Guevara's group, arriving at Ñancahuazú camp in
February 1967. Subsequently assigned to center group.
Captured October 8, 1967, at Yuro ravine while trying to rescue
Che Guevara; murdered next day.

Yon Sosa, Marco Antonio (d. 1970) – Military officer in Guatemala
who participated in failed 1960 uprising against U.S.-installed
regime. Subsequently organized November 13 Revolutionary
Movement (MR13) guerrilla front. Killed on Guatemalan border
by Mexican army in 1970.

Zamora, Oscar (1934–) – Led split from Communist Party of Bolivia
in 1964, becoming general secretary of Communist Party
(Marxist-Leninist), with Maoist political orientation. Refused to
support guerrilla movement of 1966–67. Ran for vice president
of Bolivia in 1993 as running mate of former military dictator
Hugo Banzer.

Index

Also from Pathfinder

The Changing Face of U.S. Politics

Working-Class Politics and the Trade Unions
JACK BARNES
A handbook for workers coming into the factories, mines, and mills, as they react to the uncertain life, ceaseless turmoil, and brutality of capitalism in the closing years of the twentieth century. It shows how millions of workers, as political resistance grows, will revolutionize themselves, their unions, and all of society. Also available in Spanish. $19.95

Out Now!

A Participant's Account of the Movement in the United States against the Vietnam War
FRED HALSTEAD

The story of the anti–Vietnam War movement in the United States: how it refuted Washington's rationales for the war and mobilized opposition; the political fight for a course that could organize in action the maximum number of working people, GIs, and youth and help lead the growing international opposition; how the antiwar movement, gaining momentum from the fight for Black civil rights, helped force the U.S. government to bring the troops home, thus spurring struggles for social justice and changing the political face of the United States. $30.95

Labor's Giant Step

The First Twenty Years of the CIO: 1936–55
ART PREIS

The story of the explosive labor struggles and political battles in the 1930s that built the industrial unions. And how those unions became the vanguard of a mass social movement that began transforming U.S. society. $26.95

Cosmetics, Fashions, and the Exploitation of Women

JOSEPH HANSEN, EVELYN REED,
AND MARY-ALICE WATERS

How big business promotes cosmetics to generate profits and perpetuate the inferior status of women. In her introduction, Mary-Alice Waters explains how the entry of millions of women into the workforce during and after World War II irreversibly changed U.S. society and laid the basis for the advances women have won through struggle over the last three decades. $12.95

America's Revolutionary Heritage

Marxist Essays
EDITED BY GEORGE NOVACK

Essays on the struggle by Native Americans, the first American revolution, the Civil War, the rise of industrial capitalism, and the fight for women's suffrage. $21.95

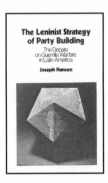

The Leninist Strategy of Party Building

The Debate on Guerrilla Warfare in Latin America
JOSEPH HANSEN

In the 1960s and '70s, revolutionists in the Americas and throughout the world debated how to apply the lessons of the Cuban revolution to struggles elsewhere. Written with polemical clarity by a participant in that debate. $26.95

Lenin's Final Fight

Speeches and Writings, 1922–23
V.I. LENIN

In the early 1920s Lenin waged a political battle in the leadership of the Communist Party of the USSR to maintain the course that had enabled the workers and peasants to overthrow the old tsarist empire, carry out the first successful socialist revolution, and begin building a world communist movement. The issues posed in his political fight remain at the heart of world politics today. Several items appear in English for the first time. Also available in Spanish. $19.95

The Communist Manifesto

KARL MARX AND FREDERICK ENGELS

Founding document of the modern work-ing-class movement, published in 1848. Explains how capitalism arose as a specific stage in the economic development of class society and how it will be superseded by socialism through worldwide revolutionary action by the working class. Also available in Spanish. $3.95

The History of the Russian Revolution

LEON TROTSKY

The social, economic, and political dynamics of the first socialist revolution, explained by one of the principal leaders of this victorious struggle which changed the course of history in the twentieth century. Unabridged edition, 3 vols. $35.95

On the Paris Commune

KARL MARX AND FREDERICK ENGELS

"Storming heaven," Marx wrote, the "proletariat for the first time held political power" in Paris for three months in 1871 and the international workers struggle "entered upon a new stage." Writings, letters, and speeches on the Paris Commune. $15.95

Imperialism: The Highest Stage of Capitalism

V.I. LENIN

"I trust that this pamphlet will help the reader to understand the fundamental economic question, that of the economic essence of imperialism," Lenin wrote in 1917. "For unless this is studied, it will be impossible to understand and appraise modern war and modern politics." Also available in Spanish. $3.95

The First Ten Years of American Communism

Report of a Participant
JAMES P. CANNON

An account of the early years of the U.S. communist movement, by one of its founding leaders. $19.95

New International
A MAGAZINE OF MARXIST POLITICS AND THEORY

New International no. 10
Imperialism's March toward Fascism and War *by Jack Barnes* • What the 1987 Stock Market Crash Foretold • Defending Cuba, Defending Cuba's Socialist Revolution *by Mary-Alice Waters* • The Curve of Capitalist Development *by Leon Trotsky*
$14.00

New International no. 7
Opening Guns of World War III: Washington's Assault on Iraq *by Jack Barnes* • 1945: When U.S. troops said "No"! *by Mary-Alice Waters* • Lessons from the Iran-Iraq War *by Samad Sharif*
$12.00

New International no. 6
The Second Assassination of Maurice Bishop *by Steve Clark* • Washington's 50-year Domestic Contra Operation *by Larry Seigle* • Land, Labor, and the Canadian Revolution *by Michel Dugré* • Renewal or Death: Cuba's Rectification Process, *two speeches by Fidel Castro*
$10.00

New International no. 9

The Triumph of the Nicaraguan Revolution • Washington's Contra War and the Challenge of Forging Proletarian Leadership • The Political Degeneration of the FSLN and the Demise of the Workers and Farmers Government
$14.00

New International no. 3

Communism and the Fight for a Popular Revolutionary Government: 1848 to Today *by Mary-Alice Waters* • 'A Nose for Power': Preparing the Nicaraguan Revolution *by Tomás Borge* • National Liberation and Socialism in the Americas *by Manuel Piñeiro*
$8.00

New International no. 5

The Coming Revolution in South Africa *by Jack Barnes* • The Future Belongs to the Majority *by Oliver Tambo* • Why Cuban Volunteers Are in Angola, *two speeches by Fidel Castro*
$9.00

THE CUBAN REVOLUTION

IN DEFENSE OF SOCIALISM
*Four speeches on the 30th anniversary
of the Cuban revolution*
Fidel Castro

Not only is economic and social progress possible
without the dog-eat-dog competition of capitalism,
Castro argues, but socialism remains the only way
forward for humanity. Also discusses Cuba's role in
the struggle against the apartheid regime in
southern Africa. $13.95

CUBA'S INTERNATIONALIST FOREIGN POLICY
Fidel Castro

Castro discusses the historic importance of the anticapitalist revolutions in
1979 in Grenada and Nicaragua; Cuba's internationalist missions in Angola
and Ethiopia; relations with the U.S. government and with Cubans living
in the United States; the fight within the Nonaligned Movement to forge
a front of struggle against imperialist exploitation; and the proletarian
internationalism that has guided the foreign policy of the Cuban
government since the 1959 revolution. $20.95

BUILDING SOCIALISM IN CUBA
Fidel Castro

Speeches spanning more than two decades trace the fight of the
revolutionary vanguard to deepen the proletarian course of the Cuban
revolution. $20.95

DYNAMICS OF THE CUBAN REVOLUTION
A Marxist Appreciation
Joseph Hansen

How did the Cuban revolution come about? Why
does it represent, as Joseph Hansen puts it, an
"unbearable challenge" to U.S. imperialism? What
political challenges has it confronted? Analysis and
debates written as the revolution advanced. $20.95

HOW FAR WE SLAVES HAVE COME!
South Africa and Cuba in Today's World
Nelson Mandela, Fidel Castro

Speaking together in Cuba in 1991, Mandela and Castro discuss the
unique relationship and example of the struggles of the South African
and Cuban peoples. Also available in Spanish. $8.95

Available from Pathfinder

AND WORLD POLITICS

THE SECOND DECLARATION OF HAVANA

In 1962, as the example of Cuba's socialist revolution spread throughout the Americas, the workers and farmers of Cuba issued their uncompromising call for a continent-wide revolutionary struggle. Also available in Spanish, French, and Greek. $4.50

THOMAS SANKARA SPEAKS

The Burkina Faso Revolution, 1983–87
The leader of the Burkina Faso revolution recounts how peasants and workers in this West African country began confronting hunger, illiteracy, and economic backwardness prior to the 1987 coup in which Sankara was murdered. Also available in French. $18.95

FIDEL CASTRO'S POLITICAL STRATEGY: FROM MONCADA TO VICTORY

Featuring *History Will Absolve Me* by Fidel Castro
Marta Harnecker, Fidel Castro

Traces the political course along which Fidel Castro organized the movement that culminated in the 1959 victory of the workers and farmers in Cuba over the U.S.-backed Batista dictatorship. Contains the full text of "History Will Absolve Me," Fidel Castro's reconstruction of his 1953 courtroom speech explaining the political and social goals of the revolution. $13.95

Ernesto Che Guevara

Episodes of the Cuban Revolutionary War, 1956–58

Ernesto Che Guevara

Ernesto Che Guevara, Argentine by birth, became a central leader of the Cuban revolution and one of the outstanding communists of the 20th century. This book is his firsthand account of the military campaigns and political events that culminated in the January 1959 popular insurrection that overthrew the U.S.-backed dictatorship in Cuba. With clarity and humor, Guevara describes his own political education. He explains how the struggle transformed the men and women of the Rebel Army and July 26 Movement led by Fidel Castro. And how these combatants forged a political leadership capable of guiding millions of workers and peasants to open the socialist revolution in the Americas. Guevara's Episodes appears here complete for the first time in English. Introduction by Mary-Alice Waters. $23.95

Che Guevara Speaks

Selected Speeches and Writings

"A faithful reflection of Che as he was, or, better, as he developed" —from the preface by Joseph Hansen. Includes works not available elsewhere in English. $12.95

Socialism and Man in Cuba

Ernesto Che Guevara and Fidel Castro

Guevara's best-known presentation of the political tasks and challenges in leading the transition from capitalism to socialism. Includes Castro's 1987 speech on the 20th anniversary of Guevara's death. Also available in Spanish, French, Farsi, and Swedish. $3.50